Assessing Student Learning

Assessing Student Learning

A Common Sense Guide

SECOND EDITION

LINDA SUSKIE

FOREWORD BY TRUDY W. BANTA

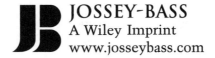

JOSSEY-BASS
A Wiley Imprint
www.josseybass.com

Published by Jossey-Bass
A Wiley Imprint
989 Market Street, San Francisco, CA 94103-1741—www.josseybass.com

Jossey-Bass books and products are available through most bookstores. To contact Jossey-Bass directly call our Customer Care Department within the U.S. at 800-956-7739, outside the U.S. at 317-572-3986, or fax 317-572-4002.

Jossey-Bass also publishes its books in a variety of electronic formats. Some content that appears in print may not be available in electronic books.

Library of Congress Cataloging-in-Publication Data
Suskie, Linda A.
    Assessing student learning : a common sense guide / Linda Suskie. — 2nd ed.
      p. cm.
  Includes bibliographical references and index.
  ISBN 978-0-470-28964-8 (pbk.)
    1. College students—Rating of. 2. Educational tests and measurements. I. Title.
  LB2336.S87 2009+
  378.1'66—dc22
                                                      2008053148

Printed in the United States of America
SECOND EDITION
PB Printing 10 9 8 7 6 5 4 3

The Jossey-Bass
Higher and Adult Education Series

CONTENTS

*To my husband, Steve, and our children, Melissa and Michael, whose love
and support made this book possible; and
To the thousands of college and university faculty, administrators,
and staff members whose passion for excellence in teaching and learning
continually inspires me*

ABOUT THE AUTHOR

Linda Suskie is a vice president at the Middle States Commission on Higher Education, an accreditor of colleges and universities in the mid-Atlantic region of the United States. Prior positions include serving as associate vice president for assessment and institutional research at Towson University and as director of the American Association for Higher Education's Assessment Forum. Her over thirty years of experience in college and university administration include work in assessment, institutional research, strategic planning, and quality management.

Suskie is an internationally recognized speaker, writer, educator, and consultant on a broad variety of higher education assessment topics. She has been an active member of numerous higher education professional organizations and groups and contributes frequently to books and journals.

Suskie has taught graduate courses in assessment and educational research methods and undergraduate courses in writing, statistics, and developmental mathematics. She holds a bachelor's degree in quantitative studies from Johns Hopkins University and a master's degree in educational measurement and statistics from the University of Iowa.

FOREWORD

Linda Suskie is one of the busiest assessment consultants in the country today—and for good reason. She confers with faculty groups on campuses, responds to individual e-mail messages and to questions posed on listservs, and makes keynote addresses tailored to the needs and interests of those in her audience. And at the same time she is imparting knowledge, experience, and wisdom, she is listening carefully to the content of the questions and comments she is receiving. Later she reflects on what she has heard and may adjust her thinking about an issue. At the very least, she adds yet another example to her rich repository so that she will have a new response and another illustration the next time she hears a familiar question.

Suskie's thoughtful, reflective approach to continuous improvement in her work in assessment, as well as her generosity in sharing her experience with others, is apparent in this second edition of *Assessing Student Learning: A Common Sense Guide*. Instead of simply updating the references and some of the content in the original, she undertook an extensive reorganization that makes this edition an even more valuable resource.

As Suskie points out in the Introduction, this book is "short on background and theory." It is not intended to advance the state-of-the-art in cognitive psychology, organizational development, program evaluation, curriculum design, pedagogical theory, or educational measurement, all of which underlie the practice of outcomes assessment in higher education. Instead she has used clear, accessible language to illustrate as no other current work does how concepts from these disparate bodies of knowledge come together to create a new branch of assessment applied in college and university settings. The book provides an excellent introduction for the faculty and administrators who consider themselves assessment novices, but nevertheless have been charged with the responsibility of implementing assessment in a classroom, department, division, or institution. It also provides definitions of terms and a treasure trove of concrete examples of learning outcomes, measurement instruments, and essential campus resources that experienced assessment practitioners can use as they orient colleagues who are brand new to assessment. Most sections of the book can stand alone, particularly since they contain references to other chapters that delve more deeply into certain points. As a consequence, a campus assessment coordinator might refer colleagues to a chapter or section at a time as questions arise.

Evaluation, a concept some use interchangeably with outcomes assessment, is at the highest level of cognitive complexity. Thus, no one who is being introduced to assessment in higher education need apologize for seeking an explanation of it that cuts through the jargon used by theorists and illustrates its relevance to one's own work. Suskie's common sense approach does just that.

I read the Suskie manuscript from the perspective of an instructor who introduces graduate students to outcomes assessment. I wondered if I might adopt this as a text for my own course as well as recommend it to others. I have reached a positive conclusion. Graduate students resemble any other audience that is new to assessment. They need a work that will make complex new concepts understandable. I don't know of another book that contains such an extensive set of definitions for as many of the concepts that undergird assessment as does this one. Suskie's list of references is extensive and up-to-date, and she has woven illustrations from the work of others skillfully into her own narrative. Finally, the "Time to Think, Discuss, and Practice" section at the end of each chapter gives instructors some excellent jumping-off points for advance assignments or for classroom conversations and activities.

Many of the ideas Suskie includes about engaging faculty, providing leadership, selecting measuring instruments, and situating assessment in valued institutional processes so that it will be viewed more favorably are covered in other work. But Suskie gives readers a more fulsome explanation and a richer set of examples than others. Cases in point include her chapters on writing goals and objectives for learning, designing rubrics, and writing test items. Sections that really make this book unique include those on sampling, benchmarking, and presenting findings. In addition, her training and experience in educational measurement are apparent throughout the book as she offers insights and cautions about quantitative and qualitative approaches to measurement in general, and standardized tests in particular.

Few, if any, of the other books and articles on outcomes assessment in higher education that have appeared since 1985 are really out of date. Good ideas about organizing for assessment, collecting data, reporting findings, and using findings to guide improvement are as useful today as before. But in addition to detailed treatment of all these dimensions of assessment, this book contains current information about accountability and instrument design and selection that is not to be found in the earlier works. It brings together the best of the past and the present in a single volume.

Trudy W. Banta
Professor of Higher Education and Senior Advisor to the
Chancellor for Academic Planning and Evaluation
Indiana University–Purdue University Indianapolis

PREFACE

When Jim Anker, the publisher of the first edition of this book, approached me about writing a second edition, I figured that I'd update the References and a few chapters and be done. The first edition was based, after all, on an enduring common sense approach to assessment that hasn't changed materially since the first edition was published in 2004.

But just like anyone else with a passion for teaching and learning—and using assessment results to inform teaching practice—I never do the same thing twice. In my workshops and presentations, I continually use participant feedback to rethink what I'm doing, and I ended up doing the same with this second edition. The myriad questions and comments from the thousands of faculty and staff I've met at workshops, presentations, and campus visits over the past five years have made me rethink how to explain assessment, emphasize different aspects of assessment, and develop new models and structures for approaching assessment.

We've concurrently seen dramatic changes in the world of higher education in the five years since the first edition was published. As more colleges and universities have moved from launching assessment to refining it, they are running into new challenges. And increased pressures for accountability are raising new issues.

So I ended up not with the minor editing I originally envisioned but a complete reorganization and rewrite of the first edition, with expanded attention to some new and emerging topics:

- *How can we get our colleagues on board with assessment?* The first edition's chapter on assessment culture was essentially a laundry list of ideas without much structure. To help readers see the forest for the trees of this difficult topic, I have renamed the chapter, "The Keys to a Culture of Assessment: Tangible Value and Respect," and reorganized it around those two themes.

- *How do we get things organized?* The first edition's chapter on creating an assessment plan is now somewhat dated because more campuses have already created initial (or second or third) assessment plans. But campuses are still wrestling with getting everything organized in a truly functional fashion. So I have replaced the chapter on assessment planning with a new one on organizing assessment. The new chapter presents many of the same concepts but arranges them more meaningfully and usefully.

- *Do we need an assessment director? Do we need to invest in special assessment software?* I've added a new chapter, "Supporting Assessment Efforts with Time, Infrastructure, and Resources," that focuses on helping faculty and staff find time and providing staffing, resources, and infrastructure. This chapter includes new material on the characteristics of an effective assessment coordinator and choosing assessment technologies.

- *We're confused by all the assessment jargon.* To help orient readers who are new to assessment and its vocabulary, I've moved the first edition's chapter on choosing an assessment strategy—really a glossary of assessment terms—to the beginning of the book. I've also added additional material on assessment terminology to other chapters.

- *How can we assess attitudes and values?* I have merged the two chapters on reflection and surveys into a new chapter on assessing attitudes, values, and the like. The new chapter begins with an overview that brings material scattered among several chapters in the first edition into a new framework.

- *What do we do with our assessment results?* I've significantly expanded the last part of the book on understanding and using results. To help those who don't normally deal with numbers, the chapter on summarizing results spends more time on simple tools like tallies, percentages, and aggregated scores. The chapter on using results now addresses using results to inform planning and budgeting, as well as to improve teaching and learning.

- *What the heck is going on with accountability?* A new chapter, "Why Are You Assessing Student Learning?" discusses external audiences and accountability more thoroughly. I have also rewritten the chapter on sharing results to emphasize the need to understand your audiences and tell your story in terms that the audiences can grasp and use. This chapter specifically addresses sharing results with public audiences.

- *What's all the talk about value-added and comparability?* Another new chapter, "Setting Benchmarks or Standards," discusses comparable and value-added assessments more thoroughly than in the previous edition and presents eight other ways to set benchmarks and standards.

- *Our past assessment efforts have sputtered and died. How can we keep this one going?* Yet another new chapter, "Keeping the Momentum Going," pulls together strategies for valuing assessment efforts, monitoring assessment efforts, offering feedback, and reflecting on assessment progress.

I've made some other changes as well. To help readers who use this book as a reference, I've converted many of the bulleted lists in the first edition into tables that are easier to find and use. I've done quite a bit of reorganizing and rewriting to improve flow, remove redundancies, and provide more thorough and integrated discussions. I've also updated and replaced some of the exercises concluding each chapter. And I did update the References as I originally envisioned!

Linda Suskie
November 2008

ACKNOWLEDGMENTS

Some of the material in this book is adapted from my earlier book, *Questionnaire Survey Research: What Works*, published by the Association for Institutional Research. I am grateful to the association for permission to adapt this material. I also thank my daughter Melissa for writing the deliberately less-than-sterling essay in Exhibit 9.9.

This book would not exist without three mentors who shepherded me on my lifelong assessment adventure. Julian Stanley introduced me to the fascinating world of educational testing and measurement when I was an undergraduate at Johns Hopkins University. Bob Forsyth and other faculty affiliated with the Iowa Testing Programs at the University of Iowa gave me a solid graduate education on the principles of educational testing and measurement—principles that endure over thirty years later. And Ted Marchese challenged and inspired me to aim to make a national impact when I was director of the Assessment Forum at the American Association for Higher Education.

This book would not be in your hands without the guidance, advice, and support of many wonderful colleagues across the country. Assessment practitioners and scholars are the nicest, friendliest, and most supportive people in the world! For this second edition, I particularly want to acknowledge, with deep gratitude, the wise counsel and suggestions of Virginia Anderson, Towson University; Marilee Bresciani, San Diego State University; Peter Gray, United States Naval Academy; Elizabeth Jones, West Virginia University; Susan Kahn, Indiana University–Purdue University Indianapolis; Jodi Levine Laufgraben, Temple University; and James Limbaugh, Angelo State University, on various aspects of this book. Special bouquets of gratitude go to Elizabeth Paul, The College of New Jersey, and Ephraim Schechter, HigherEdAssessment.com, who painstakingly read entire chapters and offered detailed, insightful feedback. This book would not be half what it is without the contributions of these distinguished assessment practitioners and scholars.

INTRODUCTION

Interest in assessing student learning at colleges and universities—
and the need to learn how to do it—skyrocketed in the final two
decades of the twentieth century and continues to grow in the
twenty-first century. In the United States, accrediting organizations
have increasingly rigorous requirements that institutions and programs assess how well they are achieving their goals for student
learning. Concurrently, the higher education community is growing increasingly committed to creating learning-centered environments in which faculty and staff work actively to help students
learn, and the assessment of student learning is essential to understanding and gauging the success of these efforts. Both trends have
created a need for straightforward, sensible guidance on how to
assess student learning.

Purpose and Intended Audience

Several years ago, someone commented on the value of my workshops to the "But how do we *do* it?" crowd. The phrase has stayed
with me, and it is the root of this book. Yes, we in higher education
are theorists and scholars, with an inherent interest in whys and
wherefores, but there are times when all we need and want is simple, practical advice on how to do our jobs. Providing that advice is
the purpose of this book.

This second edition of *Assessing Student Learning: A Common
Sense Guide* is designed to summarize current thinking on the
practice of assessment in a comprehensive, accessible, and useful
fashion for those without formal experience in assessing student

learning. Short on background and theory and long on practical advice, this is a plain-spoken, informally written book designed to provide sensible guidance on virtually all aspects of assessment to four audiences: assessment newcomers, experienced assessment practitioners, faculty and others involved in student learning, and students in graduate courses on higher education assessment.

Scope and Treatment: A Common Sense Approach to Assessment

This book is called *A Common Sense Guide* because its premise is that effective assessment is based on simple, common sense principles. Because every institution and program is unique and therefore requires a somewhat unique approach to assessment, this book presents readers not with a prescriptive cookbook approach but with well-informed principles and options that they can select and adapt to their own circumstances.

This book is also based on common sense in that it recognizes that most faculty do not want to spend an excessive amount of time on assessment and are not interested in generating scholarly research from their assessment activities. The book therefore sets realistic rather than scholarly standards for good practice. It does not expect faculty to conduct extensive validation studies of the tests they write, for example, but it does expect them to take reasonable steps to ensure that their tests are of sufficient quality to generate fair and useful results, and it provides practical suggestions on how to do that.

This book has some other distinctive qualities in addition to its common sense approach. Assessment newcomers, for example, will particularly appreciate the minimal use of educational and psychometric jargon. This book discusses reliability, validity, and research design but avoids using those terms as much as possible!

This book is also unique in its comprehensive scope. It introduces readers not only to popular assessment topics such as learning outcomes, rubrics, and portfolios but also to multiple-choice tests and published instruments. Its treatment of setting benchmarks and standards is unmatched.

Because of the broad array of topics in this book, it provides introductory rather than exhaustive treatments of them. It is not (as my husband reminded me when I was in despair over ever finishing the first edition) an encyclopedia. Because this book focuses on general assessment principles applicable to a wide range of programs and situations, it does not specifically address assessment in particular situations such as student affairs programs. Similarly, it does not address the assessment of specific skills such as writing and critical thinking or assessment in special instructional settings such as online learning. If you find that a particular chapter whets your appetite and you'd like to learn more, consider the references at the end of the book and the recommended readings at the end of the chapter for more information and further resources.

Overview of the Book

Part One introduces newcomers to the vocabulary of assessment. Chapter One defines student learning assessment and explains several related concepts, such as grading, evaluation, institutional effectiveness, and accountability. It also compares assessment at the course, program, general education, and institutional levels. Chapter Two furthers the vocabulary lesson by explaining the many approaches to assessment, including direct and indirect evidence, performance assessments, and quantitative and qualitative assessments. This chapter provides a thorough discussion of the challenges of add-on assessments and offers suggestions for maximizing student participation in them. Chapter Three reviews many of the characteristics of effective, accurate, and truthful assessment strategies and discusses ethical issues. It discusses sampling strategies in some detail.

Part Two sets the stage for successful assessment activities. Chapter Four discusses the purposes of assessment, comparing assessing for improvement with assessing for accountability. It delves into the internal and external audiences for assessment results and the need to articulate the decisions that assessment results may inform. Chapter Five addresses the many strategies for building a campus assessment culture. Chapter Six discusses ways to ease the burden of assessment and support assessment work with appropriate resources and infrastructure. Chapter Seven goes through the steps of getting everything going, from reviewing where you are now to developing guidelines and working out the logistical details. This chapter includes information on curriculum mapping; collecting assessment information from alumni, employers, and others beyond students; and special challenges such as adjuncts and general education. Chapter Eight discusses the many kinds of learning goals that faculty and staff might consider and offers suggestions on identifying and articulating goals.

Part Three provides information and guidelines on a wide range of assessment tools. Chapter Nine's discussion of rubrics includes information on five rubric formats. Chapter Ten explores how to develop effective instructions to students regarding an assignment and addresses how to counter plagiarism. Chapter Eleven discusses multiple-choice questions and their variations, including matching and interpretive exercises. Chapter Twelve presents a framework of two windows—reflection and behaviors—for assessing values, attitudes, dispositions, and habits of mind, and it discusses a variety of strategies for assessing these traits. Chapter Thirteen looks at the strengths and challenges of portfolios and offers suggestions for implementing them. Chapter Fourteen examines the pros and cons of using published tests and surveys and provides guidance on how to identify and evaluate them.

Part Four addresses understanding and using assessment results. Chapter Fifteen discusses ten kinds of benchmarks and standards and the pros and cons of each. Because of recent media coverage, it gives particular attention to peer benchmarks and value-added benchmarks. Chapter Sixteen shares how to sum up results and introduces, in general terms, how to identify meaningful differences and evaluate the quality of assessment strategies. Chapter Seventeen reviews ethical principles for disseminating results and the need to understand each audience for the results. It then focuses on how to tell the story of one's results rather than present a set of dry numbers. Chapter Eighteen reviews ethical principles for appropriate use of results and reiterates the need to understand one's purpose and goals. It discusses how to address both positive and disappointing results and how to use the results to inform planning and resource allocation as well as to improve teaching. Chapter Nineteen ends the book by sharing strategies to keep the momentum going, including celebrating and honoring assessment efforts, monitoring assessment activities, providing feedback, and periodically reflecting.

Using This Book

For assessment newcomers who want to gain a general understanding of all aspects of assessment, the book's four parts go roughly sequentially through the assessment process: understanding assessment, planning the assessment process, choosing and developing appropriate tools, and using assessment results. Experienced assessment practitioners will find the book a helpful reference guide. Plenty of headings, lists, and tables, plus a thorough index, help readers find answers quickly to whatever questions they have about assessment.

While this book is designed primarily to meet the needs of those charged with planning and implementing a program or institutional assessment effort, much of the book, especially Part Three, will be of interest to anyone involved in student learning, including faculty who want to improve assessments within their classes.

This book is also designed to be suitable for professional development workshops and graduate courses in assessment. Each chapter concludes with questions and exercises for thought, discussion, and practice. No answer key is provided, because these are mostly complex questions with no simple answers! Often the conversation leading to the answers will reinforce learning more than the answers themselves.

As you read this book, keep in mind that assessment is a nascent discipline. The science of educational testing and measurement is scarcely a century old, and many of the ideas and concepts presented here have been developed only within the past two or three decades. Assessment scholars and practitioners have yet to agree on many definitions, models, and principles, and some of them may disagree with some of the ideas expressed here. As you hear conflicting ideas, use your own best judgment—your common sense, if you will—to decide what's most appropriate for your situation. You'll find that some references are not from higher education but from basic education and the business world. Each sector has much to learn from the others, and I encourage you to consider resources from outside higher education as seriously as those from within.

Assessing Student Learning

PART ONE

Understanding
Assessment

CHAPTER 1

What Is Assessment?

Some Valuable Ideas You'll Find in This Chapter

- Students learn best—and assessment works best—when education is a purposeful, integrated, collaborative experience.
- Teaching to the test may not be such a bad thing.
- Assessment is research, but it is not traditional empirical research.
- Grades alone may not tell us much about student learning, but the grading process can yield a wealth of valuable information.

Oral and written examinations have been part of education for hundreds of years, but only in the past century have the theory and science of assessment been studied systematically. Because the assessment of student learning in higher education is relatively new compared to many other fields of study, and because it has been undertaken by people from disciplines with widely differing orientations, the vocabulary of assessment is not yet standardized. (This chapter, for example, discusses several ways that the term *evaluation* is used.) This book therefore begins by defining assessment and distinguishing it from some related concepts.

Many assessment practitioners, notably Thomas Angelo (1995), have put forth definitions of assessment. Table 1.1 summarizes their work.

The four steps in Table 1.1 do not represent a once-and-done process but a continuous four-step cycle (Figure 1.1). In the fourth step, assessment results are used to review and possibly revise approaches to the other three steps, and the cycle begins anew.

Table 1.1. What Is Assessment

Assessment is the ongoing process of:

Establishing clear, measurable expected outcomes of student learning
Ensuring that students have sufficient opportunities to achieve those outcomes
Systematically gathering, analyzing, and interpreting evidence to determine how well student
   learning matches our expectations
Using the resulting information to understand and improve student learning

---

While the term *assessment* can be used broadly—we can assess any goal or outcome in any discipline or any activity—in this book, the term refers to the assessment of student learning.

What Is the Difference Between Traditional and Current Approaches to Assessment?

How are today's approaches to assessment different from the oral and written examinations that faculty have been conducting for centuries? Table 1.2 summarizes some key differences.

An important difference between contemporary and traditional thinking about assessment is that under contemporary approaches, assessment is viewed as part of an integrated, collaborative learning experience. Students learn better when their college experiences are not collections of isolated courses and activities but are purposefully designed as coherent, integrated learning experiences in which courses and out-of-class experiences build on and reinforce one another (see Table 18.3). Indeed, Gerald Graff (2008) has noted that successful colleges stress collaboration over "individual teaching brilliance" and that students find unrelated courses

Figure 1.1. Teaching, Learning, and Assessment as a Continuous Four-Step Cycle

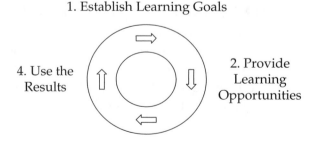

Table 1.2. Contemporary Versus Traditional Ways of Thinking About Assessment

Contemporary Approaches: Assessment is . . .	Traditional Approaches: Assessment is . . .
Carefully aligned with goals: the most important things we want students to learn (Chapter Eight)	Planned and implemented without consideration of learning goals, if any even exist
Focused on thinking and performance skills (Chapter Eight)	Often focused on memorized knowledge
Developed from research and best practices on teaching and assessment methodologies (Chapter Eighteen)	Often poor quality because faculty and staff have had few formal opportunities to learn how to design and use effective assessment strategies and tools
Used to improve teaching and learning as well as to evaluate and assign grades to individual students (Chapters Four and Eighteen)	Used only to evaluate and grade individual students, with decisions about changes to curricula and pedagogies often based on hunch and anecdote rather than solid evidence
Used to tell our story: what makes our college or program distinctive and how successful we are in meeting students' and societal needs (Chapter Seventeen)	Not used to tell that story; stories are told through anecdotes about star students rather than broader evidence from representative students

confusing. When students can see connections among their learning experiences, their learning is deeper and more lasting.

The value of education as an integrated, collaborative experience has several important implications for teaching and assessment:

- *Integrated learning goals.* There should be appropriate relationships among institutional, program, and course learning goals. This is discussed in Chapter Eight.

- *Curricular alignment.* Curricula should be designed to ensure that every student, regardless of the particular choices he or she makes in choosing a course of study, has ample opportunity to achieve every key institutional and program learning goal. This is discussed in Chapters Three and Seven.

- *Collaboration.* Learning goals, curricula, and assessments should be designed through collaboration across the college community. This is discussed in Chapter Five.

- *Embedded assessments.* An important side benefit of providing integrated learning experiences is that student learning assessments can be similarly integrated. Assessments that are embedded into individual courses (Chapter Two) can often provide information on student achievement of program goals, general education goals, and institutional goals.

What Are the Differences Among Course, Program, General Education, and Institutional Assessments?

Student learning takes place in many venues:

- Individual courses
- Academic programs, including undergraduate and graduate degree programs, certificate and other nondegree programs, and noncredit programs
- General education core curricula
- Cocurricular programs and student life programs designed to promote student learning and development
- Cohort-based programs and other special programs designed to enhance student learning, such as:
  - First-year experiences
  - Learning communities
  - Service-learning programs
  - Developmental education programs
  - Tutoring programs
  - Honors programs
  - Programs for at-risk student cohorts
  - Study-abroad programs

Assessment at the Course Level

Assessment in individual courses is typically based on the tests and assignments that contribute to the grading process. Under the contemporary approaches to assessment listed in Table 1.2, assessment at the course level means not just assigning individual grades but also reflecting on how well students as a whole are achieving the course's key learning goals. This is done by aggregating assessment results (Chapter Sixteen), such as by counting how many students answered each test question correctly. This takes time, of course, but can often be accomplished by looking at the results of just a few key assignments, generally those completed toward the end of the course.

Course assessment becomes more complicated if several faculty members are teaching multiple sections of the same course and using different tests, assignments, and other grading criteria. If the course is a prerequisite to further study or to a career, all sections should share a core of common course learning goals (Chapter Eight) that are essential to future success. (Individual faculty members may, of course, address additional goals of their own choosing beyond this common core.) It can be very helpful to come up with some common test questions (Chapter Eleven) or assignments (Chapter Ten) and develop common criteria (Chapter Nine) to evaluate these common goals.

Assessment at the Academic Program Level

Because an academic program should be integrated and greater than the sum of its parts—that is, more than a collection of courses—it may have goals and assessments that are broader than those of its courses. A course assessment might examine whether students can solve a specific kind of problem, for example, while a program assessment might examine whether students can design appropriate approaches to solving a variety of problems in the discipline.

Assessment at the academic program level can take place in a variety of ways.

Embedded course assignments.   Course assignments, especially those completed toward the end of a program, can be assessed for achievement of key program goals as well as course goals. A paper that a student writes in an advanced course, for example, can show not only what the student has learned in that course but also the writing skill that she has developed throughout the entire program of study. Embedded assessments are discussed further in Chapter Two.

Capstone experiences.   These are holistic activities that students are required or encouraged to complete as they approach the end of their program. They include theses, dissertations, oral defenses, exhibitions, performances, presentations, and research projects. Capstones help students synthesize their learning by tying together the various elements of their program and seeing the big picture. Capstones thereby promote deep, lasting learning (Table 18.3). These experiences provide a wonderful venue for program assessment because they provide a holistic portrait of what students have learned throughout their program. A senior project might be evaluated—perhaps through a rubric—for such program goals as written communication skills, critical thinking skills, information literacy skills, and research skills. If students make presentations on their projects, the presentations can be evaluated for oral communication skills as well.

Field experiences.   Many programs require students to participate in an internship, practicum, service-learning activity, student teaching assignment, or some other capstone experience in the field. If these experiences give students opportunities to practice applying the knowledge and skills they've learned in the program to real-life situations, their supervisors' ratings of their performance can be powerful evidence of the overall success of a program in achieving its major learning goals. Rubrics make it easy for supervisors to provide this information (see Exhibit 9.5).

Portfolios. Academic programs increasingly require students to compile a portfolio that demonstrates what they have learned throughout the program. Portfolios can draw a rich, full picture of student learning, but they can also be complicated and time-consuming to implement. Portfolios are discussed in Chapter Thirteen.

Published tests. Some programs require or encourage students to take a published test of what they have learned. Published tests are discussed in Chapter Fourteen.

Assessment in General Education Core Curricula

As with academic programs, a good general education core curriculum is greater than the sum of its parts. It has overarching goals and because those goals are integrated, they are the hallmark of every undergraduate's education at the college. Those goals are addressed repeatedly in multiple rather than single general education courses, and the assessment of general education focuses on those goals.

Catherine Palomba and Trudy Banta (1999) have offered three general approaches to assessing general education learning goals. One approach is to let faculty identify their own embedded assessments (Chapter Two) of the general education courses they teach. This approach gives faculty the greatest sense of ownership and may therefore generate the most useful results. But this approach makes it difficult to aggregate the results and get an overall picture of how well students are achieving general education goals across the entire college.

Another approach is to use a collegewide assessment, perhaps a portfolio, a published test of general education skills, or a capstone requirement of the general education curriculum. While this makes it easy to get an overall picture of student learning, faculty may not be able to see how the results relate to their classes or how to use the results to improve student learning. Another challenge is that college-wide assessments are often add-on assessments, and student motivation may be an issue (Chapter Two).

The third approach is for faculty teaching courses in a group of related disciplines or subjects to identify a common assessment strategy. Faculty teaching science laboratory courses, for example, might agree to include certain key elements in their rubrics for students' lab exercises.

Unless a consistent approach is mandated by an accreditor, state agency, or the like, there is usually no need to use just one approach throughout the general education curriculum. Writing might be assessed through a collegewide portfolio requirement, fine arts faculty might each develop their own assessments of the general education goal for creativity, and the science faculty might agree to include a common set of test questions on their final exams.

Assessment in Cocurricular, Student Life, and Cohort-Based Programs

Student learning takes place outside as well as within the curriculum: in first-year experiences, learning communities, other cocurricular programs, and student life programs. Wherever student learning and development are supposed to happen, there should be goals for that learning and assessments to see how well students are achieving those goals.

Many of these programs have goals to develop attitudes, values, and the like. Strategies to assess these kinds of goals are discussed in Chapter Twelve.

Assessment at the College or University Level

Many colleges have overarching learning goals for all students, regardless of major. Frequently these institutional learning goals are delivered through the general education core curriculum. If this is the case, assessment at the institutional level is synonymous with general education assessment.

But some college mission statements and strategic goals articulate institutional learning goals that are not addressed systematically in the general education curriculum. A faith-based college, for example, may have goals related to spirituality that students develop through participation in extracurricular activities rather than—or in addition to—the general education curriculum. Some colleges have a distinctive goal that students develop through both the general education curriculum and their academic major field of study. Hamilton College in Clinton, New York, for example, characterizes itself as "a national leader for teaching students to write effectively" (Trustees of Hamilton College, 2008), and it emphasizes this skill throughout its curricula.

In these circumstances, institutional learning assessment goes beyond general education assessment, but the principles for assessing general education curricula apply.

Responsibility for institutional learning assessment is often shared—or should be shared—not only among faculty but also with student development staff. Interpersonal skills are an example of an institutional goal that might be developed and assessed in the general education curriculum, majors, and student development programs. This requires communication and collaboration, as discussed in Chapter Five.

What Is the Difference Between Assessment and Grading?_____

Obviously there is a great deal of overlap between the tasks of grading and assessment, as both aim to identify what students have learned. A key difference is that grades focus on individual students, while assessment focuses on entire cohorts of students and how effectively everyone, not an individual faculty member, is helping them learn. Grades alone are usually insufficient evidence of student learning for assessment purposes (Johnstone, Ewell, & Paulson, 2001) for several reasons:

Grades alone do not usually provide meaningful information on exactly what students have and have not learned. We can conclude from a grade of B in an organic chemistry course, for example, that the student has probably learned a good deal about organic chemistry. But that grade alone cannot pinpoint what aspects of organic chemistry she has and has not mastered.

Grading and assessment criteria may (appropriately) differ. Some faculty base grades not only on evidence of what students have learned, such as tests, papers, presentations, and projects, but also on student behaviors that may or may not be related to course learning goals. Some faculty, for example, count class attendance toward a final course grade, even though students with poor attendance might nonetheless master course learning goals. Others count class participation toward the final grade, even though oral communication skills aren't a course learning goal. Some faculty downgrade assignments that are turned in late. These practices can all be appropriate classroom management strategies and grading practices, but they illustrate how grades and assessment standards might not match. A student who does not achieve major learning goals might nonetheless earn a fairly high grade by playing by the rules and fulfilling other less important grading criteria.

Conversely, a student who achieves a course's major learning goals might nonetheless earn a poor grade if she fails to do the other things expected of her.

Grading standards may be vague or inconsistent.   While many faculty base assignment and course grades on carefully conceived standards, grades can be inadequate, imprecise, and idiosyncratic, as Thomas Angelo has pointed out in the Foreword to the first edition of *Effective Grading* (Walvoord & Anderson, 1998). Faculty may say they want students to learn how to think critically but then base grades largely on tests emphasizing factual recall. Faculty teaching sections of the same course may not agree on common standards and might conceivably award different grades to the same student performance on the same assignment. Sometimes individual grading standards are so vague that a faculty member might, in theory, award an A to an essay one day and a B to the identical essay a week later.

Grades do not reflect all learning experiences.   As *Greater Expectations* (Association of American Colleges and Universities, 2002) points out, grades provide information on student performance in individual courses or course assignments. They do not provide information on how well students have learned key competencies, such as critical thinking or writing skills, holistically over an entire program. Grades also do not address what students have learned from ungraded cocurricular activities.

Do grades have a place in an assessment program?   Of course they do! Grades can be useful, albeit indirect, evidence (Chapter Two) of student learning. They can be useful *if* the grades are based on direct evidence of student learning (Chapter Two) such as tests, projects, papers, and assignments that are clearly linked to major learning goals through test blueprints (Chapter Eleven) or rubrics (Chapter Nine). *Effective Grading* (Walvoord & Anderson, 1998) gives a plethora of practical suggestions on how to tie grades more closely to explicit learning goals.

What Is the Difference Between Assessment and Teaching to the Test?

In a way, good assessment *is* teaching to the test. Assessment is part of a process that identifies what we want students to learn, provides them with good opportunities to learn those things, and then assesses whether they have learned those things. In other words, good assessment assesses "what matters most" (Angelo, 1999, p. 3).

Teaching to the test gets a bad name when tests measure something other than what we value, either because someone else has told us what to assess or because our own tests measure relatively trivial learning. As Lee Shulman (2007) has pointed out, "Assessments must be designed so that the tests are *worth* teaching to" (p. 24).

What Is the Difference Between Assessment and Evaluation?____

Evaluation is defined in a variety of ways. One perspective equates it with judgment: evaluation is using assessment information to make an informed judgment on such things as:

- Whether students have achieved the learning goals established for them

- The relative strengths and weaknesses of teaching and learning strategies

- What changes in goals and teaching-learning strategies might be appropriate

Evaluation defined this way is the last two steps of the assessment process described at the beginning of this chapter: interpreting assessment evidence (part of step 3) and using the results (step 4). This definition points out that assessment results alone only guide us; they do not dictate decisions to us. We use our best professional judgment to make appropriate decisions. This definition of evaluation thus reinforces the ownership that faculty and staff have over the assessment process.

A second conception of evaluation is that it determines the match between intended outcomes (step 1 of the assessment process) and actual outcomes (step 3 of the assessment process). Under this definition, the assessment of student learning and the evaluation of student learning could be considered virtually synonymous.

A third conception of evaluation is that it investigates and judges the quality or worth of a program, project, or other entity rather than student learning. We might evaluate an anthropology program, employee safety program, alumni program, or civic project designed to reduce criminal recidivism. Under this definition, evaluation is a broader concept than assessment. While assessment focuses on how well student learning goals are achieved, evaluation addresses how well all the major goals of a program are achieved. An anthropology program, for example, might have goals not only for student learning but also to conduct anthropological research, provide anthropological services to local museums, and conduct its affairs in a cost-effective manner. An evaluation of the program would consider not only student learning but also research activities, community service, and cost-effectiveness. Program reviews, discussed below, are an increasingly popular tool for evaluating academic programs.

What Is the Difference Between Assessment and Faculty Evaluation?

While faculty evaluations examine the impact and effectiveness of individual faculty members, assessments of student learning evaluate the collective impact of faculty, staff, and the resources that support them on students in an entire program or an entire college or university.

As discussed in Chapter Eighteen, one of the fastest ways to kill an assessment effort is to use the results to evaluate individual faculty, especially if disappointing results are used to penalize faculty. But end-of-course evaluation forms completed by students might provide useful assessment information if they are aggregated across faculty. A question about opportunities for interaction with other students may provide useful, albeit indirect (Chapter Two), program assessment information, for example.

What Is the Difference Between Assessment and Research?

Lee Upcraft and John Schuh (2002) have noted that assessment differs from traditional research in its purpose and therefore in its nature. Traditional empirical research is conducted to test theories, while assessment is a form of action research, a distinct type of research whose purpose is to inform and improve one's own practice rather than make broad generalizations. Peter Ewell (2002) has called this a craft-based rather than scientific approach. The four-step assessment cycle of establishing learning goals, providing learning opportunities, assessing student learning, and using the results mirrors the four steps of action research: plan, act, observe, and reflect.

Assessment, like any other form of action research, is disciplined and systematic and uses many of the methodologies of traditional research. But most faculty and staff lack the time and resources to design and conduct rigorous, replicable empirical research studies with impartial distance. They instead aim to keep the benefits of assessment in proportion to the time and resources devoted to them (Chapter Six). If you take the time and effort to design assessments reasonably carefully and collect corroborating evidence, your assessment results may be imperfect but will nonetheless give you information that you will be able to use with confidence to make decisions about teaching and learning. Chapters Three and Sixteen discuss strategies for doing this.

What Is the Difference Between Assessment and Program Review?

Program review is a comprehensive evaluation of an academic program that is designed both to foster improvement and demonstrate accountability (Suskie, 2006). Program reviews typically include a self-study conducted by the program's faculty and staff, a visit by one or more external reviewers, and recommendations for improvement based on the conclusions of the self-study and the reviewer. Program reviews are sometimes conducted to meet the requirements of an accreditor or state system and sometimes simply because institutional leaders find the concept appealing.

Program reviews can be a useful tool for improvement or a meaningless paper-pushing exercise, depending on how they are designed. Robert Shirley and J. Fredricks Volkwein (1978) have suggested that program reviews focus on quality, along with need, cost, and cost-effectiveness. But what is quality? As Chapter Four discusses, colleges and universities have traditionally defined quality based on inputs, including resources (such as faculty credentials and library holdings), students (such as their high school preparation), and activities (such as faculty scholarship and community service).

But quality and effectiveness increasingly are defined by how well a program is achieving its goals. Under this view of quality, a program review should focus on collecting and examining evidence of goal achievement. Because student learning is a fundamental goal of any academic program, student learning assessment should be a primary component of the program review process.

The value of program reviews depends not only on their focus but also on how they are used. At some colleges, completed program reviews are submitted, filed, and forgotten, making them a pointless exercise. But other colleges use program reviews—including assessment results—to develop plans for advancing programs and allocating resources to support achievement of those plans. Chapter Eighteen discusses using assessment results to inform planning and budgeting decisions.

What Is the Difference Between Assessing Student Learning and Assessing Institutional Effectiveness?

Accreditation organizations, governing boards, legislators, and other audiences increasingly ask colleges and universities to assess institutional effectiveness as well as student learning. What's the difference? Institutional effectiveness is how well a college or university is achieving its mission and major strategic goals. Since student learning is the heart of most college missions, the assessment of student learning is a major component of the assessment of institutional effectiveness (Figure 1.2).

But institutional effectiveness goes further, addressing other aspects of college mission, perhaps research and scholarship, community service, building a diverse community, or modeling certain values. Institutional effectiveness also addresses progress in achieving major institutional goals, which might include offering financial support to those without sufficient means to attend college, providing facilities and infrastructure that promote student learning, or developing collaborative partnerships with basic education.

Assessing institutional effectiveness thus involves assessing not only student learning but also each of these other collegewide aims through the same four-step cycle. Assessing a college mission

Figure 1.2. The Relationship of Student Learning to Institutional Effectiveness

of community service begins, for example, by developing a clear statement of the major goals of the college's community service efforts (step 1). Programs designed to achieve those goals are then implemented (step 2). The programs are next assessed to see whether they are achieving their major goals (step 3). For example, a goal to provide cultural programming to the local community might be assessed by counting attendance at cultural events and perhaps surveying local residents on how well the college meets their cultural interests. Finally, the results are used to modify the college's community service goals, programs, or assessment strategies (step 4), and the cycle begins anew.

What Is the Difference Between Assessment and Performance Indicators?

Performance indicators are quantitative measures (Chapter Two) summarizing assessment results for student learning or other aspects of college performance that are distilled down to single numbers. Student retention and graduation rates, job placement rates, racial/ethnic enrollment breakdowns, financial ratios, and student-faculty ratios are all examples of performance indicators. Busy college leaders, board members, and government policymakers often want performance indicators because they are quickly digested, even though they may present an incomplete, if not distorted, picture of effectiveness and quality.

Most performance indicators used today are not measures of student learning because most student learning assessment results are complex and cannot be distilled down to a single number. Rubrics (Chapter Nine) and surveys (Chapter Twelve), for example, usually yield results on multiple criteria.

But some student learning assessment results could be viewed as performance indicators. The percentage of students who earn at least a minimally acceptable overall score on a rubric or test, who give a particular answer to a single survey question, or who earn a certain score on a single rubric criterion are examples of possible performance indicators.

Performance indicators greatly increase the temptation to make quick judgments and decisions based on just one assessment result. As discussed in Chapter Three, assessment results are always imprecise, and no decision should be based on the results of a single assessment.

But we cannot ignore increasingly vocal calls for simple, clear assessment results that public audiences such as employers and policymakers can easily absorb and understand. Until the education community develops effective, compelling ways to summarize and communicate student learning assessment results, the temptation to look on some results as performance indicators will remain. Chapters Four and Seventeen discuss the challenges of sharing assessment results with public audiences.

What Is the Difference Between Assessment and Accountability?

Assessment is the act of evaluating student learning; accountability is using the results of assessment to demonstrate the quality of a program or college to concerned audiences. Chapter Four discusses the twin purposes of assessment: using results to improve teaching and learning and using results to be accountable to internal and external audiences.

Time to Think, Discuss, and Practice

1. Think of an assignment in a course you have taught or taken.
   - Did the assignment help students learn important goals or relatively unimportant goals of the course?
   - Might the completed assignment be evidence of student achievement of a program or college learning goal? Which goal?
2. Are the academic programs at your college required to undergo any periodic program review?
   - What are the guidelines for those reviews?
   - Is evidence of student learning part of the review?

Recommended Readings

The following readings are recommended along with the references cited in this chapter.

Allen, M. J. (2006). *Assessing general education programs.* Bolton, MA: Anker.

Calhoun, E. (1993). Action research: Three approaches. *Educational Leadership, 51*(2), 62–65.

Ewell, P. T. (2002). *An emerging scholarship: A brief history of assessment.* In T. W. Banta & Associates, *Building a scholarship of assessment* (pp. 3–25). San Francisco: Jossey-Bass.

Ewell, P. T. (2004). *The examined life: Assessment and the ends of general education.* Paper presented at the Association of American Colleges and Universities General Education and Assessment Conference, Long Beach, CA.

Joint Committee on Standards for Educational Evaluation. (1994). *The program evaluation standards* (2nd ed.). Thousand Oaks, CA: Sage.

Lake, C., Harmes, P., Guill, D., & Crist, C. (1998). *Defining assessment.* Retrieved September 16, 2008, from www.essentialschools.org/cs/resources/view/ces_res/124.

Leskes, A. (2002). Beyond confusion: An assessment glossary. *Peer Review, 4*(2/3), 42–43.

Leskes, A., & Miller, R. (2005). *General education: A self-study guide for review and assessment.* Washington, DC: Association of American Colleges and Universities.

Leskes, A., & Wright, B. (2005). *The art and science of assessing general education outcomes: A practical guide.* Washington, DC: Association of American Colleges and Universities.

Seeley, M. M. (1994). The mismatch between assessment and grading. *Educational Leadership, 52*(2), 4–6.

CHAPTER 2

How Can Student Learning Be Assessed?

Some Valuable Ideas You'll Find in This Chapter

- No assessment of knowledge, conceptual understanding, or thinking or performance skills should consist of indirect evidence alone.

- Retention and graduation rates alone don't tell us much about student learning because so many other factors can affect them.

- Motivating students to participate in add-on assessments and give them serious thought and effort is a significant challenge.

- Using a single assessment score as a gatekeeper graduation or progression requirement is an unethical use of assessment results.

- Qualitative assessments are underused and underappreciated, but they help discover problems—and solutions—that can't be found through quantitative assessments alone.

- Every assessment is inherently subjective.

The many ways to assess student learning can be overwhelming. This chapter aims to help you sort through your options by introducing you to the abundance of approaches to assessing student learning. As discussed in Chapter Three, the best assessment efforts use multiple, diverse approaches. Depending on your interests and needs, these approaches may include:

- Assessments yielding direct and indirect evidence of student learning

- Assessments of learning outcomes, processes, inputs, and context

- Performance assessments and traditional assessments

- Embedded and add-on assessments

- Local and published assessments

- Qualitative and quantitative assessments

- Objective and subjective assessments

This chapter is thus a glossary of some of the key terms used to describe assessment tools and strategies.

Direct and Indirect Evidence of Student Learning

Direct evidence of student learning is tangible, visible, self-explanatory, and compelling evidence of exactly what students have and have not learned. It might also be defined as the kind of evidence that a skeptic would accept. A skeptic might be dubious of grades or students' self-ratings as evidence that students can write well, for example. Grades might be inflated, after all, and students could have misconceptions about their skills. But a skeptic would be hard-pressed to argue with actual student writing samples, accompanied by grading criteria showing rigorous standards. Table 2.1 gives examples of direct evidence of student learning.

Indirect evidence consists of proxy signs that students are probably learning. Indirect evidence is less clear and less convincing than direct evidence. Table 2.2 gives examples of indirect evidence.

Donald Kirkpatrick and James Kirkpatrick's (2006) four levels of learning experience outcomes, summarized in Table 2.3, provide a framework for understanding indirect evidence.

Reaction, or student satisfaction, is important because dissatisfaction is a clue that students may not have learned some important things. But student satisfaction levels alone don't reveal whether they have learned what we value. Similarly, *transfer*—using what has been learned in later pursuits—is theoretically important, but some students may pursue paths that simply do not give them opportunities to use what they have learned.

Table 2.1. Examples of Direct Evidence of Student Learning

Ratings of student skills by their field experience supervisors or employers (Chapter Nine)

Scores and pass rates on appropriate licensure or certification exams such as Praxis or National Council Licensure Examination (NCLEX) or other published tests such as Major Field Tests that assess key learning outcomes (Chapter Fourteen)

Capstone experiences such as research projects, presentations, theses, dissertations, oral defenses, exhibitions, and performances, scored using a rubric (Chapter Nine)

Other written work, performances, and presentations, scored using a rubric[a] (Chapter Nine)

Portfolios of student work[a] (Chapter Thirteen)

Scores on locally designed multiple-choice or essay tests such as final examinations in key courses, qualifying examinations, and comprehensive examinations, accompanied by test blueprints (Chapter Eleven) describing what the tests assess[a]

Score gains (referred to as "value added") between entry and exit on published or local tests or writing samples[a] (Chapter Fifteen)

Observations of student behavior (such as presentations and group discussions), undertaken systematically and with notes recorded systematically[a]

Summaries and assessments of electronic class discussion threads[a] (Bauer, 2002)

Think-alouds, which ask students to think aloud as they work on a problem or assignment[a]

Classroom response systems (clickers) that allow students in their classroom seats to answer questions posed by the teacher instantly and provide an immediate picture of student understanding (Bruff, 2009)

Feedback from computer-simulated tasks such as information on patterns of action, decisions, and branches[a]

Student reflections on their values, attitudes, and beliefs (Chapter Twelve), if developing those are intended outcomes of the program[a]

---

[a]Especially suitable for assessing general education core curricula (Chapter One).

Table 2.2. Examples of Indirect Evidence of Student Learning

Course grades (Chapter One) and grade distributions[a]

Assignment grades, if not accompanied by a rubric or scoring criteria (Chapter One)[a]

Retention and graduation rates

For four-year programs, *admission rates into graduate programs* and graduation rates from those programs

For two-year programs, *admission rates into four-year colleges* and graduation rates from those programs

Scores on tests required for further study (such as Graduate Record Examinations) that evaluate skills learned over a lifetime

Quality and reputation of graduate and four-year programs into which alumni are accepted

Placement rates of graduates into appropriate career positions and starting salaries

Alumni perceptions of their career responsibilities and satisfaction

Student ratings of their knowledge and skills and reflections on what they have learned over the course of the program (Chapter Twelve)[a]

Questions on end-of-course student evaluation forms that ask about the course rather than the instructor[a]

Student, alumni, and employer satisfaction with learning, collected through surveys, exit interviews, or focus groups (Chapter Twelve)[a]

Voluntary gifts from alumni and employers

Student participation rates in faculty research, publications, and conference presentations

Honors, awards, and scholarships earned by students and alumni

---

[a]Especially suitable for assessing general education core curricula (Chapter One).

Table 2.3. The Kirkpatricks' Four Levels of Learning Experience Outcomes

1.	Reaction	Student satisfaction with the learning experience.
2.	Learning	What students have learned as a result of the learning experience.
3.	Transfer	Students' use of what they have learned in later pursuits: further study, on the job, community service, and so on.
4.	Results	How what students have learned is helping them achieve their goals and our goals for them. These goals may include persistence through graduation, obtaining and advancing through positions for which they've prepared, admission to appropriate programs of advanced study, and achievement of other life goals that they've identified for themselves

Source: Reprinted with permission of the publisher. From *Evaluating Training Programs, Third Edition,* copyright© 2006 by Donald L. Kirkpatrick and James D. Kirkpatrick, Berrett-Koehler Publishers, Inc., San Francisco, CA. All rights reserved. www.bkconnection.com.

Results—retention, graduation, and placement rates and the like—are also important outcomes, but they don't tell us exactly what students have and haven't learned. If we know, for example, that 95 percent of the graduates of a teacher education program find jobs as teachers, we can conclude that they have probably learned important things, because they're attractive to employers, but we can't tell from this statistic alone exactly what they have and haven't learned.

An even greater concern with results like graduation and placements rates is that it is hard to tie the effect of a particular course, program, or other learning experience to these kinds of outcomes. There are too many possible mitigating factors. A 95 percent teacher placement rate, for example, may be due as much to a regional shortage of teachers as to the quality of a teacher preparation program. Recent downturns in the banking and finance industries have meant that many well-prepared graduates of finance programs have been unable to find jobs. The reason has been a shift in the economy that had nothing to do with the quality of the students' finance programs or what they learned.

Reaction, transfer, and results are thus all indirect evidence of student learning. While goals for persistence, transfer, and job placement can be important and should be monitored, assessment efforts should include direct evidence of student learning (the Kirkpatricks' second level): the knowledge, skills, attitudes, and habits of mind that students need to persist, graduate, transfer, obtain jobs, and otherwise succeed in their life pursuits. No assessment of knowledge, conceptual understanding, or thinking or performance skills should consist of indirect evidence alone.

Indirect evidence can nonetheless be an important part of an assessment program. Information on learning processes, discussed in the next section, can be especially useful indirect evidence. Many attitudes and values can be assessed only with indirect evidence (Chapter Twelve). Because indirect evidence is less convincing, it is especially important to use multiple measures to corroborate it (Chapter Three).

Assessments of Learning Outcomes, Processes, Inputs, and Context

Information on learning outcomes can be the most compelling evidence of student learning, but it alone may not help explain why students are or are not learning. Look at learning processes, inputs, and context as well as outcomes in order to understand what is happening and how we might improve student learning.

Assessments of Learning Outcomes

Most direct evidence of student learning focuses on learning *outcomes:* the knowledge, skills, attitudes, and habits of mind that students have and take with them when they successfully complete a course or program. Assessments of learning outcomes are often what some people call *summative* assessments: the kind obtained at the end of a course or program.

Assessments of learning outcomes are of interest to many external audiences (Chapter Four) including accreditors, employers, and policymakers. But even if these interests are put aside, assessments of learning outcomes can be a good starting point for an assessment effort. If students are graduating with the competencies you want them to have, there may be no need to spend additional time and effort drilling down further into their learning experiences. But if you're disappointed with the results, move to assessments of processes, inputs, and contexts as needed to help you understand why and how students are learning and not learning.

The key drawback of outcomes assessments is that because these assessments occur at the end of the course or program, students may not receive any feedback on their performance other than possibly an overall grade, and faculty and staff may not be able to use the results to improve those students' learning. As Lee Shulman (2007) has observed, "the later the assessment, the later the knowledge of results, and the less likely it is that the assessments will yield information that can guide instruction and learning" (p. 24). But while outcomes assessments may be too late to help current students, they can certainly be used to make changes affecting subsequent students, and in this way they can be formative, as discussed below.

Assessments of Learning Processes

In the past few decades, research has identified a number of learning processes, such as time on task and active learning opportunities, that help students learn effectively (Table 18.3). Evidence of these learning processes is thus important, albeit indirect, evidence that students are probably learning important things. Evidence that students spend a lot of time writing is, for example, an indication that students are learning how to write, although of course the evidence is not as compelling as actual samples of student writing.

Assessments of learning processes are nonetheless an important component of many assessment efforts because they can help us understand why students are or are not learning. If we learn through an assessment of student learning outcomes that students aren't writing as well as we would like, we can understand why by looking at when and how they learn how to write throughout the program.

The other key benefit of assessments of learning processes is that they are often what some call *formative* assessments: those undertaken while student learning is taking place rather than at the end of a course or program. Because formative assessments are done midstream, faculty and staff can use them to improve the learning of current students by making immediate changes to classroom activities and assignments and by giving students prompt feedback on their strengths and weaknesses.

Table 2.4 gives examples of assessments of learning processes. *Classroom Assessment Techniques* (Angelo & Cross, 1993) offers many other suggestions.

Assessments of Learning Inputs

Learning *inputs* are the things in place before learning processes begin that might affect the processes and outcomes. They can yield insight into why students are or are not learning. Students may not do well in a math class into which they've been incorrectly placed. They may not learn current laboratory techniques if they work in ill-equipped labs. Table 2.5 gives examples of learning input evidence.

Assessments of Learning Context

Learning *context* refers to the environment in which the learning process takes place, particularly those aspects that might affect learning processes and outcomes. Employer needs are an example of context that affects technical, vocational, and professional

Table 2.4. Examples of Evidence of Learning Processes That Promote
Student Learning

Transcripts, catalogue descriptions, and course syllabi, which can be analyzed for evidence of such things as program coherence and opportunities for active and collaborative learning[a]

Journals and logs maintained by students documenting such things as time spent on course work; interactions with faculty, staff, and other students; and the nature and frequency of library use[a] (Chapter Twelve)

Interviews and focus groups with students, asking them why they achieve some learning goals well and others less well[a] (Chapter Twelve)

Counts of out-of-class interactions between faculty and students[a]

Counts of programs that disseminate lists of the program's major learning goals to all students in the program

Counts of courses whose syllabi list the course's major learning goals[a]

Counts of courses whose stated learning goals include thinking skills (Chapter Eight), as well as basic understanding[a]

Documentation of the match between course or program learning goals and assessments[a]

Counts of courses whose final grades are based at least in part on assessments of thinking skills as well as basic understanding[a]

Ratio of performance assessments (discussed later in this chapter) to paper-and-pencil tests[a]

Proportions of class time spent in active learning[a]

Counts of courses with collaborative learning opportunities[a]

Counts of courses with service-learning opportunities or the number of student hours spent in service-learning activities[a]

Library activity in the program's disciplines,[a] such as number of books in the discipline that have been checked out, number of online database searches that have been conducted, and number of online journal articles in the discipline that have been accessed

Counts of student majors participating in relevant cocurricular activities, such as the percentage of biology majors participating in the Environmental Club

Voluntary student attendance at disciplinary seminars and conferences and other intellectual and cultural events relevant to a program

[a] Especially suitable for assessing general education core curricula (Chapter One).

curricula. If faculty don't consider this context and don't design curricula that give students the skills that employers need, their graduates won't be able to find jobs. Table 2.6 gives examples of information on learning context or environment.

Performance Assessments and Traditional Assessments_____

Traditional assessments are the kinds of tests that have been around for decades, if not centuries: multiple-choice tests, essay tests, and oral examinations. They are usually designed only to collect assessment information, not give students a learning opportunity. Students typically complete traditional assessments in controlled, timed examination settings.

Table 2.5. Examples of Evidence of Learning Inputs That Affect Student Learning

Students' high school records, including curriculum, grades, and rank in class[a]

SAT or ACT scores

Placement test scores[a]

If the college or program admits transfer students, *transfer articulation policies* and agreements with other colleges[a]

Library holdings in the program's or general education requirement's disciplines[a]

Faculty credentials, such as the percentage holding terminal degrees in their discipline[a]

Opportunities and expenditures for faculty and staff professional development on teaching and learning[a]

Funding for academic programs

Student-faculty ratio, average class size, or ratio of students to full-time faculty[a]

Instructional facilities, technologies, and materials[a]

Number and dollar value of grants awarded for improving student learning[a]

[a]Especially suitable for assessing general education core curricula (Chapter One).

Performance assessments ask students to demonstrate their skills rather than relate what they've learned through traditional tests. Writing assignments, projects, laboratory and studio assignments, and performances are examples. Performance assessments are sometimes called *alternative assessments* because they are alternatives to traditional multiple-choice and blue book tests. Performance assessments that ask students to do real-life tasks, such as analyzing case studies with bona-fide data, conducting realistic laboratory experiments, or completing internships are called *authentic assessments.* Performance assessments have two components: the assignment or prompt that tells students what is expected of them (Chapter Ten) and a scoring guide or rubric (Chapter Nine) used to evaluate completed work.

Performance assessments are increasingly popular because they merge learning and assessment. Students learn while they are working on performance assessments, unlike traditional testing periods during which they often learn nothing. Authentic assessments have the additional advantage of giving students realistic learning situations in which they solve messy real-world problems with many acceptable answers rather than fabricated problems for which there is only one correct answer.

While essay test questions and oral examinations have been characterized here as traditional assessments, in reality they straddle the line between traditional and performance assessments. They are traditional in the sense that they are usually not designed to give students a learning opportunity and because their timed setting with limited access to resources often doesn't mimic the real world. They are performance assessments, however, because they

Table 2.6. Examples of Evidence of Learning Context That Affects Student Learning

Prospective students' interest in the college, program, or course[a]

Prospective employers' demand for graduates of the college or program[a]

Needs and expectations of prospective employers and graduate programs[a]

Perceptions of the college or program by employers and other public audiences

Characteristics and comparative strengths and weaknesses of competing colleges, programs, and courses[a]

Regional and national trends in the discipline[a]

The regional climate for higher education, including public and private support for higher education[a]

[a]Especially suitable for assessing general education core curricula (Chapter One).

ask students to perform skills such as writing, critical thinking, and speaking.

Embedded and Add-On Assessments

Embedded assessments are program, general education, or institutional assessments that are embedded into course work. In other words, they are course assessments that do double duty, providing information not only on what students have learned in the course but also on their progress in achieving program or institutional goals.

Because embedded assessments are typically designed locally by faculty and staff, they match up well with local learning goals. They therefore yield information that faculty and staff value and are likely to use to improve teaching and learning. Embedded assessments also generally require less extra work than add-on assessments. Convincing students to participate in assessment activities is not an issue.

To keep program and institutional assessment processes manageable, embedded assessments are typically examined for achievement of program or institutional goals in only a few courses. Progress in achieving program goals might be examined only in the courses that students take just before graduation. Progress in achieving general education goals might be examined only in general education courses with high enrollment. Chapters Five and Six offer more suggestions for keeping assessment manageable.

Sometimes embedded assessments cannot answer all key questions about student learning across a program or college. Embedded assessments that are locally designed, for example, cannot give insight into how students compare to those in peer programs or colleges. In these kinds of situations, students may be asked to participate in ungraded *add-on* assessments beyond course requirements. Students might assemble a portfolio throughout their program (Chapter Thirteen) or, as they prepare to graduate, take a published test (Chapter Fourteen) or participate in a survey or focus group (Chapter Twelve).

The major challenge with most add-on assessments—indeed, their major drawback—is convincing students not only to participate in them but also to give the assessment tasks serious thought and effort. There is no magic answer to this. There is no foolproof incentive, and what entices some students will not entice others. Because of this limitation, add-on assessments, while potentially useful under some circumstances, should never be the centerpiece of an assessment program.

How can you maximize participation rates in add-on assessments? The following four factors probably have the most effect (Suskie, 1996):

Four Factors Affecting Participation Rates in Add-On Assessments

1. *The nature of the assessment.* A short survey asking for simple, nonthreatening opinions will generally get a higher participation rate than a test that requires three hours on a Saturday morning and a good deal of careful thought and effort.

2. *The people you are assessing.* Students who have been dismissed from your college will be less likely to participate in a survey, for example, than students who are currently enrolled in good standing.

3. *How important the assessment appears.* If the assessment appears important, your participants' contribution will seem more worthwhile and they'll be more likely to participate.

4. *How considerate you are of your participants.* Recognize that you have no right to expect anyone to go to the trouble of taking an optional test or spending time in a focus group and that your participants are doing you a great favor when they do. If you show your appreciation by doing all you can to minimize their trouble and make their job as easy as possible, they will be much more likely to participate and give you sound, useful information.

Usually not much can be done about the first two factors. You may not be able to affect the fundamental nature of the assessment or the students who must be contacted. But you can address the last two factors—making the assessment appear important and being considerate of your participants—and thereby maximize your participation rate. The following strategies may help.

Make participation in the assessment a requirement of a program or course (typically a capstone course).   This is the most effective participation incentive (Ekman & Pelletier, 2008), although it will not necessarily compel students to give the assessment their best effort. If you decide to do this, put the requirement in writing, and draw it to the attention of students entering the course or program.

Sometimes an add-on test or portfolio can be scored quickly enough that the results could conceivably be factored into a course grade. While this would be a powerful incentive for students to give the assessment their best effort, it may be an inappropriate use of results, because add-on assessments are designed to assess what has been learned throughout the student's program and not just in a particular course. Course grades should reflect course learning goals.

Convince participants of the importance of the assessment activity.   Explain how participation will make an impact on something significant that participants understand and appreciate. Include in the assessment questions or tasks that participants will find interesting and important. Cultivate a strong campus culture of assessment (Chapter Five) in which students continually hear from their professors and campus leaders as well as posters, advertisements, and announcements that add-on assessment activities are inherent, valued parts of the academic program, not superfluous extras. And make the official sponsor of the assessment someone respected and important (sad to say, this may not be you!). Provide someone's name and contact information should your participants have questions about the assessment (this may be you!).

Appeal to participants' self-interest.   Answer their unspoken question, "What's in this for me?" Explain how the results will benefit participants directly or some cause or issue about which they are concerned. Offer to send participants a summary of the results that will let them see the impact of their efforts. Give students feedback on their strengths and weaknesses, how they compare to their peers, and how their participation is leading to tangible improvements. Also guarantee unconditional confidentiality. If you are using assessments with code numbers or other identifying information, explain why. Stress that you will look only at aggregated responses.

Be sensitive to survey fatigue. Ask yourself if you really need to conduct an add-on assessment. If you are considering a survey, interview, or focus group, check with others at your college who might be planning something similar. Sometimes you can piggyback on another survey, adding a few questions to it rather than creating a separate survey. Or everyone can plan to survey different samples so that no one receives more than one survey.

Minimize the inconvenience of the assessment activity. If the assessment cannot be completed online at the participants' convenience, schedule it at a convenient time and place—not before a holiday or during finals week, for example—and give participants plenty of advance notice. If it's not possible to conduct the assessment during regularly scheduled class time in appropriate courses, consider conducting the assessment on several days, at several times, so students can find an assessment period that they can attend regardless of their other obligations. Some colleges schedule an assessment day once each term or year when no regular classes are held so students can participate in assessment activities.

Keep the assessment short. The shorter the assessment, survey, or interview, the more considerate you are of your participants' time and the higher the participation rate. Try to keep any paper survey to no more than one page, a telephone interview to no more than five minutes, and a focus group or in-person interview to no more than thirty minutes. Review the questions posed in Chapter Four about the purpose of the assessment, and make sure that it focuses only on critical learning goals and issues.

Keep the assessment clear. Participants shouldn't have to spend time trying to figure out what the assessment is really looking for or how to use necessary technologies such as navigating through a Web site. If possible, try out the assessment with a small group of students to be sure the guidelines and questions are truly clear and the technologies easy to use.

Provide a material incentive to encourage students to participate. Consider these possibilities:

- A token incentive enclosed with every invitation (perhaps a pencil, window decal, or coupon for a free ice cream cone), because it can create a sense of obligation
- A material incentive to students who participate, such as cash, a complementary meal, or a gift certificate

- Perks that are highly prized but have little or no direct cost, such as registration or housing preference, a parking space in a prime lot, or extra graduation tickets
- Entering the names of those participating in random drawings for significant prizes such as laptops

The effectiveness of material incentives varies dramatically, depending on campus culture, student values, and the assessment itself. Free pizza might work beautifully with some students and be a dismal failure with others. The key is to find an incentive that is particularly appealing to your students. Sometimes a campus-specific item, such as a T-shirt with logo or tickets to a popular campus event, works best. With other students, a more generic incentive, such as a complimentary meal or a gift certificate to an online store, is more effective. And if the time and thought contributed are significant, a check compensating students for their time may be necessary.

Ask some students to suggest incentives that would convince them to participate, and consider trying out incentives with small groups of students before launching a full-scale assessment. You may want to use some special incentives only with subgroups of students whose participation rates are historically low.

Allow students to include assessment results in their credentials at their discretion.   This is especially effective if prospective employers or graduate programs value the assessment. Some students may find that they can strengthen their job prospects or graduate school applications by including items from their portfolios or by having their academic record note that they scored at, say, the eighty-seventh percentile on a nationally recognized exam. Include scores in student credentials only if the student so chooses, or students who think they will do poorly will be unlikely to participate.

Give top scorers or the first students to return a survey some kind of recognition.   Students earning exceptional scores on important assessments might receive an award, a seal on their diplomas, or a notation on their transcripts. Or they might be offered one of the no-cost perks mentioned earlier. Keep in mind, however, that offering incentives to top scorers or the first students to return a survey may not motivate students who are late to check their e-mail or think they have no chance of earning a top score.

While it may be tempting to ensure student participation in an add-on assessment by establishing a minimum score as a graduation or progression requirement, single scores should never be the sole basis of any major decision such as retention or graduation.

Using a single assessment score as a gatekeeper graduation or progression requirement is an unethical use of assessment results. Minimum scores may be used as graduation or progression requirements only if students have multiple opportunities to complete the assessment successfully and have an alternative means of demonstrating competence, such as submitting a portfolio of their work for evaluation by a faculty-staff panel.

Brainstorm all possible reasons for people not to participate. Then do all you can to overcome those obstacles.

Local and Published Assessments

Local assessments are those created by faculty and staff at a college; *published* instruments are those published by an organization external to the college and used by a number of colleges. Chapter Fourteen discusses the pros and cons of published instruments. A combination of locally designed and published assessments generally provides a fuller picture of student learning than either alone.

Quantitative and Qualitative Assessments

Quantitative assessments use structured, predetermined response options that can be summarized into meaningful numbers and analyzed statistically. Test scores (Chapter Eleven), rubric scores (Chapter Nine), survey ratings (Chapter Twelve), and performance indicators (Chapter One) are all examples of quantitative evidence. Quantitative assessments are more common than qualitative, probably because many assessment practitioners are more familiar with quantitative techniques, some accreditors require quantitative evidence of student learning, and some public audiences find quantitative results more convincing.

Qualitative assessments use flexible, naturalistic methods and are usually analyzed by looking for recurring patterns and themes. Reflective writing, online class discussion threads, and notes from interviews, focus groups, and observations are examples. The key difference between qualitative assessments and informal, anecdotal observations is that qualitative assessments are systematic and structured. Students are routinely evaluated using common criteria.

Qualitative assessments are underused and underappreciated in many assessment circles. Unlike quantitative assessments, which collect only predetermined information, qualitative assessments allow us to explore possibilities that we haven't considered. They can give fresh insight and help discover problems—and solutions—that can't be found through quantitative assessments alone. Qualitative assessments add a human dimension to an assessment effort, enhancing the dry tables and graphs that constitute many assessment reports with living voices. Chapter Twelve discusses qualitative assessments further.

Objective and Subjective Assessments

An *objective* assessment is one that needs no professional judgment to score correctly (although interpretation of the scores requires professional judgment). Most objective test items have only one correct answer and could be scored accurately by a reasonably competent eight year old armed with an answer key. *Subjective* assessments yield many possible answers of varying quality and require professional judgment to score.

Multiple-choice, matching, and true-false test questions (Chapter Eleven) are generally designed to be objective; most other assessments are subjective. Subjective assessments are increasingly popular for the reasons shown in Table 2.7, and objective assessments remain widely used for the reasons shown in Table 2.8.

Some people confuse quantitative with objective assessments, assuming that quantitative assessments must be objective. To the contrary, many subjective assessments yield quantitative results.

Table 2.7. Advantages of Subjective Assessments

Subjective assessments evaluate many important skills that objective tests cannot, including organization, synthesis, and problem-solving skills. Subjective assessments are the tools of choice when encouraging creativity and originality, as traditional multiple-choice tests have, by definition, only one correct response and therefore encourage convergent thinking.

Subjective assessments can assess skills directly. Many faculty and staff would agree, for example, that a writing sample is more convincing evidence of a student's writing skill than answers to multiple-choice questions on how to write. Similarly, watching a student nurse draw a blood sample provides more compelling evidence of skill than the student's answers to multiple-choice questions on how to draw blood.

Subjective assessments promote deep, lasting learning. You probably learned and remember far more from the research papers you wrote in college than from the studying you did for multiple-choice final exams.

Scoring procedures for subjective assessments allow nuances. On a subjective math test, for example, students can receive partial credit for doing part of a problem correctly, but on a multiple-choice math test, they usually receive no credit for an incorrect answer, even if they do much of their work correctly.

Table 2.8. Advantages of Objective Assessments

Students can provide a great deal of information on a broad range of learning goals in a relatively short time. Testing experts call this *efficiency.* If you want to assess a wide array of concepts and skills, a forty-five-minute multiple-choice test will yield more comprehensive information on student learning than a forty-five-minute essay test.

Objective assessments encourage broader—albeit shallower—learning than subjective assessments because of their efficiency. Asking students to write a paper on a particular poem by Wordsworth is a good choice if the learning goal is to develop a thorough understanding of that poem, but it is a poor choice if the learning goal is to develop a general understanding of Romantic poetry. For the latter goal, an objective test asking students to react to a variety of Romantic poems might be a better approach.

Objective assessments are fast and easy to score, although they are difficult and time-consuming to construct. If they are stored securely so they can be reused, the payback on the time spent writing them increases.

Objective assessment results can be summarized into a single number—a performance indicator (Chapter One)—making them appealing to those governing or funding colleges and programs.

Rubric scores (Chapter Nine), for example, are subjective ratings of student work that can be quantified and analyzed statistically.

Indeed, every assessment is inherently subjective because its directions, questions, problems, and scoring criteria are all developed through subjective, albeit expert, judgment. Not only assessments but the standards or benchmarks against which results are interpreted (Chapter Fifteen) are determined subjectively. So "objective" assessments are not necessarily more accurate or of better quality than "subjective" assessments.

Which Assessment Strategy Is Best?

Every assessment strategy has potential value. Which are best for your particular situation depends primarily on the purpose of your assessment and the learning outcomes you are assessing. Other factors, such as resource availability and campus culture, can also affect your decision. Table 2.9 gives general guidelines on when to use the assessment tools discussed in the following chapters.

Table 2.9. Assessment Strategies to Consider

If you want to . . .	Consider using . . .
Assess thinking and performance skills	Assignments or prompts (Chapter Ten) planned and evaluated using scoring guides or rubrics (Chapter Nine)
Assess knowledge, conceptual understanding, or skill in application and analysis	Multiple-choice tests (Chapter Eleven)
Assess attitudes, values, dispositions, or habits of mind	Reflective writing, surveys, focus groups, or interviews (Chapter Twelve)
Draw an overall picture of student learning	Portfolios (Chapter Thirteen)
Compare your students against peers elsewhere	Published tests or surveys (Chapter Fourteen)

Time to Think, Discuss, and Practice _____

1. A faculty member wants to assess the writing and research skills of students majoring in English literature. Brainstorm examples of the following that could be helpful in assessing these skills:

    -   Direct evidence of student learning
    -   Evidence of learning processes
    -   Qualitative evidence

2. The international studies faculty wish to interview graduating seniors on their perceptions of the program. Seniors in the program typically take many different combinations of courses in a variety of departments, so these interviews can't be conducted as a class activity. Brainstorm three approaches that the faculty might use to convince seniors to participate in an out-of-class interview.

3. Faculty in your department would like to survey recent graduates to assess their satisfaction with your program and identify areas for improvement. Assume the survey will be mailed to a random sample of recent graduates. Brainstorm three feasible strategies to maximize the participation rate.

Recommended Readings_____

The following readings are recommended along with the references cited in this chapter.

Astin, A. W. (1991). *Assessment for excellence.* New York: Macmillan.

Banta, T. W. (2006). Reliving the history of large-scale assessment in higher education. *Assessment Update, 18*(4), 3–4, 15.

Campbell, D. T., & Stanley, J. C. (1963). *Experimental and quasi-experimental designs for research.* Skokie, IL: Rand McNally.

Duvall, B. (1994). Obtaining student cooperation for assessment. In T. H. Bers & M. L. Mittler (Eds.), *Assessment testing: Myths and realities* (pp. 47–52). New Directions for Community Colleges, no. 88. San Francisco: Jossey-Bass.

Porter, S. R. (2004). Raising response rates: What works? In S. R. Porter (Ed.), *Overcoming survey research problems* (pp. 5–12). New Directions for Institutional Research, no. 121. San Francisco: Jossey-Bass.

Prus, J., & Johnson, R. (1994). A critical review of student assessment options. In T. H. Bers & M. L. Mittler (Eds.), *Assessment testing: Myths and realities* (pp. 69–83). New Directions for Community Colleges, no. 88. San Francisco: Jossey-Bass.

Stufflebeam, D. L. (2000). *The CIPP model for evaluation.* In D. L. Stufflebeam, G. F. Madaus, & T. Kellaghan (Eds.), *Evaluation models: Viewpoints on educational and human services evaluation* (2nd ed., pp. 279–318). Norwell, MA: Kluwer.

Wiggins, G. (1990). The case for authentic assessment. *Practical Assessment, Research and Evaluation, 2*(2). Retrieved September 16, 2008, from http://PAREonline.net/getvn.asp?v=2&n=2.

CHAPTER 3

What Is Good Assessment?

Some Valuable Ideas You'll Find in This Chapter

- The best assessments are those whose results are used to improve teaching and learning and inform planning and budgeting decisions.

- The greater the variety of assessment evidence, the more confidently you can make inferences about student learning.

- Students should have multiple opportunities to develop and achieve key learning goals.

- It is unfair to place full responsibility for a key program or institutional goal on one faculty member or one course.

- Assessment is a perpetual work in progress.

More than anything else, a good assessment is one whose results are used to improve teaching and learning and inform planning and budgeting decisions (Chapter Eighteen). In order for results to be used with confidence in these ways, assessments must have the four characteristics in Table 3.1.

This chapter focuses on just the first of these four criteria: designing assessments to yield reasonably accurate and truthful information on what students have learned. Chapter Four discusses assessment purpose, and Chapter Five examines ways to engage faculty and staff. Student learning goals are discussed in detail in Chapter Eight, but clear and important student learning goals are the underlying foundation of each of the other criteria

Table 3.1. The Four Characteristics of Useful Assessments

They *yield reasonably accurate and truthful information* on what students have learned, so that we can use the assessment results with confidence to make plans and decisions.

They *have a clear purpose*, so that the assessment results are valued and don't end up sitting on a shelf.

They *engage faculty and staff*, so the assessment becomes a useful part of the fabric of campus life.

They flow from and focus on *clear and important student learning goals*, so the results provide information on matters the college or university cares about.

and consequently are addressed in all of these chapters—and, indeed, throughout most of this book.

Is It Possible to Assess Completely Accurately?

No, it's not possible to determine with complete confidence exactly what students have and haven't learned, because we can't get inside their heads to find out what they truly know and what they don't. The best we can do is to look at samples of their behavior—what they write, produce, say, and perform—and from those samples try to estimate or infer what they truly know. Even under the best of circumstances, making an inference from these snapshots of behavior is bound to be at least somewhat inaccurate because of what psychometricians call *measurement error*—fluctuations in human performance that we can't completely control—such as:

- Whether a student is ill on the day she completes an assignment or takes a test

- Whether a student is preoccupied with an argument he's had and isn't focusing sufficiently to do his best

- Memory fluctuations (we all periodically blank out on key names and facts)

- Luck in whether a particular assignment or test question focuses on something a student knows well (we all learn some aspects of a subject better than others)

- Luck in guessing on multiple-choice questions

- Mental set (sometimes we have flashes of insight; sometimes we seem inexplicably in a mental rut)

A perfect assessment—one giving absolutely accurate information on what students have learned—thus does not exist. As Carol Geary Schneider and Lee Shulman (2007) have noted, "One of the most dangerous and persistent myths in American education is that the challenges of assessing student learning will be met if only the right instrument can be found" (p. vii). We must instead simply strive to make assessments sufficiently truthful that we will have reasonable confidence in our findings and can use them with enough assurance to make decisions about goals, curricula, and teaching strategies. The approaches discussed in this chapter will help.

Start with Clear and Important Goals

Assessments yield reasonably accurate, truthful results and are used only if they truly assess what we want them to assess: our learning goals for our students. This is why it is critical to begin with clear statements of the most important things you want students to learn from your course or program. Chapter Eight discusses how to articulate clear statements of student learning goals.

Next, plan your assessments carefully to make sure they assess the important goals that you've articulated. Aim not only to assess your key learning goals but to do so in a balanced, representative way. If your goals are that students understand what happened during a particular historical period and evaluate the decisions key individuals made during that period, your test should balance questions on basic conceptual understanding with questions assessing evaluation skills.

If the assessment is a test, plan the test by creating a test blueprint: a list of the key learning goals to be assessed by the test and the number of points or questions to be devoted to each learning goal (Chapter Eleven). Then write the test questions so each clearly corresponds to the learning goal you've identified for it in your test blueprint. This creates a fair, balanced test.

Similarly, before creating an assignment, write a scoring guide or rubric (Chapter Nine): a list of the key things you want students to learn by completing the assignment and to demonstrate on the completed assignment. Then write the assignment itself, making sure that it will elicit from students what you are looking for.

Finally, have clear, appropriate standards for acceptable and exemplary student performance (Chapters Nine and Fifteen). If you are evaluating student papers, for example, have a clear sense of the characteristics of outstanding, adequate, and poor work.

Use a Variety of Assessments

Because any one assessment is imperfect and imprecise, collect more than one kind of evidence of what students have learned. The greater the variety of evidence, the more confidently you can infer that students have indeed learned what you want them to. Lee Shulman (2007) calls this a "union of insufficiencies" (p. 24). Instead of assessing students solely through multiple-choice tests or writing assignments, assess them using a combination of tests, writing assignments, and other projects. One assignment might be a panel presentation, another a chart or diagram, and a third a written critique. Students might convey the essence of a novel's protagonist through a diagram, video, or oral presentation rather than only through a traditional essay. If you are assessing learning across an entire program, rather than give students just one culminating examination, look at samples of papers students have written or perhaps internship supervisors' ratings of their skills. Table 10.1 offers other suggestions for varying assignments.

Using a variety of assessments acknowledges the variety of prior knowledge, cultural experiences, and learning styles that students bring to the classroom:

- Maria is not a strong writer but can easily visualize concepts. She will better demonstrate her understanding of a complex concept if she can draw a diagram rather than write an explanation.

- Robert's culture values collaboration, and he learns more from working with others than by studying alone. He will better demonstrate his understanding if he can work with others on a group presentation rather than make a solo presentation.

- Janice is not a good test taker but is very creative. She will better demonstrate her understanding if she can create a video explaining a complex concept rather than take a test.

- Jason was home-schooled in a home without a computer, so he is still insecure using a computer. He will better demonstrate his understanding on a paper-and-pencil test than on a computer-based test.

- Leah attended a high school that stressed rote memorization and drill. She will better demonstrate her knowledge of key events in American history on a fill-in-the-blank test than in a term paper that requires critical thinking skills.

- Omar has poor test-taking skills. If question 2 stumps him, he'll likely spend the whole testing period pondering that question and never answer the remaining ones. He will better demonstrate his understanding by writing a term paper than by taking a multiple-choice test.

Thus, if all your course assignments are oral presentations, you may unfairly penalize those who have truly mastered the material but are poor speakers, unless one of your major learning goals is to strengthen oral communication skills.

As you plan multiple assessment strategies, be sure to include, if possible, direct—tangible, visible, and self-explanatory—evidence of student learning such as samples of student work. As discussed in Chapter Two, this kind of evidence is more compelling than indirect evidence such as surveys or self-ratings. Because we are preparing students to lead productive and fulfilling lives, assessments that mirror real-world experiences can be especially useful.

Multiple assessment strategies are especially important for goals to instill attitudes and values because direct evidence of these goals is often difficult or impossible to collect. Chapter Twelve discusses strategies to assess these traits.

Choose and Create Fair and Unbiased Assessment Strategies___

No one wants to use an assessment tool with obvious stereotyping or offensive material. But it's easy to use tools that inadvertently favor some students over others. The following tips minimize the possibility of inequities:

Don't rush.   Assessments yielding fair and reasonably accurate and truthful results take some time and thought to choose or create. The maxim "garbage in, garbage out" applies here. Assessments thrown together at the last minute invariably include flaws that greatly affect the fairness, accuracy, and usefulness of the results.

Aim for assignments and questions that are crystal clear.   If students find a question difficult to understand, they may answer what they think is the spirit of the question rather than the question itself, which may not match your intent. Creating clear assignments, test questions, and survey questions is discussed further in Chapters Ten, Eleven, and Twelve, respectively.

Guard against unintended bias.   A fair and unbiased assessment tool describes activities that are equally familiar to all and uses words that have common meanings to all. A test question on quantitative skills that asks students to analyze football statistics might not be fair to women, and using scenarios involving business situations may be biased against students studying the humanities, unless you are specifically assessing understanding of these topics. One way to detect some kinds of potential bias, especially in surveys and interviews, is to ask, "If someone were hoping to see the exact opposite of the results that I'm hoping for, would he or she conduct the same assessment in the same way?" If you're trying to collect information to support the need for increased funding for library materials, for example, imagine you're trying to cut back on funding (difficult though this may be for you!). Would you still ask the same questions and phrase them the same way?

Ask a variety of people with diverse perspectives to review assessment tools before implementing them. This helps make sure the tools are clear, appear to assess what you want them to, and don't favor people of a particular background. Chapter Five discusses the importance of collaboration, and here it is especially important. If you are developing an assessment for a course, share it with those teaching the same, similar, or related courses such as the next course in a sequence. You'll help promote communication on what you're all collectively trying to accomplish. If you are considering published tests or surveys, Chapter Fourteen offers questions to consider as you review them.

Try out assessment tools with a small group of students before using them on a larger scale. Consider asking some students to "think out loud" as they answer a test question; their thought processes should match those you intended. Read students' responses to make sure their answers make sense, and ask students if they found anything unclear or confusing.

Attitudes, values, and the like are particularly difficult to assess fairly and accurately. Chapter Twelve offers specific suggestions on ways to do so.

Conduct Assessments Ethically

A number of professional organizations engaged in the assessment of human performance have developed statements of ethical standards. Virtually all of these statements agree on several principles of good practice for conducting assessments. Principles of good practice for sharing and using assessment results fairly, ethically, and responsibly are discussed in Chapters Seventeen and Eighteen, respectively.

Inform Students of the Nature, Purpose, and Results of Each Assessment

Students should be fully informed about each assessment and how it fits into their overall learning experience. Peter Ewell (1996) has noted that we often operate with four curricula—designed, delivered, expectational, and experienced—that may not be congruent. Increasing this congruence through communication with students is thus not only an ethical practice but also good pedagogy. Students learn more effectively when they understand the goals, rationale, and structure of courses and programs (see Table 18.3).

Help students understand what and why they are learning by sharing answers to the questions in Table 8.6, along with your learning goals, rubrics, and test blueprints. It may be helpful to revise Web pages, catalogue descriptions, program brochures, course syllabi, and the like to make this information clear and easy to find.

If students have add-on graduation or program completion requirements, such as compiling a portfolio, completing a survey, participating in a focus group, or taking a comprehensive examination, inform them of this in writing and as early in their program as possible, as discussed in Chapter Two.

Assessment activities can be valuable learning opportunities for students only if they receive prompt, concrete feedback on their performance (Butler & McMunn, 2006). To require students to participate in an assessment activity and not give them feedback on their performance diminishes the overall value of the assessment experience and is inconsiderate of their contributions to an assessment effort.

Protect the Privacy and Dignity of Those Who Are Assessed

Take appropriate security precautions before, while, and after you conduct an assessment, and protect the confidentiality of individually identifiable information. Password-protect computer files with identifiable information, and store paper records with identifiable information in locked file cabinets. If several people are reviewing samples of student work or accessing a computer file, removing information that identifies individuals may be a wise precaution.

While it is important to protect student privacy, faculty and staff must have sufficient information to be able to do their jobs, and this can often mean sharing identifiable information. Some faculty and staff, for example, periodically hold department meetings to discuss the progress of each of the students in their program. They also consult with their colleagues about their students less formally; a faculty member concerned about a student's slipping performance might consult with the student's advisor for ideas on how to help this student get back on track. Faculty and staff are simply carrying out an important part of their responsibilities when they hold such conversations, and considering identifiable assessment results can make the conversations more fruitful.

Give Students Ample Opportunities to Learn the Skills Needed for the Assessment

The second step of the assessment process (Chapter One) is ensuring that every student in your course, program, or college has sufficient opportunity to achieve every fundamental goal that you've articulated. All students, no matter what curricular and cocurricular choices they make, deserve to have confidence that if they complete their work successfully, they will be prepared for what lies next, be it the next course in a sequence, a subsequent program, or their life work. This is called *curricular alignment* and is discussed in Chapter Seven.

If you are truly serious about ensuring that students achieve key learning goals, design the curriculum to ensure that students have multiple opportunities to develop and achieve those goals. It is simply not fair to place full responsibility for student achievement of a major goal on just one assignment, one faculty member, or one required course.

Multiple learning opportunities in courses. We all learn best with practice (see Table 18.3), so give students repeated, purposeful opportunities to learn the major concepts and skills that they will be assessed and graded on. If one of your course goals is that students develop an appreciation of other cultures, for example, include in your syllabus several assignments and classwork specifically designed to help students develop this appreciation.

Multiple learning opportunities in programs. Students should have repeated opportunities to achieve major program goals throughout the program. If a program goal is that students write effectively, for example, the curriculum should ensure that all students, regardless of curricular choices, take multiple courses in which they learn how the discipline defines good writing, learn how to write in the discipline, and receive constructive feedback on their writing.

Multiple learning opportunities for institutional goals. If an institutional goal is to instill a commitment to community service, for example, curricula and degree requirements should ensure that every student, regardless of major or extracurricular involvement, has ample opportunity to develop this commitment before graduation. Simply offering service opportunities that students may or may not participate in, at their option, will not suffice.

Use proven pedagogies. Give students plenty of practice and feedback, and find ways to engage and encourage them. Positive contact with faculty greatly influences the performance of some students.

Evaluate Student Work Fairly, Equitably, and Consistently

No matter how carefully assessments are constructed, most remain essentially subjective (Chapter Two) and thus prone to unintentional evaluation errors and biases, as discussed at the beginning of this chapter. Rubrics (Chapter Nine) can help ensure fair, consistent evaluation of student work, but they are nonetheless subject to scoring errors and biases such as those in Table 3.2.

Table 3.3 suggests strategies to minimize scoring errors and biases and achieve greater scoring consistency. Some of these strategies are easier said than done, of course, and following all these steps can be time-consuming and expensive. (Faculty and staff

Table 3.2. Examples of Scoring Errors

Leniency errors occur when faculty and staff judge student work better than most of their colleagues would judge it.

Generosity errors occur when faculty and staff tend to use only the high end of the rating scale.

Severity errors occur when faculty and staff tend to use only the low end of the rating scale.

Central tendency errors occur when faculty and staff tend to avoid both extremes of the rating scale.

Halo effect bias occurs when faculty and staff let their general impression of a student influence their scores, perhaps giving higher scores to a student who seeks extra help or lower scores to a student who is quiet in class.

Contamination effect bias occurs when faculty and staff let irrelevant student characteristics (such as handwriting or ethnic background) influence their scores.

Similar-to-me effect bias occurs when faculty and staff give higher scores to students whom they see as similar to themselves, such as students who share their research interests.

First-impression effect bias occurs when faculty and staff's early opinions distort their overall judgment. A student who presents her outstanding research in a sloppy poster display might suffer from first-impression effect bias, as might a student whose generally excellent essay opens with a poorly constructed sentence.

Contrast effect bias occurs when faculty and staff compare a student against other students instead of against established standards. Faculty might give a rating of "unacceptable" to the worst paper they read, even though the paper meets stated minimally acceptable standards.

Rater drift occurs when faculty and staff unintentionally redefine scoring criteria over time. As faculty and staff tire while scoring student work, some get grumpy and more stringent, while others skim student work more quickly and score more leniently.

Table 3.3. Strategies to Minimize Scoring Errors and Biases

Consider using a descriptive rubric (Chapter Nine)—one that describes student achievement at each of the rubric's performance levels.

Remove or obscure identifying information from student work before it is scored. This is called *blind scoring.*

Practice scoring consistently when faculty and staff are scoring student work together. First, discuss and come to agreement on the meaning of each performance level. Then score a few samples of student work, share your scores, and discuss and resolve any differences in your ratings. Once you're reasonably sure that you're all interpreting the rubric consistently, you can begin the actual scoring.

Have each sample of student work scored independently by at least two faculty or staff members. If those two disagree on any sample of student work, have that work scored by a third person to break the tie.

Rescore the first few samples when scoring many samples of student work to guard against rater drift.

Periodically schedule a refresher scoring practice session when faculty and staff are scoring large numbers of papers, in which they all compare their scores and discuss and resolve any emerging differences.

may expect extra compensation for spending hours or days scoring student work beyond that in the courses they teach.) To decide if these steps are worthwhile, consider the following questions.

Do we have a problem with scoring errors and bias? Look at the scores that faculty and staff are awarding. Are they reasonably consistent across faculty and staff, or are some faculty and staff more lenient or more stringent than the majority? If there may be reason for concern, do a spot check: ask a faculty or staff member or two to rescore—blind—a few student work samples to verify that there is indeed a problem with consistency.

What are the consequences of scoring errors or bias? If the scores are simply part of several pieces of information used to inform faculty and staff about teaching and learning successes and concerns, it may not be worthwhile to invest time and resources in rigorously eliminating scoring errors and bias. But if the scores are used to help make major decisions, such as whether students graduate or whether a program continues to be funded, ensuring accurate, consistent scoring becomes extremely important.

Are the scores of sufficient quality that we can use them with confidence for their intended purpose? If you don't think so, you may need to increase your investment in scoring accuracy and consistency.

Look at Enough Evidence_____

Obviously, the more assessment evidence you collect and consider, the greater confidence you will have in your conclusions about student learning. Faculty and staff who look at three hundred essays will have more confidence in their conclusions about student writing skills than those who look at ten essays. But more evidence means more precious time spent collecting and examining it, so an important question is, "How much evidence is enough?"

Should You Collect Evidence from Everyone or Just a Sample?

The temptation to ask only samples of students to participate in assessments of program or institutional goals is strong. Published test and surveys such as the Collegiate Learning Assessment (Council for Aid to Education, 2006) and the National Survey of Student Engagement (Indiana University, 2007) can be quite expensive, and the cost of administering them to everyone may be unaffordable. While the direct costs of locally designed surveys, focus groups, and interviews are not as high, the time needed to administer these to all students may be prohibitive.

Another reason to ask only samples of students to participate is that a representative sample can yield information that is almost as accurate as information from everyone. Consider that professional pollsters, trying to determine the opinions of millions of people, rarely survey more than a thousand people. If you've seen the results of such surveys, you may have noticed that pollsters note an error margin of about 3 percent. This means that if a pollster finds, for example, that 76 percent of the public think an elected official is doing a good job, the pollster is very sure (actually 95 percent sure) that if everyone could be surveyed, between 73 percent and 79 percent (76 percent plus and minus 3 percent) would say that the official is doing a good job.

The drawback of asking only a sample of students to participate is that, because participation is obviously not required, it can be very difficult to convince students to participate. Even if they do, they may not give the assessment their best thought and effort. Chapter Two discusses strategies to motivate students to participate in voluntary add-on assessments. If possible, a better strategy than inviting a sample of students to participate in an assessment is to require all students to participate and then choose a representative sample to examine.

How Much Evidence Should You Look At?

The sample size you choose depends on how great an error margin you're willing to tolerate. Table 3.4 lists the error margins of various sample sizes.

While professional pollsters often aim for samples of about a thousand people, with an error margin of 3 percent, unless your assessments may lead to major (read expensive) changes, a sample of no more than three or four hundred is probably sufficient. What if that many is still too large to be practical? What if faculty and staff have the time to score only, say, fifty or a hundred essays? You can use smaller sample sizes—whatever number you think is feasible—if you recognize that your error margin will be larger. If the assessment will likely lead only to minor changes, such as adjusting the curriculum of a course or two, a smaller sample may be fine. Consider looking at sequential samples. Start with a representative sample of, say, ten essays. Then look at another representative sample of ten essays to see if they add any new insight. If they do, look at a third sample of ten essays. Eventually you will look at a sample of ten essays that adds no new insight, and at that point, you may conclude that you have looked at enough essays.

What if you have a very small program or college? Obviously, you don't need to examine 300 papers if you have only 250 students in your course or program. Table 3.5 lists the sample sizes needed for a 5 percent error margin from some relatively small groups of students.

The ultimate answer to, "How much evidence is enough?" is to use your common sense. Collect enough evidence to feel reasonably confident that you have a representative sample of what your students have learned and can do. The sample should be large enough and representative enough that you can use the results with confidence to make decisions about a course or program. And take careful steps to ensure the accuracy and truthfulness of your assessment findings.

Table 3.4. Error Margins of Various Sample Sizes

Random Sample Size	Error Margin
9,604	1%
2,401	2%
1,067	3%
600	4%
384	5%
264	6%
196	7%

Table 3.5. Sample Sizes Needed from Small Groups for 5 Percent Error Margins

Number of Students You Are Sampling From	Random Sample Size
1,000	278
500	217
350	184
200	132
100	80
50	44

What Is an Acceptable Participation Rate?

Just because you invite students to participate in a survey doesn't mean that they will all do so. In this age of survey fatigue, it is not uncommon to have a participation rate of only 25 percent—or less—of those invited. How high a participation rate should you aim for?

This question has both simple and complex answers. The simple answer is that survey experts have traditionally aimed to have 70 to 80 percent of those contacted participate in a survey or interview and have considered a 50 percent participation rate minimally adequate. The complex answer is that the quality of participants is more important than the quantity. In other words, having participants who are truly representative of the group from which you are sampling can be more important evidence of your assessment's credibility than its participation rate.

Imagine that faculty and staff at two large universities, each graduating about eight thousand students annually, want to learn about their seniors' self-perceptions of their thinking skills. Faculty and staff at Eastern State University send a survey to all eight thousand seniors, of which 400 are returned. Faculty and staff at Western State University send a survey to a random sample of six hundred seniors. They make strong efforts to convince students to complete and return the survey and, as a result, 360 are returned.

Which is the better approach? While more students completed Eastern State's survey, its response rate is only 5 percent. This makes it unlikely that the respondents represent all seniors. Some cohorts may be underrepresented (perhaps students in certain majors or students with certain experiences), which calls the value of the survey into question. Western State's survey yields a more respectable 60 percent return rate, which gives more confidence that the respondents are a good cross-section of all seniors, even though the number of returned surveys is smaller. Furthermore, Western State's approach may be more cost-effective;

it may be less expensive to survey six hundred students intensively than eight thousand scattershot. Relatively small-scale assessments with high participation rates may thus yield more credible results than larger assessments with low participation rates.

No matter what your participation rate is, collect demographic information on the participants. When you share the results, report the participation rate and describe how representative the participants are of the group you're surveying (Chapter Sixteen), so audience members can judge for themselves how credible the survey results are.

How Might You Choose a Representative Sample?

Samples can be selected in a variety of ways. Here are three ways particularly appropriate for student learning assessment.

"Simple" random samples. These kinds of samples, in which every student has an equal chance of being selected, are a straightforward way to ensure that the sample is representative of all students. A simple random sample might be drawn by writing every student's name on a separate slip of paper, putting all the slips in a bag, shaking the bag, and drawing out as many names as you need. This can be done electronically by using software to generate a random sample. If such software isn't available (check with technical support staff), select students based on the last few digits of their student identification numbers, because the last digits are usually randomly distributed. If you have 250 students and wish to examine writing samples from 50 (20 percent) of them, for example, you could choose all students whose student identification numbers end in, say, 4 or 5 (20 percent of all possible digits 0 through 9).

Simple random samples aren't always practical. If you want to administer an in-class survey, for example, it wouldn't be feasible to choose a random sample of the entire student body, go to every class, and ask just the sampled students in each class to complete the survey while the rest of the students sit idle. If a simple random sample is not realistic, other kinds of samples are possible.

Cluster random samples. These kinds of samples are taken by choosing a random sample of subgroups of students and then collecting information from everyone in those subgroups. You could take a random sample of first-year writing classes, for example, and then assess essays written by everyone in those classes. Or you could take a random sample of floors in the residence halls and interview everyone on those floors.

Purposeful or judgment samples. These kinds of samples are carefully but not randomly chosen so that, in your judgment, they are representative of the students you are assessing. Suppose that you want to assess essays written by students in first-year writing classes and would like to select a random sample of classes. Unfortunately, you know that while some faculty will gladly cooperate, others will decline to provide you with copies of student essays. You can still obtain a good sample of essays by choosing, from those classes with cooperating faculty, a sample of classes that meet on various days and at various times and seem, in your judgment, to represent a good cross-section of all first-year writing classes.

Or suppose that you want to assess student learning in general education science courses. While students may meet this requirement by taking any of seventeen courses, 80 percent take one of just two courses: Introductory Biology and Introductory Geology. Collecting assessment information from just these two courses will be far simpler and more cost-effective than collecting information from all seventeen courses and will give useful information on 80 percent of your students.

Keep in mind that if you must use a small or nonrandom sample or have a low participation rate, it's especially important to collect information showing that your sample is representative of students in general.

Consider Assessment a Perpetual Work in Progress

Good assessments are not once-and-done affairs. They are part of an ongoing, organized, and systematized effort to understand and improve teaching and learning.

When assessment is truly systematized, some assessment activity is happening every year. Assessments conducted just once every five or ten years take more time in the long run because there is a good chance that no one will remember, find the documentation for, or understand the rationale behind the last assessment. This means far more time is spent planning and designing a new assessment—in essence, reinventing the wheel. Imagine trying to balance your checking account once a year rather than every month or your students cramming for a final rather than studying over an entire term, and you can see how difficult and frustrating infrequent assessments can be compared to those conducted routinely.

"Systematized" does not necessarily mean doing exactly the same thing, semester after semester or year after year. Some good synonyms are *progressive, iterative,* and *spiraled.* As David Hollowell,

Michael Middaugh, and Elizabeth Sibolski (2006) have noted, a "planning document is not an immutable course of actions" (p. 7). As the needs of your students evolve in a rapidly changing world, so will your goals, curricula, teaching methods, and assessment practices. There is no point in repeating assessments that have become outdated or no longer provide new insight, so periodically take time to sit back with your colleagues and evaluate your assessment efforts and their outcomes. Chapter Nineteen discusses this further.

Should You Document Evidence of the Quality of Your Assessment Methods?

The answer depends on how the results will be used. An assessment used to make minor curricular modifications does not need thorough evidence of its quality. But assessments that help determine placement of incoming students, whether expensive modifications should be implemented, or whether a program should be terminated need more compelling evidence of their quality. Assessments whose findings are likely to be challenged (Chapter Seventeen) also need evidence of their quality.

Obviously the more rigorous and extensive your assessment evidence is, the more compelling it is, but also the more time-consuming it is to collect and evaluate. So balance the need for quality with the need for cost-effectiveness.

One important way to document the quality of assessments is to keep records of everything that has been done to maximize assessment quality. This can include reviews of assessment tools by others, tryouts of assessment strategies, rubrics used to score student work, blind scorings by colleagues, and the other strategies discussed in this chapter. Should you decide to take further steps to evaluate the quality of your assessment activities, Chapter Sixteen discusses how to do so.

The Role of Institutional Review Boards in Assessment

Title 45, Part 46 of the Code of Federal Regulations (U.S. Department of Health and Human Services, 2005) describes federal policy for the protection of human research subjects. The regulations stipulate that colleges must establish institutional review boards (IRBs) to ensure that research protects and poses no significant risk or threat to the rights and welfare of human subjects. There are three levels of review: full review (which requires appearing before the entire IRB), expedited review (in which at least one member of the IRB reviews the research plan), and exempted from review (under which the research plan must still be sent to the IRB).

The regulations define research as "a systematic investigation, including research development, testing, and evaluation, designed to develop or contribute to generalizable knowledge." Two kinds of research activities are exempt from the policy. One is research conducted in educational settings involving normal educational practices, such as research on instructional strategies or the effectiveness of teaching methods. The other exemption is for research involving the use of educational tests, surveys, interviews, and observations. The only exception to this second exemption is when the information obtained can be linked to the subjects *and* any disclosure of their responses places them at risk of liability or might damage their financial standing, employability, or reputation.

Should an assessment effort come under IRB review? Some colleges take the position that their assessment activities are "action research" (Chapter One), designed only to inform local teaching and learning practices and not to develop or contribute to generalizable knowledge. Under this position, faculty and staff are not engaged in research as defined by this policy, the assessment activities are exempt from the policy, and there is no reason to involve the IRB.

Some colleges take the position that they conduct assessments in established educational settings involving normal educational practices, or the assessments involve educational tests, surveys, and interviews that do not place subjects at risk. Under this position, assessment programs are exempt from this policy and there is no reason to involve the IRB.

Some other colleges require that assessment plans be submitted to the IRB with a formal request for exemption. Still other colleges take the position that assessment activities should undergo review. The rationale is that even though most assessments are not designed to contribute to generalizable knowledge, faculty and staff may decide later to share what they have learned with professional colleagues in a conference or journal.

When an assessment plan undergoes IRB review, the IRB requires the activities to meet the following criteria:

- Risks to subjects are minimized.
- Risks to subjects are reasonable.
- Selection of subjects is equitable.
- Informed consent is sought and documented.
- Adequate provisions are in place to ensure subjects' safety, protect their privacy, and maintain confidentiality.

Some colleges that require IRB review of assessment activities take the position that assessment activities pose minimal risk to subjects—no more than that "ordinarily encountered in daily life"—and therefore qualify for expedited review.

Obviously interpretations of the federal regulations vary, and there is no clear consensus on the role of IRBs in assessment programs. Ask the chair of your IRB for your college's interpretation.

Time to Think, Discuss, and Practice_____

1. The history faculty are assessing students' writing skills by evaluating senior theses for organization, focus, style, and mechanics.

   • Brainstorm three ways that the faculty might help ensure that this assessment will give them accurate, truthful information.

   • What might the faculty do to protect the privacy of the students and their professors as they conduct this assessment?

2. One of the goals of Mackenzie College's general education curriculum is for students to develop a tolerance for perspectives other than their own. Brainstorm three survey questions faculty might ask that you think would yield unbiased results.

3. The business program at Calvert College requires every student to compile a portfolio of his or her work. The program's ten faculty would like to assess student learning by examining a sample of portfolios from its two hundred graduating students. It takes about twenty-five minutes to review each portfolio. How many portfolios would you recommend that the faculty examine? Why?

Recommended Readings_____

The following readings are recommended along with the references cited in this chapter.

American Association for Higher Education. (1992). *Nine principles of good practice for assessing student learning.* Sterling, VA: Stylus.

Association of American Colleges and Universities. (2008). *Project on accreditation and assessment: Criteria for recognizing "good practice" in assessing liberal education as collaborative and integrative.* Washington, DC: Author.

Badger, E. (1999). Finding one's voice: A model for more equitable assessment. In A. L. Nettles & M. T. Nettles (Eds.), *Measuring up: Challenges minorities face in educational assessment* (pp. 53–69). Norwell, MA: Kluwer.

Campbell, D. T., & Fiske, D. W. (1959). Convergent and discriminant validation by the multitrait–multimethod matrix. *Psychological Bulletin, 56*(2), 81–105.

Joint Committee on Standards for Educational Evaluation. (1994). *The program evaluation standards: How to assess evaluations of educational programs* (2nd ed.). Thousand Oaks, CA: Sage.

Joint Committee on Testing Practices. (2004). *Code of fair testing practices in education.* Washington, DC: Author.

Krejcie, R., & Morgan, D. (1970). Determining sample size for research activities. *Educational and Psychological Measurement, 30*(3), 607–610.

National Council on Measurement in Education. (1995). *Code of professional responsibilities in educational measurement.* Madison, WI: Author.

National Research Council. (1993). *Leadership statement of nine principles on equity in educational testing and assessment.* Washington, DC: Author.

Parkes, J. (2000). The relationship between the reliability and cost of performance assessments. *Education Policy Analysis Archives, 8*(16). Retrieved September 16, 2008, from http://epaa.asu.edu/epaa/v8n16/.

Scheaffer, R. L., Mendenhall, W., & Ott, L. (1990). *Elementary survey sampling* (4th ed.). Boston: PWS-Kent.

Shavelson, R. J., & Huang, L. (2003). Responding responsibly to the frenzy to assess learning in higher education. *Change, 35*(1), 10–19.

PART TWO

Planning for Assessment Success

CHAPTER 4

Why Are You Assessing Student Learning?

Some Valuable Ideas You'll Find in This Chapter

- Don't undertake any assessments without a clear understanding of who will use the results and the decisions that the results will inform.
- One of the benefits of assessment is that it brings neglected issues to the forefront of campus conversations.
- Assessment is not a fad. Calls to be accountable for how public and private dollars are spent are not going to go away, and neither is the movement to be more effective in helping students learn.

At too many colleges, assessment results have ended up sitting on a shelf. They may have been disseminated in some form or briefly discussed in a meeting, but they have never really been used in any meaningful way. Why? Invariably the campus plunged into assessment without thinking first about why it was conducting the assessment, who needed the results, and what decisions the results would inform. If you want your assessment to be truly useful, consider the questions in this chapter before you plan an assessment strategy.

What Is Your Purpose: Improvement, Accountability, or Both?

Colleges and universities increasingly are emphasizing the assessment of student learning for two primary reasons:

- *Improvement.* Assessment can help improve the quality of teaching, learning, programs and services, and planning and decision making.

- *Accountability.* Assessment can validate current programs, services, and teaching and learning efforts and thereby secure continued support for them by demonstrating their effectiveness to concerned audiences. In other words, assessment can demonstrate accountability to these audiences.

Understanding these dual purposes will help you clarify your own aims.

Improving Educational Programs and Practices

Many of today's faculty are dedicated teachers who want to do the best possible job helping their students learn—and want and need feedback in order to do so. They are part of a revolution in higher education that Robert Barr and John Tagg (1995) have described as a new paradigm for teaching and learning.

Barr and Tagg have posited that faculty have traditionally viewed their responsibility as providing instruction rather than fostering student learning. Under this traditional, or teaching-centered, paradigm, faculty teach primarily by presenting lectures and assigning readings. Faculty teaching under this paradigm believe that if students don't learn the material and thereby earn a poor grade, the fault lies with the students, not themselves. Such faculty feel no sense of responsibility to reach out to students and help them learn.

Today faculty and staff increasingly follow a learning-centered paradigm. The paradigm draws on significant research (Chapter Eighteen) demonstrating that students learn more effectively when, among other things, they are actively involved in self-directed learning, they view their professor more as a guide than as a remote authority, and they receive frequent and prompt feedback on their work. Under this paradigm, faculty and staff are more directly involved in helping students learn. Of course, there will always be some unmotivated students who are cavalier about fulfilling their responsibilities and deserve to fail. But faculty and staff with a learning-centered orientation assume that if a significant number of their students do not achieve their learning goals, their curricula and teaching methods share at least some of the responsibility.

The purpose of assessment has expanded under this new paradigm. Under the teaching-centered model, the major, if not sole, purpose of assessment has been to assign student grades. Under the learning-centered paradigm, assessment is also used to improve curricula and pedagogies to bring about even greater learning. Assessment helps accomplish this in several ways:

Assessment helps students learn more effectively. This is because:

- The clear expectations that good assessment requires help students understand where they should focus their learning time and energies.
- Assessment, especially the grading process, motivates students to do their best.
- Assessment feedback helps students understand their strengths and weaknesses.

Assessment activities bring faculty and staff together to discuss important issues. Assessment leads faculty and staff to discuss what they teach, why, and their standards and expectations. In other words, assessment encourages faculty and staff to undertake a collaborative approach to teaching. Chapter Five discusses the importance of collaboration further.

Assessment activities help faculty and staff see how courses link together. Assessment encourages the formation of coherent, integrated programs. It helps faculty see how the courses they teach contribute to student success in subsequent pursuits. Chapter One discusses the importance of curricular coherence.

Assessment results provide feedback. Such feedback is essential to helping faculty and staff understand what is and is not working and decide what changes, if any, are warranted. The kinds of decisions that assessment results can inform are discussed later in this chapter.

Assessment brings neglected issues to the forefront. Some colleges have problems that have been swept under the carpet far too long: outdated general education curricula, a dysfunctional governance system, a fragmented and incoherent curriculum, or outmoded pedagogies. Launching an assessment effort often requires addressing issues that probably should have been tackled long ago. Some people find that assessment processes are even more useful than their products: these initial conversations and work yield greater benefits than the eventual assessment results.

Assessment helps faculty and staff make better decisions and use limited resources more wisely. At too many colleges, decisions are based more on hunches, intuition, anecdote, and lore than on solid evidence. Assessment increases the likelihood of making appropriate decisions and directing scarce resources where they are most needed.

Does assessment really improve student learning? In a word, no. As Carol Geary Schneider and Lee Shulman (2007) have noted, "Assessment all by itself is an insufficient condition for powerful learning and improvement" (p. viii). It is not the assessment itself but how faculty, staff, and institutional leaders use it that leads to improvements in student learning.

But does assessment have even this impact? Do the uses that are made of it indeed lead to better student learning? Systematic evidence is scant, although two important contributions are studies by Lisa Lattuca, Patrick Terenzini, and J. Fredricks Volkwein (2006) and Marvin Peterson and Marne Einarson (2001). Several other books (for example, Banta, Lund, Black, & Oblander, 1996; Bresciani, 2006, 2007) have compiled case studies in which assessment results have led to improvements in teaching and learning.

There is a good reason for this scarcity of evidence. As discussed in Chapter One, assessment is action research, not experimental research. While it is systematic, it is context specific rather than generalizable, informal rather than rigorous, and designed to inform individual rather than general practice. It thus does not have the precision, rigor, or generalizability of experimental research. These defining characteristics make it difficult to substantiate the overall impact of assessment.

Consider, for example, a group of faculty who assess their students' analysis skills with a simple rating scale or rubric (Chapter Nine) that they've devised to evaluate student papers. They're not satisfied with the results of their assessment, so they introduce a new problem-based learning pedagogy. The students' subsequent papers, evaluated using the same rubric, are much better. The faculty did their work carefully enough that they have confidence in the improvement they are seeing in their work. They have documented evidence that assessment has led to improved student learning.

But this is not experimental research. The faculty did not randomly assign students to the two cohorts of classes, and they did not adjust statistically for mitigating factors (perhaps the second group of students enrolled with better analytical skills). Indeed, the prospect of this kind of quantitative experimental design and analysis might scare some faculty off!

So this is not the kind of work that the faculty will publish in a peer-reviewed journal or present at a professional conference. And there is no way that the hundreds, if not thousands, of these kinds of success stories can be aggregated as meaningful research. But as many campus assessment coordinators can attest, these things are happening, in very individualized ways, every day.

Improving Planning and Decision Making

At many colleges and universities, decisions have been based on hunch, gut instinct, or anecdotal evidence. But resources are now so scarce and initiatives so expensive that we cannot afford to spend a dime without reasonable assurance that the investment will yield worthwhile dividends. This means basing decisions on systematic evidence garnered through assessment. Chapter Eighteen discusses using assessment results to inform planning and resource allocation, and Chapters Five and Nineteen emphasize the importance of doing so in fostering and maintaining a culture of assessment.

Accountability: Validating Programs and Practices

The second major reason to assess student learning is accountability: demonstrating the effectiveness of teaching and learning efforts, programs, and services to a variety of audiences. But what does *effectiveness* mean in this context? David Leveille (2005) has explained that accountability is "a systematic method to assure those inside and outside the higher education system that colleges and universities—and students—are moving toward desired goals" (p. 10). Assessment does this by documenting how effectively a course, program, or college achieves its goals, as first discussed in Chapter One.

Why is there increased demand for accountability? Calls for colleges and universities to demonstrate their effectiveness and be accountable to public audiences have skyrocketed in recent years. One driving force in the United States has been the federal government, which sets conditions that accrediting organizations must meet in order to be recognized by the U.S. Department of Education. American accrediting organizations have always required colleges and universities to provide evidence of their quality, but prior to the mid-1980s, this evidence largely consisted of resources and other inputs into the teaching and learning process: number of books in the library, number of faculty holding doctorates, number of dollars spent on academic programs, and so on. The assumption was that if these resources were in place, learning and other desired outcomes were bound to happen.

The federal government changed this approach in the mid-1980s when it mandated that accrediting organizations must require colleges and universities to provide evidence that they are achieving their missions through outcomes, not just inputs. Since the mission of all colleges and universities includes the education of students, colleges and universities must now provide evidence that students are achieving whatever learning goals the colleges have established. In 2006, the Commission on the Future of Higher Education, known as the Spellings Commission because it was appointed by U.S. Secretary of Education Margaret Spellings, vigorously endorsed this requirement (U.S. Department of Education, 2006).

Another force driving the accountability movement is increasingly constrained resources. Governing boards, legislators, and others funding higher education are taking a more business-like approach and asking whether their investments are yielding appropriate dividends. They are asking colleges and universities to provide substantive evidence that the investments yield significant results. Judith Eaton (2007) has noted that government, charities, religious institutions, and corporations are all being held increasingly accountable. She has argued that in this climate, it is "more and more difficult for colleges and universities, which spend hundreds of billions of public and private dollars annually, to argue persuasively that they should not be more accountable for what they produce with those dollars" (p. 21).

Will assessment ever go away? Is assessment another higher education fad that we can simply ride out? It's not likely. One obvious reason is that calls for greater accountability—and the U.S. regulations that have flowed from them—aren't likely to go away, and they may even accelerate. To be blunt, the American higher education community is now on borrowed time. If American colleges and universities assemble compelling evidence of student learning now, demonstrating though assessment that their students graduate with important skills such as writing, critical thinking, and analysis, they have a much better chance of warding off inappropriate mandates and are far more likely to receive the support they need. If they do not do so, the risk of an external mandate dictating what and how to assess—and in a useless, burdensome fashion—is very real.

An even more important reason, however, is that higher education's sharpened focus on helping students learn is likely to remain. Assessment is a critical tool to help ensure that teaching and learning in colleges and universities are the best that they can be.

Challenges in demonstrating accountability. Too often we in higher education and our audiences lack clear consensus on college, program, and even course goals. Not only may faculty and staff disagree among themselves about the key aims of a particular program, but public audiences may disagree with them even more. Faculty and staff may agree, for example, that they want students to develop a rich appreciation of the arts, while some public audiences may care only about job-related skills, delivered as inexpensively as possible.

Another challenge with demonstrating accountability is that many audiences want information on effectiveness in the form of an overall snapshot rather than the detailed feedback that students, faculty, and administrators find useful. Some public audiences may want a single test score on student writing performance, for example, while faculty and staff may prefer student portfolios of written work that give comprehensive feedback on student strengths and weaknesses and provide meaningful clues on how to improve teaching and support. Chapter One discusses performance indicators, which are quick snapshots of institutional performance.

Both of these challenges call for better communication both within a college community and with its external audiences. Understanding and communicating with assessment audiences is discussed below and in Chapter Seventeen.

Reconciling These Disparate Purposes

On the surface, the two major purposes of assessment—improvement and accountability—look very different and appear to call for different strategies. Assessing for public accountability seems to call for aggregated information on strengths, while assessing for improvement seems to call for detailed information on weaknesses. But these two purposes can be reconciled by planning assessments that yield detailed information on both strengths and weaknesses. The detailed information on weaknesses can be used for improvement, of course, while the detailed information on successes can build morale and reduce fears that any negative results will be used punitively (Chapter Five).

At the same time, detailed results can be aggregated into summaries that tell the story of successes for accountability purposes. As discussed in Chapter Seventeen, even weaknesses can be spun into a story of success by focusing on the changes and improvements being made to address disappointing results.

Who Will Use Your Findings?_____

Chapter Three began by noting that the fundamental characteristic of good assessment is yielding useful information that can help make worthwhile decisions. Assessment planning thus requires a clear understanding of who will use the findings to make these decisions. Table 4.1 lists some possibilities.

Once you've determined your assessment audiences, consider talking to representatives of them or at least people who are familiar with them, so you can design assessments that will meet their needs. Try to answer the following questions:

What are your audiences' perspectives? Do they understand your course, program, or college, or do they see it only in terms of their own roles and responsibilities? Do they have any prejudices or biases regarding your course, program, or college? Do they appreciate its history, values, culture, and environment? Are they aware of its strengths and weaknesses? Do they understand how your assessment might affect their responsibilities, actions, and decisions?

What are your audiences' needs and priorities? What matters to them? What do they value? Are they concerned with improvement, accountability, or both? What kind of support and help do

Table 4.1. Audiences for Assessment Results

Internal Audiences Largely Interested in Improvement
You (an individual faculty or staff member)
Faculty and staff
Assessment steering committee members

Audiences Interested in Both Improvement and Accountability
Campus leaders
Governing board members
Accreditation organizations
Alumni

Public Audiences Largely Interested in Accountability
Government officials and policymakers
Prospective students and their families
Foundations, alumni, and other donors
Prospective employers
Taxpayers and the public at large

they need from your assessment effort? Is their most pressing need for more resources, more attention, or more respect? Do they want support for the status quo or for initiating change?

Are your audiences' needs and expectations changing?   Many accreditors, for example, have far more rigorous expectations for assessment than they did just a few years ago.

What Decisions Will Your Assessment Results Inform?

One of the most important things to learn about assessment audiences is the decisions they need to make and the information they need in order to make those decisions. Table 4.2 lists examples of questions that may be of interest to your audiences. Tables 15.1 and Table 17.2 provide additional questions.

Table 4.2. Questions and Decisions That Assessment Results Might Inform

Audience	Questions of Particular Interest
Internal Audiences Largely Interested in Improvement	
You (an individual faculty or staff member)	Are my students learning the most important things I want them to learn? Are they learning what they need to succeed in their future endeavors?
	If they're not learning some important things, what are the stumbling points? How might I change my curriculum or teaching strategies to help them learn more effectively?
	Might new pedagogies or new technologies lead to improved student learning?
Faculty and staff	Are our students learning the most important things we want them to learn in this course or program? Are they learning what they need to succeed in their future endeavors?
	Are we getting better at helping our students learn? Do recent innovations, such as moves to online learning or learning communities, help students learn more effectively?
	If our students are not learning some important things, what are the stumbling points? How might we change what we're doing to help them learn more effectively?
	Might new pedagogies or new technologies lead to improved student learning? Would new or increased resources help students learn more effectively? Where and how would those resources have the greatest impact on student learning?
	Is this program of appropriate quality and value?
	Should we support proposed changes to it?

(Continued)

Table 4.2. (*Continued*)

Audience	Questions of Particular Interest
Audiences Interested in Both Improvement and Accountability (Validation)	
Campus leaders	Is this program of appropriate quality and value?
	Is it effective in achieving its goals? Are students successful?
	Is it operating efficiently?
	Might new pedagogies or new technologies lead to improved student learning? Would new or increased resources help students learn more effectively? Where and how would those resources have the greatest impact on student learning?
	Should we support proposed changes to this program?
Governing board members	Is this program or college of appropriate quality and value?
	Is it operating efficiently?
	Should we support proposed changes to it?
Accreditation organizations	Is this program or college of appropriate quality and value?
	Is it effective in achieving its goals? Are students successful?
Alumni	Is this program or college worthy of our investment and support?
Public Audiences Largely Interested in Accountability (Validation)	
Government officials and policymakers	Is this college worthy of our investment and support?
	How much does an education here cost to students and their families? Is it affordable to them?
	Are students successful in graduating, transferring to other colleges, and finding appropriate jobs?
	Is this college operating efficiently?
	Is it meeting regional or national needs?
	Do underrepresented students have sufficient access to an education at this college? Are they successful here?
Prospective students and their families	How much will this education cost? Is it affordable to me?
	Will this college be a good fit with my background, interests, and needs? What kinds of students enroll here?
	Are students successful in graduating, transferring to other colleges, and finding appropriate jobs?
Foundations and other donors	Is this program or college worthy of our investment or support?
	Is it effective in achieving its goals? Are students successful?
	Is it operating efficiently?
Prospective employers	Are this college's students graduating with the knowledge and skills we need in our employees?
Taxpayers and the public at large	Is this college worthy of our investment and support?
	Is this college operating efficiently?

Responding to External Pressures to Use a Particular Assessment

In the United States, recent public conversations on accountability have resulted in pressures and mandates on some colleges to adopt a particular assessment measure or strategy. Public colleges and universities may have mandates from their state or system offices to use a particular published instrument. Some colleges and universities belong to associations that are pressing their members to use particular instruments or report results publicly in particular ways. Other colleges belong to consortia that decide to use particular assessment strategies that some members find inappropriate.

We all feel resentful if we're not involved in a decision affecting us or if our voices aren't heeded. So our instinctive reaction to these kinds of pressures and mandates is to criticize them as inappropriate. But blunt criticisms may yield a defensive posture from the decision makers, leading to an impasse and ill feelings all around. So consider the alternative responses in Table 4.3.

If your campus is not under external pressures or mandates now, it may well be in the future. The best defense is a good offense, so start now to develop and use effective, appropriate assessment measures so that when the specter of external pressures or mandates arises, you can say, "We're already doing this, and we're doing it well, and here's the evidence."

Table 4.3. Responding to External Pressures and Mandates

Educate yourself. Why was this mandate or pressure imposed? Was it a well-intended but knee-jerk response to the threat of a worse mandate, or was it promoting some personal or political agenda?

Be open-minded. It's always possible that the mandated assessment measure or strategy may have value even if you weren't involved in the decision. Try it, and see how it works.

See if you can educate those exerting the mandate or pressure. Most educational leaders, government policymakers, business leaders, and other public audiences are uninformed about the complex topic of assessment. What can you do to help them learn how to choose, develop, and use appropriate assessment strategies? Can you try to educate your campus leaders and ask them to carry the message forward?

Use the mandate as an opportunity to launch needed conversations. If a mandated assessment of quantitative skills focuses on skills that you and your colleagues consider inappropriate, use the assessment as an opportunity to launch discussions on articulating the kinds of quantitative skills that you should teach and assess.

Show that another assessment is better by using it in tandem with the mandated assessment. Yes, this means more work in the short run, but it may well lead to a saner use of assessment resources in the long run.

Give the mandate some time. The truly ill-considered ones are often unwieldy and will fall on their faces soon enough. Be ready with a better conceived and more appropriate alternative when they do.

Recognize that we all share blame for the pickle we're in. If external audiences don't understand what we are doing and how well we are doing it, we have only ourselves to blame for not conveying our effectiveness in terms that others can grasp easily and quickly. If an external audience requires an inappropriate assessment, it is only because we haven't convinced them that we are already assessing student learning meaningfully and appropriately. Chapter Seventeen discusses strategies for sharing assessment results with external audiences.

Time to Think, Discuss, and Practice_____

1. Does each of these faculty have a learning-centered or a teaching-centered approach? Why do you think so?

   - In Dr. Alfred's classes, term papers are due on the last day of class. He grades them during the following week, and students can pick them up when the next term begins.

   - Dr. Berger wants students to discover principles on their own through homework problems rather than absorb them through a lecture.

   - Dr. Cowell views her job teaching calculus as identifying which students should continue as math majors and which should not.

   - Dr. Dietz views his job as designing a learning environment for his students.

2. The teacher education faculty at Cape May College require students to compile portfolios documenting achievement of the program's key learning goals. They assess the portfolios using a rubric (Chapter Nine).

   - Identify three possible audiences for the results of this assessment.

   - Is each audience interested in improvement, accountability, or both?

   - For each audience, brainstorm a decision that the audience might need to make that these results might inform.

Recommended Readings _____

The following readings are recommended along with the references cited in this chapter.

Association of American Colleges and Universities. (2004). *Our students' best work: A framework for accountability worthy of our mission.* Washington, DC: Author.

Association of American Colleges and Universities & Council for Higher Education Accreditation. (2008). *New leadership for student learning and accountability: A statement of principles, commitment to action.* Washington, DC: Authors.

Banta, T. W. (2007). Can assessment for accountability complement assessment for improvement? *Peer Review, 9*(2), 9–12.

Business–Higher Education Forum. (2004). *Public accountability for student learning in higher education: Issues and options.* Washington, DC: American Council on Education.

Callan, P. M., & Finney, J. E. (2002). Assessing educational capital: An imperative for policy. *Change, 34*(4), 25–31.

Crist, C., Guill, D., Harmes, P., & Lake, C. (1998). *Purposes of assessment.* Retrieved September 16, 2008, from www.essentialschools.org/cs/resources/view/ces_res/126.

CHAPTER 5

The Keys to a Culture of Assessment: Tangible Value and Respect

Some Valuable Ideas You'll Find in This Chapter

- Pervasive, ongoing assessment happens only when campus leaders are actively committed to it and when faculty are empowered as assessment leaders.

- There is no magic formula to creating a culture of assessment. What works on any campus depends on its culture, history, and values.

- Being flexible in requirements, expectations, and approaches is one of the keys to assessment success.

- Assessment is more likely to happen at campuses that actively encourage and value risk-taking behaviors.

- Offer curriculum development grants to help faculty and staff find time to address disappointing assessment results, thereby addressing the fear that such results will be used punitively.

- Academic freedom doesn't relieve faculty of their responsibility to ensure that all students have sufficient opportunity to achieve the goals that faculty collectively agree are essential.

- Don't expect to get everyone onboard.

The movement to assess student learning in higher education has been around for roughly a quarter of a century. Why, then, is there still resistance to assessment on many campuses? Marilee Bresciani (2006) suggests two underlying reasons: the value and importance

Table 5.1. Four Keys to Fostering a Culture of Assessment

Value campus culture and history.

Respect and empower people, especially faculty.

Value innovation and risk taking, especially in improving teaching.

Value assessment efforts, especially by supporting them with appropriate resources and infrastructure (Chapter Six) and using the results to inform important decisions on important goals (Chapter Eighteen).

of assessment are not understood, and assessment activities are not supported with appropriate resources. A third reason may be added to these: fear of and resistance to change.

How can these sources of resistance be countered and a culture of assessment fostered? The keys are value and respect, as summarized in Table 5.1. Value and respect must be more than just words, however. In order to have maximum impact, they must be conveyed through actions and resources.

The Critical Role of Campus Leaders

While there are many reasons that some colleges are engaged in assessment and others are not, assessment practitioners and scholars have found that one factor predominates: *if campus leaders are truly and actively committed to assessment, assessment gets done, and done well.* If campus leaders—especially the chief academic officer (vice president for academic affairs, provost, or dean) and the chief executive officer (president or chancellor)—aren't onboard, there may be pockets of assessment efforts across campus, but assessment doesn't permeate campus culture. Indeed, the vast majority of strategies offered in this chapter can be implemented only with the active and strong support of campus leaders.

Table 5.2 lists some of the ways that engaged, committed campus leaders foster a culture of assessment. Most of these strategies are discussed in the rest of this chapter.

Value Campus Culture and History

Campus cultures, histories, values, and personalities differ, and therefore so do the root causes of resistance to assessment. Consider these hypothetical (but realistic) examples:

- Everyone at Rehoboth College feels so overworked that they resent the added burden of assessment.

Table 5.2. How Campus Leaders Can Foster a Culture of Assessment

---

Value campus culture and history.

Promote a culture of respect for diversity in what people do, what they value, and their perspectives.

Focus campus resources and energies on the fundamental mission of most colleges and universities: teaching and learning.

Respect and empower people: faculty, staff, and students.

Recognize and reward faculty and staff who collaborate to build a community with a common understanding of what is important for students to learn and a curriculum with a purposeful structure.

Establish communication channels with those working on assessment, and use those channels to promote and facilitate assessment.

Charge faculty with assessment leadership (Chapter Six).

Encourage flexible rather than rigid approaches.

Value innovation and risk taking, especially in improving teaching and learning.

Encourage and reward efforts to improve teaching and learning.

Encourage and reward faculty and staff who engage in the scholarship of teaching.

Hire the right people: those with documented success in creating learning-centered environments.

Encourage risk taking and exhibit patience when changes in curricula and pedagogies initially fail.

Value assessment efforts.

Use assessment results to inform important decisions on important goals, and do so ethically and appropriately (Chapter Eighteen).

Take the time to acquaint yourself with current thinking on the principles and practices of assessment.

Understand why assessment is important, and have a personal commitment to it.

Inspire interest in assessment across campus through a clear vision of assessment that you share enthusiastically with others.

Establish a sense of urgency, making clear why assessment is a priority and why it must be taken seriously.

Talk up assessment in your formal remarks and informal conversations with faculty, students, and staff, explaining how assessment will benefit your college, individual programs, and individual faculty and staff members.

Provide incentives, resources, infrastructure, and support for assessment efforts (Chapter Six). Sponsor consultants, speakers, and forums on assessment, and support these programs with your active presence. Make assessment efforts a highlighted component of performance reviews of those who report to you.

Recognize and honor assessment efforts in tangible ways (Chapter Nine).

- At Northern University, research is emphasized far more than good teaching, so few people are interested in assessing—or improving—student learning.

- Manheim College has a long history of discord and disrespect between the faculty and administration, so there is a high level of suspicion that unsatisfactory assessment results will be acted on punitively, with promotions denied and programs terminated.

- Mount Joy College is highly selective, largely because of its long-standing elite reputation, and consequently there's an unspoken worry that assessment results may show that the college isn't quite as special as it purports to be.

Because each of these colleges and universities has a different root cause of resistance to assessment, each will need different strategies to address that resistance. There's thus no magic formula for fostering a culture of assessment. This chapter provides a grab bag of ideas that may or may not work on your campus. You'll need to understand and respect your campus culture in order to choose the strategies that will be most helpful.

Focus on and Value Teaching and Learning

Some faculty and staff consider assessment a "four-letter word": just bring up the term, and you may hear mental doors closing. But if your college or university values teaching and learning and you focus conversations not on assessment but on helping students learn, faculty and staff who are enthusiastic teachers will readily see that assessment is just a tool to bring about better teaching and learning. Their enthusiasm may bring others onboard.

Focus, then, on cultivating a culture of learning rather than one of assessment per se. In the early stages of introducing assessment to faculty and staff, focus conversations not on the "A-word" but on concepts such as goal setting, curriculum design, and teaching methods. Then gradually introduce the concept of assessment as a tool for facilitating these conversations ("How can we tell whether our curriculum is working?"). If your campus has a professional development center (often called a teaching-learning center) to help faculty and staff improve their teaching techniques, consider affiliating the assessment coordinator with that center, as suggested in Chapter Six. This conveys visibly that assessment is simply a means to improve teaching and learning.

Start with successes. Many faculty and staff have an instinctive sense of their programs' strengths. They have ready answers to questions such as, "What makes the graduates of your program so good?" or "Why are they in demand by employers or more advanced academic programs?" Faculty in one program might be confident that their students graduate with outstanding research skills, while those in another program might be proud of their students' technology skills. Assessment can't begin and end with only good news, of course, because one of its fundamental purposes is to improve student learning, which means identifying weaknesses as well as strengths. But encouraging faculty and staff to focus initially on assessing the strongest aspects of their programs can create a win-win situation:

- Faculty and staff instincts about the program are validated with solid information.

- Students in the program see evidence that they are really learning what is important.

- Prospective students are attracted to the program because they see evidence that they will learn things that are valued and important.

- College administrators use the good news to convince alumni, foundations, and other donors to invest in the program.

- Faculty and staff fears that assessment results will be used punitively are abated. Even if subsequent assessments yield disappointing results, those results will be balanced by the good news of the initial assessment results.

Hire the right people. Virtually every college is experiencing considerable faculty turnover as those hired a generation ago are now retiring. Faculty vacancies are a great opportunity to move substantively on promoting a learning-centered—and assessment— environment. Give hiring preference to faculty candidates with documented success in creating learning-centered environments for their students and using assessment to strengthen teaching and learning. Rather than ask faculty candidates to deliver a sample lecture, ask them to give a teaching demonstration. Then give hiring preference to those whose demonstrations have clear learning goals and thoughtful learning strategies that facilitate active learning.

Learn from Campus History, Including Past Assessment Experiences

Today it's the rare college or university that is starting an assessment effort from scratch. But previous assessment efforts at many colleges have often consisted of only a brief burst of activity shortly before an accreditation review that died immediately thereafter, perhaps because of turnover in campus or assessment leadership or a shifting focus to other priorities. Talk about past experiences, both good and bad. What went well, what didn't, and why? How can you build on those experiences and stop reinventing the wheel? Taking stock of past assessment efforts is discussed in Chapter Nineteen, and Exhibits 19.4 and 19.5 are examples of templates that might facilitate this review. A survey of faculty and staff on their views of teaching, assessment, and change might also be helpful.

It's also the rare college or university where everyone is at the same stage with assessment. Often programs with specialized accreditation are further along than other programs. What assessment activities are persisting today, which ones aren't, and why? Talk to faculty and staff for whom assessment is a natural part of life to see how their experiences might help those who are just getting started.

It can also be helpful to think of some other initiative that's been launched successfully at your college, such as a first-year-experience program, a service-learning initiative, or a reform of the general education curriculum. How was campus buy-in achieved with that initiative? You may be able to emulate or adapt what worked then.

Respect Underlying Values

Many people approach a new project with more enthusiasm if they find it inherently interesting, useful, and stimulating. So help faculty and staff focus on assessment efforts that will meet their needs and give them useful information for important decisions. Thomas Angelo (2000) has a wonderful phrase for this: "A vision worth working toward" (p. 3). Encourage faculty and staff to articulate their visions and values, and use assessment to answer the questions in which they're most interested. Perhaps they are tired of their program's image as mediocre and want to start aggressively countering this notion with solid evidence. Perhaps they are convinced that smaller classes would lead to more effective learning but need evidence to justify this to campus leaders. Perhaps they are frustrated with their students' inadequate writing skills and want to learn how best to improve those skills.

Every college community also has collective values, some made explicit in a mission statement, others implicit. One mission statement might promote specific religious values, while another promotes civic responsibility. At some colleges, collaboration is a highly prized but unstated value, while at others, individual autonomy is valued but again unstated. Clarifying your college's underlying values and understanding how they might affect assessment efforts can help foster success. A college that values community service, for example, might find an assessment of service-learning activities a particularly effective way to engage faculty and staff. At a college that values collaboration, involving a relatively large number of faculty and staff in the development of appropriate policies and procedures might be critical to assessment success. And research universities might find that faculty are especially interested in advancing—and assessing—the research skills of their students.

Respect and Empower People

Identifying whom to involve in articulating learning goals, identifying and designing assessment strategies, and discussing and using the results depends to a degree on campus culture, mission, and history. But assessment is usually not done well unless faculty, student life staff, and students all contribute to these tasks and feel that they are respected and empowered members of the assessment process.

Respect What Everyone Has Been Doing

Some faculty and staff fear that assessment means that someone else will decide that much of what they have been doing their whole lives—what they teach, how they teach it, and how they assess it—is wrong. It's thus important to emphasize the many things that faculty and staff do well and especially that many faculty and staff are already meeting expectations for assessment. As Chapter Six suggests, begin by focusing initially on assessment information already on hand.

Be Flexible

Faculty and staff should be able to make appropriate choices and decisions about what to assess, how to assess, and how to use the results. This gives them a sense of control that creates a better climate for assessment. Beginning with a bottom-up approach, in which faculty and staff establish their own diverse assessment structures, processes, and tools, generally works better than a top-down approach under which everyone must follow a prescribed structure. When faculty and staff start this way, they're likely to soon see the value of greater consistency and then buy in to stronger structures.

Remember that the primary purpose of assessment is to help faculty and staff improve student learning, and if bending the rules encourages them to achieve that end, be willing to do so. While you may expect all programs to submit annual assessment reports (Chapter Nineteen), perhaps you can be flexible on the date they are due. Give faculty and staff a selection of dates spread over the academic year, and let them choose the date that works best for them. And although you may have an established format for annual assessment reports, perhaps faculty and staff who already use or prefer another format can submit it that way. Those who must submit an assessment report to a state agency or specialized accreditor can simply submit relevant portions of that report rather than rewrite it into your format.

Also be willing to adapt assessment schedules to meet evolving needs. Suppose that focus groups show high levels of student satisfaction but senior theses show poor organizational skills. You may want to put the focus groups on a back burner, conducting them only once every three years just to make sure student satisfaction isn't slipping. At the same time, begin reviewing theses every term to monitor the effectiveness of efforts to strengthen organizational skills.

Empower Faculty as Assessment Leaders

Because assessment is part of the teaching and learning process, faculty should guide assessment activities just as they guide the curriculum and student learning. David Hollowell, Michael Middaugh, and Elizabeth Sibolski (2006) have put this bluntly: "First and foremost, assessment of student learning outcomes must be owned by the faculty" (p. 93).

Colleges are increasingly finding that the best way to empower faculty is to charge a committee, composed largely or wholly of faculty and integrated into the campus governance structure, with providing leadership for assessment activities. Chapter Six discusses this further.

Involve Students

Involving students in assessment activities has two major benefits: it engages them more actively in their own learning, and it helps faculty and staff plan, implement, and use assessments more effectively.

Engaging students in their learning. Research is showing that students learn more effectively when they are actively involved in their learning (Table 18.3). This includes their thinking actively about:

- The intended goals of their education
- What they should learn from an assignment and how the assignment helps them achieve major course or program goals
- How they should spend their study time and where they should focus their efforts as they work on an assignment
- The characteristics of excellent work and the performance level to which they should strive

Table 5.3. How Students Can Contribute to Assessment Work

Students can assist with:

Identifying the purposes of assessment (Chapter Four) and helping to ensure that assessments are relevant and worthwhile

Articulating learning goals (Chapter Eight) and helping to ensure that students see learning goals as important and valuable

Identifying appropriate assessment strategies (Part Three)

Designing or reviewing drafts of local assessment strategies and tools such as rubrics (Chapter Nine), assignments (Chapter Ten), surveys (Chapter Twelve), and portfolios (Chapter Thirteen)

Researching and selecting published tests and surveys (Chapter Fourteen)

Identifying incentives for students to participate meaningfully in add-on assessments (Chapter Two)

Reviewing logistical plans for assessments to make sure they are feasible and not unduly burdensome to students (Chapter Seven)

Advising on how to share results with students (Chapter Seventeen)

Reviewing results and discussing their implications (Chapter Eighteen)

Informing students fully about assessment and how it fits into their overall learning experience helps them engage in these kinds of reflective thinking. But consider going even further. Rather than merely inform students, create a richer learning experience by involving them in the following assessment-related tasks:

- Articulating their own learning goals for a project or program of study (Chapter Eight)

- Discussing appropriate assessment strategies for particular learning goals (Part Three)

- Discussing the characteristics of an effective assignment, perhaps by helping to draft a rubric or commenting on a draft of one (Chapter Nine)

- Choosing what goes into a portfolio (Chapter Thirteen)

- Understanding the results of their assessments and using the results to learn more effectively in the future (Part Four)

Helping to plan, implement, and use assessments effectively. Engaging students in assessment work adds a fresh and vital perspective. As the primary consumers of the teaching process, students can keep us focused on fundamental questions such as why we do things the way we do. Table 5.3 lists some of the ways that students can contribute to assessment efforts.

If you're not sure why students performed poorly on a particular assessment, ask them! In an appropriate class or other setting, ask them honestly, "A lot of you got that test question wrong or did poorly on that assignment. We didn't think it would be that hard. Why it was so difficult?" Students will give surprisingly perceptive and useful replies!

Value Campuswide Collaboration

Collaboration is essential to assessment success for several reasons. Perhaps most important is the need for students to have purposeful, coherent, and integrated educational experiences (Chapter One). Such experiences, and the assessment of them, cannot happen without a community that has a common understanding of what is important for students to learn and a curriculum with a purposeful structure. This common understanding cannot develop without collaboration.

Another benefit of collaboration is the variety of perspectives brought to the table. Some of us are more task and detail oriented, while others have a more global, theoretical orientation. Writing effective goals and developing assessment strategies requires both perspectives: the ability to see both the big final destination and the specific, detailed steps to get there. If you tend toward one orientation, working with someone of the opposite perspective is helpful.

Collaboration also contributes to a sense of ownership of the assessment process. Excluded faculty, staff, and students may characterize an assessment strategy as poor quality and inappropriate for their programs, and the ensuing debate can make it impossible to use the results to improve student learning experiences. Collaboration helps ensure the successful implementation of the assessment strategy and, most important, the effective use of the results.

Collaboration can improve all phases of the assessment process. As I noted in Chapter Three, it is very helpful to ask people with varying backgrounds and perspectives to review assessment tools such as rubrics or scoring guides, assignments, locally developed tests, published tests, and surveys. Collaboration is also helpful when identifying assessment purposes and audiences (Chapter Four); articulating learning goals, especially collegewide goals, general education goals, and cocurricular goals; planning and implementing assessment processes (Chapter Seven); and using assessment results effectively and appropriately (Part Four).

Because student learning takes place outside as well as within courses and academic programs, collaboration should reach across the entire campus community. Faculty, student development staff, and students are vital participants. Other administrators and staff, alumni, and advisory boards can be important contributors to assessment discussions as well.

What About Academic Freedom?

While some might argue that establishing common learning goals or assessment strategies flies in the face of academic freedom, there is little basis for such claims. The American Association of University Professors' 1940 "Statement of Principles on Academic Freedom and Tenure" states, "Teachers are entitled to freedom in the classroom in discussing their subject" (p. 1). The statement does not give faculty autonomy in choosing their subject or deciding how to assess student learning.

Academic freedom thus does not absolve faculty of their responsibility to ensure that all students in their program, regardless of the particular courses or sections in which they enroll, have sufficient opportunity to achieve those goals that the faculty collectively agree are essential. Faculty share collective responsibility for ensuring that students leave courses and programs consistently prepared for whatever comes afterward: further study, a career, or other pursuits. Academic freedom also does not relieve faculty of the obligation to assess student learning of their subject appropriately.

This does not mean, however, that all faculty must teach identical curricula and use identical pedagogies or identical assessments. As Marilee Bresciani (2006) has stated, "Excellence in student learning can be demanded without telling a faculty member how to achieve or how to evaluate it. Such a demand is not a violation of academic freedom" (p. 133). Once the faculty in a program agree on key common learning goals, individual faculty members can choose additional goals for their own classes and decide how best to help students in their classes achieve all goals, both common and unique.

Value Innovation and Risk Taking, Especially in Improving Teaching

People may be resistant to assessment because it carries the prospect of learning that something isn't working as well as it should. This means that something needs to be changed to fix the problem. Because "the fundamental human impulse [is] to protect the familiar" (Meacham, 2008, p. 4), many people are resistant to change. Table 5.4 summarizes some of the many reasons for resistance to change.

How, then, can colleges and universities turn around the mind-sets of resistance to change and create cultures that value innovation and risk taking?

Table 5.4. Sources of Resistance to Change

Some people are satisfied with the status quo. Some faculty are reasonably good teachers, with good evaluations from students and peers and a good life in general. They're not interested in stretching to achieve even greater excellence. Their attitude is, "If it ain't broke, don't fix it."

Some don't see the relevance of an initiative to them and therefore try to ignore it. Some faculty, for example, are more engaged in their research than in the undergraduates they teach and are not interested in improving their teaching or their department's curricula.

Some are old-timers who have seen many new initiatives come and go over the years. They're convinced that if they just wait, assessment too will fade away.

Some think they will need to learn and use new skills that will be difficult to master. Some are uncomfortable with technology, for example. They worry that assessment means learning how to design and administer computer-based tests and surveys. Others are "mathphobic" and worry that they'll have to figure out how to use spreadsheets and analyze mounds of data.

Others feel threatened by a new initiative. A faculty member who teaches with entertaining but lightweight lectures might feel threatened by the prospect of assessing students' critical thinking skills. A faculty member who prizes her independence might feel threatened by the prospect of developing common learning outcomes collaboratively with her colleagues.

Some people have misconceptions about a new initiative. Some faculty fear that assessment means they'll be told exactly what and how to teach. Others worry that less-than-positive assessment results will hurt their promotion or tenure prospects.

The prospect of change means the prospect of more work, and few people want more work.

Value, Respect, and Reward Efforts to Improve Teaching

Most colleges and universities prize teaching excellence, but relatively few tangibly value efforts to improve teaching effectiveness. One way to encourage faculty to improve their teaching is to give those efforts strong consideration when making decisions about tenure, promotion, and merit pay, even if the efforts initially fail. Another way is to provide curriculum development grants to fund improvements in curricula and teaching methods indicated by assessment results. What better way to counter the suspicion that negative assessment results will be used punitively than to "reward" poor results with grants to address the identified challenges? Faculty and staff are essentially paid for poor results!

Value, Respect, and Reward Reasonable Risk Taking

As discussed in Chapter One, assessment is a form of action research: a process of trial-and-error experimentation in creating new assessment strategies and using the results to modify curricula and teaching methods. Despite the best efforts of faculty and staff, sometimes a new assessment strategy yields little useful information, and sometimes a change in curriculum or pedagogy is initially a failure.

Rather than deny a faculty or staff member's bid for promotion because of a lack of progress in assessment or a drop in student evaluations of teaching, foster "a climate that rewards change and experimentation" (Smith, 2004, p. 33). Exhibit patience, and wait for the kinks to be worked out. Some campuses, for example, do not evaluate faculty teaching a redesigned course for the first semester or two, giving faculty time to refine the design.

Regard Assessment Results as Evidence of Teaching Effectiveness

Many colleges base faculty tenure, promotion, and merit pay decisions at least in part on teaching effectiveness, which is often judged largely by student evaluations of teaching and perhaps peer observation of a class. Student evaluations and peer observations may be helpful indicators of teaching effectiveness, but an even better indicator of good teaching is whether students have learned what they're supposed to—a strong argument to allow faculty to include assessment results from their classes as evidence of teaching effectiveness.

Does this contradict a suggestion in Table 18.1 that assessment results should *not* be used to penalize individuals? Not if you are careful to distinguish between student learning in a faculty member's *individual* classes, which could be factored in promotion and similar decisions, with student learning provided by *many* faculty and staff across multisection courses, programs, general education, and the college. Student learning across these broad venues is not the responsibility of any one faculty member and should not be tied to decisions about individual performance.

It may also be helpful to make voluntary the inclusion of assessment results in tenure, promotion, and merit applications. Faculty can be encouraged to include assessment results along with other evidence of teaching effectiveness, without being compelled to include specified results.

Encourage Assessment as a Form of Scholarship

Scholarship, another factor often considered in decisions on faculty tenure, promotion, and merit pay, is traditionally defined as what Ernest Boyer (1990) called scholarship of discovery: making an original, often research-based contribution to a discipline's body of knowledge. Boyer proposed expanding this conceptualization to encompass other forms of scholarship, including the scholarship of teaching: the systematic development, through careful research, of new and better ways to help students learn a discipline's concepts and skills.

To be considered true scholarship, the scholarship of teaching requires faculty to document the effectiveness of their teaching through the assessment of student learning and to publish or present their findings in a peer-reviewed forum (Diamond, 2008). Valuing the scholarship of teaching as a form of scholarship can thus stimulate interest in assessment.

Table 5.5 lists some venues for publishing scholarship on the assessment of student learning.

Table 5.5. Opportunities to Publish Scholarship on Assessing Student Learning in Higher Education

General Interest Higher Education Journals and Publications	Journals on Teaching in a Specific Discipline
American Educational Research Journal	American Biology Teacher
American Journal of Evaluation	Biochemical Education
Applied Measurement in Education	Chemical Engineering Education
Assessment and Evaluation in Higher Education	College Composition and Communication
Assessment in Education: Principles, Policy and Practice	College Mathematics Journal
Assessment Update	Communication Education
Change	History Teacher
College Teaching	Journal of Accounting Education
Community College Journal of Research and Practice	Journal of Agricultural Education
Computer Supported Cooperative Work: The Journal of Collaborative Computing	Journal of Chemical Education
Education Policy Analysis Archives	Journal of College Science Teaching
Educational Action Research	Journal of Criminal Justice Education
Educational Evaluation and Policy Analysis	Journal of Economic Education
Educational Research	Journal of Engineering Education
Innovations in Education and Teaching International	Journal of Environmental Education
Innovative Higher Education	Journal of Geography in Higher Education
Interactive Learning Research	Journal of Geoscience Education
International Journal for the Scholarship of Teaching and Learning	Journal of Health Education
Journal of College Student Retention	Journal of Management Education
Journal of Educational Measurement	Journal of Marketing Education
Journal of Graduate Teaching Assistant Development	Journal of Nursing Education
Journal of Higher Education	Journal of Social Work Education
Journal of Student Centered Learning	Journal of Teaching in Physical Education
Journal on Excellence in College Teaching	Journal of Teaching in Social Work
Liberal Education	Journal of Teaching Writing
National Teaching and Learning Forum	Journalism and Mass Communication Educator
New Directions for Program Evaluation	Mathematics and Computer Education
New Directions for Teaching and Learning	Mathematics Teacher

New Directions for Higher Education
Peer Review
Practical Assessment, Research, and Evaluation
Research in Higher Education

Teaching Professor

Teaching Excellence

Physics Teacher
Research in Collegiate Mathematics Education
Research on Science Teaching
*Research Strategies: A Journal of Library
    Concepts and Instruction*
*Schole: A Journal of Leisure Studies and
    Recreation Education*
Studies in Higher Education
Teaching English in the Two-Year College
Teaching in Higher Education
Teaching of Psychology
Teaching Philosophy
Teaching Sociology
*Trends and Issues in Postsecondary English
    Studies*

Don't Expect to Get Everyone Onboard

Cultural change is rarely rapid, and there are invariably pockets of stubborn resistance. It may be virtually impossible to engage some individuals in assessment. Accept them, and don't be discouraged. Just as many new academic programs and other initiatives are launched without 100 percent faculty and staff buy-in, you don't need to get every faculty and staff member onboard for assessment to happen. Focus your energies on faculty and staff who are skeptical but intrigued by assessment, as well as those who are enthused about assessment, and you'll see good progress.

Value Assessment Efforts

Another way to foster a culture of assessment is to value work on assessment in tangible ways. Three strategies are particularly helpful here:

Use assessment results to inform important decisions on important goals.   Chapter Three notes that the fundamental characteristic of good assessments is that they are used. We all like to know that our work is making a difference, so a vital way to keep assessment momentum is to make sure the results are used meaningfully and appropriately. A culture of assessment is, at its heart, a culture of evidence-based planning and decision making, in which plans and resource allocations are routinely based on systematic evidence rather than hunch or gut instinct. If assessment results are used to improve teaching and learning and inform important planning and budgeting decisions, faculty who care about their teaching, student learning, and their programs will be more inclined to participate. Using assessment results—and doing so ethically and appropriately—is discussed in Chapter Eighteen.

Support assessment with appropriate resources and infrastructure. Communicate the value of assessment by supporting it in the ways described in Chapter Six, including respecting everyone's time and providing resources such as an assessment coordinator and opportunities to learn about assessment.

Celebrate and honor assessment efforts. Faculty and staff reluctant to engage in assessment may rightly ask, "What's in it for me?" Chapter Six discusses tangible incentives to encourage involvement in assessment, and Chapter Nineteen suggests ways to create convincing, meaningful rewards that recognize and honor faculty and staff who are making strong, systematized assessment efforts and thus contributing meaningfully to improved student learning.

Time to Think, Discuss, and Practice

1. The president of a community college wants faculty and staff to develop an assessment plan for the college's general education curriculum. Brainstorm three ways she might realistically help create a positive, supportive climate for this project.

2. The assistant provost of a research university knows that the university must do a lot more with assessment in order to meet accreditation requirements, but the president and provost are focused on the university's research mission. They give assessment lip service because they don't want accreditation problems, but they are really not particularly interested in assessing student learning. Brainstorm three things that the assistant provost might do, in the absence of campus leaders' visible support, to help promote a culture of assessment.

Recommended Readings

The following readings are recommended along with the references cited in this chapter.

Banta, T. W. (2005). Leaders' views on engaging stakeholders in assessment. *Assessment Update, 17*(6), 3, 15–16.

Banta, T. W. (2005). What draws campus leaders to embrace outcomes assessment? *Assessment Update, 17*(5), 3, 14–15.

Banta, T. W., & Lefebvre, L. A. (2001). *Effective practices for academic leaders: Leading change through assessment.* Sterling, VA: Stylus.

Brown, F. W., & Moshavi, D. (2002). Herding academic cats: Faculty reactions to transformational and contingent reward leadership by department chairs. *Journal of Leadership Studies, 8*(3), 79–93.

Brown, K. (2001). Community college strategies: Why aren't faculty jumping on the assessment bandwagon—and what can be done to encourage their involvement? *Assessment Update, 13*(2), 8–9, 16.

Eckel, P., Green, M., & Hill, B. (2001). *On change: Riding the waves of change: Insights from transforming institutions.* Washington, DC: American Council on Education.

Grunwald, H., & Peterson, M. W. (2003). Factors that promote faculty involvement in and satisfaction with institutional and classroom student assessment. *Research in Higher Education, 44*(2), 173–204.

Kotter, J. P. (1995). Leading change: Why transformation efforts fail. *Harvard Business Review, 73*(2), 59–68.

Kuh, G. D., Kinzie, J., Schuh, J. H., & Whitt, E. J. (2005). Never let it rest: Lessons about student success from strong-performing colleges and universities. *Change, 37*(4), 44–51.

Leviton, L. C. (2003). Commentary: Engaging the community in evaluation: Bumpy, time consuming, and important. *American Journal of Evaluation, 24*(1), 85–90.

Peterson, M. W., & Augustine, C. H. (2000). Organizational practices enhancing the influence of student assessment information in academic decisions. *Research in Higher Education, 41*(1), 21–52.

Schneider, C. G., & Shoenberg, R. (1999). Habits hard to break: How persistent features of campus life frustrate curricular reform. *Change, 31*(2), 30–35.

Stufflebeam, D. L. (2002). *Institutionalizing evaluation checklist.* Retrieved September 16, 2008, from www.wmich.edu/evalctr/checklists/institutionalizingeval.pdf.

Tromp, S. A., & Ruben, B. D. (2004). *Strategic planning in higher education: A guide for leaders.* Washington, DC: National Association of College and University Business Officers.

Wergin, J. F. (2003). *Departments that work: Creating and sustaining cultures of excellence in academic programs.* Bolton, MA: Anker.

CHAPTER 6

Supporting Assessment Efforts with Time, Infrastructure, and Resources

---

Some Valuable Ideas You'll Find in This Chapter

- If assessment is to be pervasive and sustained, it must be cost-effective, yielding benefits that justify the time and expense put into it.
- You don't have to do everything at once.
- When in doubt, choose simpler assessment strategies.
- The most important traits in an assessment coordinator are sensitivity, open-mindedness, flexibility, and a passion for teaching and learning.
- The decision to invest in assessment technologies should be led by the people who will use them: faculty and staff on the assessment front lines.

Although assessment efforts need not be costly, they do require an investment of time, guidance, and support. Chapter Five emphasizes that the keys to assessment success are value and respect. Certainly an important way to convey value and respect is through supporting assessment efforts with appropriate time, infrastructure, and resources.

Value Everyone's Time _____

One of the most common concerns that faculty and staff express about assessment is, "But when I am supposed to find the time to do this?" People who already feel overwhelmed with their responsibilities see any innovation, including assessment, as just one more thing they have to do on top of everything else, with their time already stretched too thin. Here are some strategies for minimizing the burden of assessment on faculty and staff.

Set Priorities

Because we want students to learn, grow, and develop in so many ways, the prospect of assessing every aim can be overwhelming at first glance. Calm your fears by recognizing at the outset that you don't immediately need to assess everything that you want students to learn. It's better to do a few assessments well than many poorly.

Start small. Because quick results can help build enthusiasm for assessment, encourage faculty and staff to begin with small-scale assessment projects that they can expand later. Don't ask them to wait until they have a full, approved plan in place to begin collecting assessment information. If faculty and staff want to try a portfolio (Chapter Thirteen), encourage them to include initially just a couple of examples of student work that assess one or two key learning goals. Once the faculty and staff are comfortable with new assessment tools and processes and have worked out logistical kinks, they can gradually expand the scope of their assessment efforts.

Start by focusing on important goals. Begin by assessing only those learning goals that you and your colleagues feel are most important—perhaps no more than three to six. Once you are comfortable assessing them, you can begin assessing others.

Start with the easier assessments. Focus initially on assessing those aspects of a program that you can assess most effortlessly. It might be easier, for example, for faculty to agree on how to assess technology skills than on how to assess creative thinking. As discussed in Chapter Twelve, recognize that some important goals may be difficult or impossible to assess; acknowledge and honor them, but put them aside for now.

Focus on assessment tools and strategies that yield the greatest dividends for the time and resources invested. Rubrics

(Chapter Nine) speed up the process of evaluating student papers and projects and yield a wealth of useful information. Minute papers (Chapter Twelve) are so simple that faculty and staff can implement them virtually immediately, and they yield wonderful insight into student learning.

Stop Doing Something Else

If faculty and staff are told they must continue to do everything else while they tackle assessment, the implicit message is that everything else is more important than assessment—in other words, assessment really isn't all that important.

An important way to build a culture of assessment is thus finding ways to relieve faculty and staff of less critical responsibilities as they embark on assessment. Surely there is some committee or some other project whose work can be suspended for a semester or year without things falling apart. Faculty and staff launching assessment efforts might be exempted from committee service or writing the usual annual report of department activities, for example. If your campus has a process of ongoing academic program review (Chapters One and Nineteen), consider streamlining it to deemphasize the elements that are relatively tangential to student learning. Also consider giving released time to faculty and staff who are launching particularly time-consuming assessment projects outside their normal purview, such as the assessment of a major institutional or general education goal.

If you are assessing student learning in a course, consider dropping or shortening the midterm examination to give you more time to assess student projects. Or move some of your more straightforward lectures online for students to read on their own, creating more class time for students to collaborate on assignments and for you to review assignments with individual students. Or move your tests online, freeing up class time for other kinds of assessments such as group presentations.

Keep Things Simple

The more complicated assessments are, the more precious time they consume. Keep things as simple as possible!

Start with what you have.   Maximize the use of existing information before creating or purchasing new tools (Chapter Seven).

Conduct only useful assessments.   The most important characteristic of good assessments is that they are used to inform important decisions on important goals (Chapter Three). Don't undertake any assessment unless you have a clear sense of the audiences for its results and how the results will inform important decisions (Chapter Four).

Have realistic expectations for quality.   In some ways, it might be wonderful if assessments consistently met the standards for publication in peer-reviewed research journals. But realistically, most faculty and staff don't have the time—or interest—to do this.

As discussed in Chapter One, assessment is a form of action research. Although it is disciplined and systematic, it is inherently imperfect, so don't expect perfection. Aim not for replicable, generalizable research but for results that are simply good enough and relevant enough to use with confidence to make decisions about teaching and learning in your course, program, or college.

Limit the volume of assessment information collected from students.   Perhaps a two-page abstract will help them improve their writing skills as much as a twenty-page term paper—and give you just as much assessment information. As Chapter Ten suggests, consider carefully whether the time that students put into your assignment—and that you put into grading or otherwise assessing it—yields a proportionate payoff in terms of their learning.

Look at samples rather than censuses of student work.   If students maintain journals in your course, for example (Chapter Twelve), spot-check a sample of them (Chapter Three) each week rather than read them all. If all students in your program complete a senior thesis, evaluate just a sample of them for information literacy skills.

Stagger assessments.   Stagger the due dates for course assignments so each class turns in its assignments a few weeks apart and you're not overwhelmed with papers at any one point in the term. Similarly, stagger program assessments across a multiyear period. A three-year assessment cycle might include a review of student portfolios every first year, a survey of alumni every second year, and exit interviews of graduating students every third. Use no more than a three-year cycle, however. Anything longer will lead to assessment being conducted in fits and starts, with no one remembering what was done before or everyone therefore regularly reinventing the wheel.

Keep paperwork minimal.   Most colleges need regular reports from faculty and staff on how student learning is being assessed for a variety of purposes. Chapter Nineteen offers suggestions to keep these reports short, simple, and meaningful.

Provide Appropriate Resources

Assessment need not be expensive, but it does have resource and infrastructure requirements. As you identify resource needs, keep in mind that if assessment is to be pervasive and sustained, it must be cost-effective, yielding benefits that justify the time and expense put into it. The business world's concept of return on investment applies here. Assessments should yield dividends—improvements in student learning experiences—sufficiently worthwhile to justify the investment. Assessment is like putting together a jigsaw puzzle when we don't have enough time to assemble the entire puzzle. We want to put together just enough pieces to get a reasonably good sense of what the completed picture looks like.

If a particular resource to support assessment—say, a published instrument or a software package—is especially costly in terms of time or dollars, ask yourself how likely it is to lead to significant changes and improvements in how, what, or why students learn. If dramatic benefits aren't probable, the expenditure is probably not worthwhile.

Faculty Leadership Through the Campus Governance System

Colleges are increasingly finding that the best way to empower faculty to lead assessment (Chapter Five) is to charge a committee composed largely or wholly of faculty with providing leadership for assessment activities. This can be accomplished in a variety of ways:

- Charge a new, separate committee solely with providing leadership for assessment activities.
- Ask an existing committee, such as a curriculum committee, to include assessment leadership within its responsibilities.
- Establish two assessment committees: one for student learning assessment and one for other aspects of institutional effectiveness (Chapter One).
- At a large university, establish separate assessment committees for each school or college.
- If there are multiple assessment committees, make them subcommittees of a campuswide oversight committee.

No matter where an assessment committee is situated, don't make it an ad hoc committee or one that sits outside the established governance structure, reporting to an institutional leader. Incorporating an assessment committee into the governance structure sends a powerful message that assessment is not a fad but a permanent part of the fabric of campus life. Consider making the student learning assessment committee part of the faculty governance structure—perhaps a standing committee of the faculty senate. This conveys that the faculty are responsible for leading student learning assessment.

Assessment committee functions. The functions of a committee charged with leading assessment will vary from one campus to another, depending on campus culture, mission, history, and governance structure. Table 6.1 lists some possibilities.

Assessment committee composition. The key traits of effective assessment committee members are sensitivity, open-mindedness, flexibility, and a passion for teaching and learning. Aim for selection processes that will yield committee members with these traits. Committee members can be elected or appointed by their peers, a campus governance body such as a faculty senate, or their union or collective bargaining unit, if there is one. Sometimes a combination of volunteer, elected, and appointed members provides the best mix of skills and traits.

Faculty are essential members of any assessment committee—perhaps except for a committee charged only with assessment in administrative units—because their membership conveys the faculty's leadership in the college's primary mission: student learning. Try to

Table 6.1. Possible Functions of a Committee Charged with Leading Assessment

Conduct periodic audits of assessment practices and available assessment information (Chapter Seven).

Establish, review, and update assessment policies and guidelines (Chapter Seven).

Develop and review a communications plan to keep faculty and staff informed of assessment expectations, resources, and so on.

Advise the assessment coordinator on organizing and implementing assessment (Chapter Seven).

Help promote a culture of assessment by serving as assessment advocates and sponsoring and supporting professional development opportunities.

Propose other appropriate strategies to promote a culture of assessment (Chapter Seven).

Review and offer constructive feedback on reports of assessment activities (Chapter Nineteen).

Review the results of collegewide assessments such as student surveys, and advise on their dissemination.

Evaluate overall campus assessment efforts (Chapter Nineteen), and develop or recommend appropriate modifications.

ensure that faculty are drawn from a representative cross-section of disciplines.

Including representatives of student development staff and student support staff helps convey the important message that student learning occurs outside as well as within the classroom. Other administrators may also be helpful members, especially if the committee is charged not only with student learning assessment but also with assessing other aspects of institutional effectiveness (Chapter One).

Students may be represented on this committee, but this is not essential. There are many other, perhaps more meaningful, ways for students to contribute (Chapter Five).

The assessment coordinator discussed in the next section is an ex officio member but not the chair. This conveys tangibly that the assessment coordinator's role is one of support, not leadership, and that assessment is everyone's responsibility.

Assessment Coordination and Support

It's the increasingly rare college that can launch a successful campuswide assessment effort without an assessment champion. More and more colleges need someone whose full- or part-time responsibilities include coordinating what everyone is doing, prodding the reluctant ones, and assisting those who are struggling. Larger and more complex colleges and universities often need a full-time assessment coordinator. Smaller colleges may find that it's sufficient to ask a faculty member or administrator to assume responsibility for coordinating assessment on a part-time basis.

What kind of person is best to coordinate an assessment effort? The following characteristics are critical, and they apply to assessment steering committee members as well:

Sensitivity and open-mindedness. Effective assessment coordinators develop successful working relationships with faculty and staff from a broad range of disciplines, values, and perspectives. In order to do this, they listen to and learn from faculty and staff with different experiences, priorities, values, and points of view. They are sensitive to cultural differences—not just campus culture and disciplinary cultures but also the cultures of people working in, say, student development programs or international programs.

Flexibility. Effective assessment coordinators encourage faculty and staff to choose from a variety of assessment approaches and processes rather than foist a uniform model on everyone. They promote bottom-up rather than top-down approaches that foster faculty and staff ownership and engagement (Chapter Five). Rather than continue to enforce past assessment processes and expectations rigidly, they adapt past processes to meet current needs. They recognize that assessment will not proceed across campus in lock-step fashion; some departments and programs will take longer than others, and some may require more intense guidance and support.

A passion for teaching and learning. The credibility of assessment coordinators is greatly enhanced if they have teaching experience, even if only as a part-time adjunct. This experience allows them to empathize through experience with faculty workloads, student characteristics, and the effectiveness and frustrations of various assessment strategies. Assessment coordinators have even more influence if they show a passionate enthusiasm for teaching and for seeing students learn.

Recognized expertise. Effective assessment coordinators demonstrate enough expertise in contemporary thinking on teaching, learning, and assessment to have credibility and respect with faculty, staff, and campus leaders. They understand assessment thoroughly enough to recognize that there are many legitimate ways to approach it. They are willing to acknowledge that they don't have all the answers and are willing to learn. They know how to find answers to emerging assessment questions, whether through published literature, online searches, or networking with peers.

Technical, analytical, and social science research skills, while helpful, are not absolutely necessary in an assessment coordinator. Indeed, some excellent assessment coordinators come from disciplines that do not emphasize these skills. Campuses that invest in assessment technologies do need staff who can support those technologies, as discussed later in this chapter, but this support need not come directly from the assessment coordinator.

Where should the assessment coordinator be located within the campus organization? While this depends on campus culture, history, and personalities, an assessment coordinator ideally reports directly to a campus leader who is respected by the campus community, values assessment and is ready to use assessment results in important and appropriate ways (Chapter Eighteen).

Increasing numbers of colleges now have faculty professional development (teaching-learning) centers to help faculty improve their teaching. Wherever the assessment coordinator is located within the campus organization, it is helpful to have a clear connection between the coordinator and the professional development center.

The assessment coordinator and professional development center can cosponsor professional development events on topics such as teaching and assessing critical thinking skills or using assessment results to improve curricula and pedagogies. Such affiliations help faculty and staff to see that assessment is simply part of the teaching-learning process.

Opportunities to Learn About Assessment

Many faculty and staff have no formal training and little opportunity to learn about instructional design, teaching techniques, human development, or assessment methods. The typical faculty member has few, if any, occasions to learn how to create an assignment, write a multiple-choice test, or grade an essay. Helping faculty and staff develop their assessment skills makes the assessment process far less formidable. Misconceptions about assessment abound, and professional development resources should focus on addressing the most common misconceptions on campus.

Because faculty and staff differ in their needs and preferences, offer a variety of opportunities for them to learn how to do assessment. Consider the following:

- On-campus professional development resources, such as:
  - An assessment Web site with brief readings, guides, examples, and links to off-campus resources
  - A campus assessment newsletter or a column in the employee newsletter
  - Books, journals, and video recordings
- On-campus professional development programs, such as:
  - Workshops
  - Speakers
  - Brown bag lunch discussions
- Sponsored attendance at off-campus assessment conferences, institutes, and workshops, perhaps followed with a brown bag lunch discussion or newsletter article in which participants share what they learned
- Access to faculty, staff, or consultants who can answer questions on specific aspects of assessment such as testing, surveys, focus groups, and statistics

Incentives

Why should a good and busy faculty or staff member add assessment to an already full plate of work? The answer is to create convincing, meaningful, and ongoing incentives to encourage faculty and staff to make strong, systematized assessment efforts. Incentives are a powerful way to convey that assessment efforts are valued and respected, and value and respect are the keys to fostering a culture of assessment (Chapter Five).

Most assessment activities should be viewed as a normal part of teaching activities or other responsibilities that do not merit extra compensation. But sometimes special funds can be used to encourage participation in extraordinary assessment activities. Budget supplements, stipends, mini-grants, or extra compensation can encourage faculty and staff to help read and score large numbers of student papers or projects, spend unusual amounts of time on assessment, or initiate significant assessment efforts on their own. Curricular development grants (Chapter Five) can encourage faculty to use assessment results to improve teaching and learning.

Recognition and Rewards for Assessment Efforts

One of the keys to assessment success is to let faculty and staff know in tangible, meaningful ways that their assessment efforts are valued. Many ways to do this have little direct cost, if any (see Table 19.1). Funds might be needed for annual events such as an awards program, an assessment luncheon, or an assessment fair and for refreshments for assessment meetings and scoring sessions.

Technical Support

Some colleges and universities find it worthwhile to invest in technologies to support assessment activities, along with technical and support staff to help with the mundane but essential tasks of collecting, processing, and analyzing assessment results. Software to support assessment can help with a number of tasks, including the following:

- Creating scannable bubble sheet tests or surveys
- Creating online tests or surveys
- Creating scripts and response entry forms for computer-assisted telephone surveys
- Making audiovisual recordings of student presentations and performances
- Maintaining student portfolios online
- Entering, processing, and analyzing assessment results
- Maintaining assessment plans, results, and other records

There are literally dozens of vendors of these technologies, and choosing one can be overwhelming. Table 6.2 suggests some steps to make sure a technology investment is a wise one.

Table 6.2. Steps in Choosing Assessment Technologies

Give a leadership role in the decision to the people who will use the product: faculty and staff on the assessment front lines. Make them, not the information technology staff, the drivers in identifying and choosing technologies.

Identify your needs. There's no point in investing in expensive technologies to maintain assessment reports if the reports generated through word processing are working fine for everyone. Similarly, there is no point in investing in statistical analysis software if no one wants to do anything more than tally results.

Identify the purpose of the technologies you are exploring. Is the primary aim to ease the time and effort that faculty and staff spend compiling and analyzing assessment results? Or is it to help students synthesize their learning by reviewing their work in a portfolio (Chapter Thirteen)? Or is it to help public audiences quickly grasp your college's story (Chapter Seventeen)?

Clarify the requirements and expectations of your accreditor and other external audiences (Chapter Four). Although a few accreditors expect assessment information to be compiled and presented in a particular way (for example, in online student portfolios), most do not require or expect that colleges invest in or use particular technologies to meet accreditation requirements.

Clarify how you plan to use the technologies. Will all departments be required to use the technology, for example, or will they be able to use it or not at their option? It's generally wise to encourage but not require faculty and staff to use new technologies. The early adopters can serve as advocates to their more reluctant colleagues.

Consider whether faculty and staff are ready to embrace the technologies being considered. Will faculty and staff welcome this technology as solving a pervasive problem, or will they view the need to learn how to use it as simply another assessment-related burden?

Consider whether your campus has the staff support to implement the technology successfully. Many software packages cannot be implemented without the ongoing support of someone with technological expertise.

Identify potential vendors. This can be done through conference exhibits and presentations, published literature, colleagues, and online searches and discussion lists.

Ask vendors for references—colleges currently using their technologies—and contact the colleges' assessment coordinators directly to ask them about their experiences:

How much does the technology cost: both the initial purchase price and annual fees?

How widely is it being used at your college? Which departments and programs are using it?

Are faculty and staff using it themselves? If not, who uses it?

Which features are being used?

How user friendly is the technology?

How much training and staff support have faculty and staff needed to use the technology?

How well does the technology interface with other technologies used on campus? For example, how well does it interface with technologies that faculty and staff use to support online learning or to record student grades?

Does the technology have any particular hardware or software requirements? Does it require, for example, that personal computers use a particular operating system, have a certain amount of memory, or use a particular Internet browser?

What kind of support is needed from information technology staff to use and maintain the technology?

If you could make this decision over again, would you still buy this package? Why or why not?

Ask vendors for demonstrations of the technology. These are often available online.

Consider the balance of costs versus benefits. Many assessment technologies run well into tens or even hundreds of thousands of dollars, plus the costs of local training and staff support. This is a major investment, so make sure you have a clear sense of the payoffs and whether they are worth the costs.

Take your time making a decision. Before investing in any technology, do a trial run of your assessments and reports using paper forms, word processing, or spreadsheets. The experience will help faculty and staff understand their goals and needs, perhaps come to realize that better technologies will make their lives easier and the process more useful, and make a more appropriate technology choice.

Published Instruments

Some published tests and surveys cost thousands of dollars. Incentives for students to participate in them and in other add-on assessments can increase the total cost significantly. Published tests and surveys are discussed in Chapter Fourteen; incentives for students to participate in add-on assessments are discussed in Chapter Two.

Time to Think, Discuss, and Practice

1. Identify committees at your college or university whose work might be put on hiatus for a year to free up time for assessment. What would be the adverse impacts, if any, of such a hiatus?

2. What might be a suitable membership composition of an assessment steering committee at your institution? Justify your choices, and reflect on what they tell you about your institution's values and culture.

3. What are the three biggest things that faculty and staff at your college or university most need or want to learn about assessment?

   - Do you feel you can answer this question reasonably accurately, or do you need to conduct a needs assessment?

   - What might be done to help them learn those things? Do your ideas have any budgetary implications?

Recommended Readings

The following reading is recommended along with the references cited in this chapter.

Primary Research Group. (2008). *Survey of assessment practices in higher education.* New York: Author.

CHAPTER 7

Organizing an Assessment Process

Some Valuable Ideas You'll Find in This Chapter

- There's no point in assessing something that students don't have an opportunity to learn, so curricular review is an important step in the assessment process.

- Students' peers and field experience supervisors can be good sources of assessment information, but it can be difficult to get good-quality assessment information from students who leave before graduating and alumni.

- General education assessment is not fundamentally different from program assessment, as long as steps are taken to foster a culture of assessment in general education.

Any undertaking benefits from some kind of plan. Even a shopping trip can be more successful if you start with some notes on what you want to buy and which stores you want to visit. Assessment is no different; it will be more effective and successful if you plan your work.

Because assessment is most likely to succeed under faculty leadership, faculty should take the leadership in addressing the planning and organizational matters discussed in this chapter. The usual mechanism for doing this is through a committee composed largely or wholly of faculty and charged with assessment leadership, as discussed in Chapter Six.

The Cornerstones: Purpose, Audience, Culture, and Support ___

Assessment planning begins by laying the four cornerstones of a foundation for success discussed in Chapters Four, Five, and Six:

- A clear understanding of why are you assessing student learning
- An understanding of the audiences for your assessment findings and the decisions that your results will inform
- A supportive climate for assessment
- Adequate resources to support assessment efforts

Once you have laid these cornerstones, you can organize your assessment effort.

Take Stock of Curricula and Learning Opportunities ___

There's no point in assessing something that students don't have an opportunity to learn. Chapter Three discusses the importance of ensuring that every student, regardless of curricular and cocurricular choices, has sufficient opportunity to achieve every key goal. As that chapter emphasizes, this means giving students multiple opportunities to achieve essential goals, because it is unfair to place full responsibility for a fundamental goal on one faculty member or one course.

Several tools can be helpful in reviewing your curriculum to ensure this curricular alignment. Sometimes the insight they provide is so eye-opening that it leads to fairly swift changes in curricula and teaching methods. When this happens, the assessment process leads to significant improvements in teaching and learning even before any assessments have been conducted!

Curriculum Mapping

A good way to analyze learning opportunities in a program or general education curriculum is to map its learning goals (Chapter Eight) against its courses. Create a grid listing your college's, program's, or general education curriculum's key learning goals down the left side and courses and other curricular requirements across the top. Then ask faculty to check the goals that are addressed in each course or requirement that they teach. If you suspect that some faculty may overstate what their courses cover, ask them to check off only those goals that are addressed in tests, classwork, or assignments that are graded. Exhibit 7.1 is an example of a curriculum map.

Exhibit 7.1. An Example of a Curriculum Map for a Five-Unit Program on Assessment

Learning Goal: Participants will be able to:	Organizing for Assessment Unit	Organizational Development and Cultural Change Unit	Assessment Tools and Strategies Unit	Understanding and Using Assessment Results Unit	General Education and Accreditation Unit
Organize and budget for assessment	X				X
Inventory existing assessment activities	X				
Assess institutional effectiveness	X	X		X	
Relate institutional effectiveness to planning and budgeting	X	X			
Promote planned change and diffusion of innovation		X			
Create a culture of assessment		X	X		X
Lead assessment efforts		X			
Articulate clear learning objectives			X	X	X
Locate and evaluate published tests			X		X
Create in-house assessment instruments			X		X
Set targets for assessment results				X	X
Collect, summarize, and communicate assessment results			X	X	
Use assessment results for improvement		X		X	X
Use information technologies and course management systems for assessment				X	
Assess student learning in general education curricula					X
Meet accreditation and accountability expectations		X	X		X

Source: With the permission of the faculty of the 2008 Association for Institutional Research Assessment Institute: Marilee Bresciani, Peter Gray, Joseph Hoey, Paula Krist, Sharron Ronco, Linda Suskie, and Kimberly Thompson.

Now step back and look at the completed grid. You may find that some important learning goals that should be addressed throughout the curriculum are addressed in just one or two courses, and then only minimally. Other important learning goals may not be addressed anywhere or in only one or two elective courses that relatively few students take. And some relatively minor goals may suffer from overkill, taking up time in too many classes that could be devoted to other important goals that need increased attention.

In the example in Exhibit 7.1, most goals are addressed in at least two units, and some especially critical goals are addressed in three. These were deliberate decisions by faculty planning the program to ensure that participants have multiple opportunities to achieve the program's key goals.

Transcript Analysis

Students can often fulfill some college, program, or general education requirements by choosing courses from lists. If so, it can be helpful to review a sample of transcripts of graduating students to learn which courses they choose and when they take them. This analysis can help answer questions such as these:

- Which courses do students usually take to fulfill college, general education, or program requirements?
- When do they take them: in the intended sequence or, say, by postponing a fundamental course such as mathematics or public speaking until just before graduation?
- Are students achieving a general education goal through courses in their majors?

Syllabus Analysis

Reviewing samples of relevant syllabi can help determine if students have enough assignments and classwork to achieve each of the intended learning goals of the course, including the program, general education, or institutional learning goals that the course is intended to support.

This review should not be a once-and-done activity. As faculty, curricula, learning technologies, and societal needs change, so may course curricula, and a course that addressed key learning goals a few years ago may no longer do so. Ideally, all courses should be reviewed on a regular basis—perhaps every five years or so—to make sure they continue to address the key goals of the program or general education curriculum that they are part of.

This review is easier if all syllabi are required or expected to list their course learning goals and, if the course is part of a program or general education curriculum, the broader goals that the course helps foster. Better yet is a chart or grid in each syllabus that lists not only relevant learning goals but also the class assignments that help students achieve each goal. This is because students learn more effectively when they understand the purpose of their assignments (see Table 18.3).

Improving the Alignment Between Learning Goals and Curricula

Once your review of a college, program, or general education curriculum is completed, you may find that it does not align well with its intended learning goals. Some students may be able to graduate without taking any courses that address some key concepts, skills, or competencies. Perhaps students can graduate without having taken any general education courses that address information literacy skills.

Or you may find that students have only minimal opportunity—say, in just one course—to achieve a key learning goal. Perhaps the quantitative skills expected of graduates of a particular academic program are addressed in only one course, and students frequently postpone that course until the final semester before they graduate, giving them insufficient opportunities to practice and improve their quantitative skills.

In these situations, you and your colleagues will need to decide whether to develop a new curriculum that better aligns with key learning goals—a potentially long, difficult, and contentious process—or tinker with the curriculum you have. Suppose you find, for example, that most, but not all, of the courses that can fulfill the general education social sciences requirement address critical thinking skills. The easiest approach might be to ask faculty into incorporate development of critical thinking skills into the remaining general education social science courses—or remove those courses from the list.

Take Stock of Available Assessment Information _____

One of the keys to fostering a culture of assessment is to respect everyone's time (Chapter Six). An important way to make sure time is used wisely is to build on what's already happening rather than engaging in unnecessarily duplicative work. Chapter Five discusses learning from campus history, including experiences with assessment. It's also helpful to take stock of assessment information on hand and available from external resources.

What Assessment Information Is Already on Hand?

Every college and university has some assessment information on hand. Ask your colleagues:

- How do we know that our students are successful? How do we know that they are indeed learning what we value?
- Are our conclusions based on solid evidence or on hunches and anecdotes?
- How would we convince board members, employers, and other audiences that graduating students have in fact learned these things?
- If we're not sure if our students have achieved our goals, do we at least have some clues?

Even if available assessment information is incomplete or isn't rigorous, it may still yield hints about what's working and what might be improved. Table 7.1 gives examples of information that may already be on hand.

It's one thing to collect assessment information and another to use it to improve student learning. Once you have a sense of assessment information on hand, your next question is how, if at all, that information has been used to improve teaching and learning. Do faculty and staff use their evaluations of student capstone projects simply to assign grades or also to identify ways to improve curricula and pedagogies? Have campus leaders acted on student survey results or simply seen the reports and continued with business as usual? Chapter Eighteen discusses how to use assessment results effectively and appropriately.

Table 7.1. Examples of Assessment Information That May Already Be on Hand

Scores on published tests, such as tests for placement, certification, or licensure
Ratings of students by field experience supervisors
Assessment information assembled to meet specialized accreditation requirements
Grading criteria and grades or scores on locally developed tests and assignments
Retention and graduation rates
Placement rates of graduates into appropriate careers or subsequent academic programs
Surveys of students and alumni
Course syllabi, which can be analyzed for learning outcomes, active learning opportunities, and assessment methods
Student transcripts, which can be analyzed for course enrollment patterns
End-of-course student evaluation forms, which can be reviewed for questions that ask about the course rather than the instructor
Counts of students participating in cocurricular, extracurricular, and service-learning activities
Library circulation statistics, including uses of online and electronic library resources

What Have Others Done?

Faculty and staff everywhere have made tremendous strides in recent decades in developing new and improved strategies to assess student learning. It never makes sense to reinvent the wheel, so capitalize on the work of others by researching current thinking on how each learning goal might be assessed. Review published literature, search online, contact relevant professional associations, attend assessment conferences, and talk to colleagues on your campus and elsewhere. Posting a query on an appropriate discussion list may generate good ideas and models.

Set Parameters

In all likelihood, your review of past and current assessment practices and information will identify some gaps. While you may have good information on hand regarding some learning goals, you may need to organize and document it better in order to use it. And you may have inadequate evidence on other learning goals and no information on still others.

Everyone will need guidance on what, if anything, they need to do differently (as well as what they're doing right) to build on current assessment practices and create a truly pervasive culture of ongoing, sustained assessment that meets the principles of good practice in Chapter Three. While structure is helpful, flexibility is even more so, as discussed in Chapter Five. Faculty and staff need sufficient guidance to understand what they are to do without being overwhelmed with excessive rules, forms, and bureaucracy.

Define Key Terms

As faculty and staff are introduced to the concept of assessment, many won't be familiar with the term or will have conflicting or misinformed ideas about what it means. Having a locally accepted definition of *assessment,* along with definitions of some other potentially fuzzy terms such as *goal* (Chapter Eight), *standard* (Chapter Fifteen), and *rubric* (Chapter Nine), may help prevent confusion or disagreement over exactly what is and is not expected. Chapters One and Two provide more information on defining assessment and some related terms.

Develop a Local Statement of Principles of Good Assessment Practice

Faculty and staff engaged in assessment need to be reassured of campus support for their efforts and that assessments will be conducted and used ethically and appropriately. Consider developing a local statement of principles of good assessment practice that describes characteristics of good assessment and the college's commitment to fostering successful assessment practices. Such a statement might proclaim, for example, that assessment results will not be used punitively.

While the principles of good practice discussed in Chapter Three are a good starting point for developing a local statement, it's usually not a good idea to adopt an existing statement wholesale. Your campus culture undoubtedly has unique perspectives, values, and concerns that should be addressed through a local statement. If faculty and staff are unionized, for example, a local statement might relate assessment expectations to contractual rights and responsibilities.

Just as students deserve to know the grading criteria for their assignments and what kinds of work will earn an A, faculty and staff deserve clear guidelines on the kinds of assessment practices that are considered exceptional, adequate, and inadequate on your campus. Exhibit 19.3 is an example of a rubric that provides this guidance.

Provide Guidelines on What Everyone Is to Do

Any task is less daunting if we understand exactly what we are to do, and assessment is no exception. We joke that students' most common questions about an assignment are, "How long should it be? When is it due?" but many of us find our work easier to accomplish if we have similar structure and guidelines. An effective assessment program gives faculty and staff clear expectations and guidance on precisely what they are to do. Logistical expectations are discussed later in this chapter; expectations for written assessment reports are discussed in Chapter Nineteen.

Identify Who Beyond Students Might Provide Assessment Information

Students are, of course, the fundamental source of assessment information. But others may also provide information on student learning.

Students' Peers

Student evaluations of their peers' presentations, drafts, and other assignments can be important parts of both learning and assessment.

Peer evaluations help the students who are being evaluated by adding the insight of people (fellow students) with different perspectives from their professor. Peer evaluations of contributions to collaborative learning activities can motivate the evaluated students to participate fully and effectively in them, especially if the evaluations count in some way toward final grades.

Peer evaluations also help the students who are doing the evaluations, because the act of evaluating peer work can strengthen critical thinking skills and help students understand faculty expectations.

Peer evaluations help with the assessment process as well. If learning goals include the development of interpersonal skills such as leadership or collaboration, peer evaluations can add a dimension that faculty and staff may not be able to view directly. Students achieve these goals by working with their peers, after all, while faculty and staff simply observe them.

Students can evaluate their peers' work by completing rubrics or rating scales (Chapters Nine and Twelve) or by providing structured observations (Chapter Nine). Exhibit 9.4 is an example of a rating scale for evaluating peer group members.

A significant shortcoming of peer evaluations is that they can be subject to biases and errors (Chapter Three) because they're transparent—that is, it's obvious which evaluations are positive or negative. Students may downrate a fellow student with good skills and traits simply because they don't like him. Because of the potential for inaccuracies, use peer evaluations cautiously:

- Ask students to evaluate specific behaviors rather than the overall performance of their peers. Asking students, "Did this student complete his or her share of the group's work on time?" will yield more accurate information than, "Was this student an effective group member?"

- Use peer evaluations in conjunction with more direct evidence of the traits being evaluated.

- If you are counting peer evaluations toward course grades, weight them minimally (perhaps no more than 5 percent).

Alumni

Alumni can contribute assessment information by describing their postgraduation experiences and their views of their education at your college. They can share, for example, how well they think their academic program prepared them for their current position or enriched their life. Indeed, some faculty and staff argue that attitudes, values, and the like (Chapter Twelve) take years to develop, and therefore the only way to assess them is to contact alumni many years from now and see if their education has indeed affected them in the ways we hope.

It's not always practical or meaningful to contact alumni, of course. It can be extraordinarily difficult to get a representative sample of alumni to participate in any assessment. It can be equally difficult to separate the impact of a course, program, or college from the impact of postgraduate experiences. Alumni may develop a passion for lifelong learning not through the academic program at their undergraduate institution but through postgraduate study or a mentor at work. And by the time we assess alumni, especially if we want to see how they are living their lives a number of years after they graduate, we may be assessing obsolete learning goals, a curriculum no longer offered, and long-retired faculty and staff, a pointless task.

But the aphorism, "As the twig is bent, so grows the tree," can be helpful here. If we want alumni to be passionate, lifelong learners, it's not unreasonable to expect students to start displaying relevant traits before they graduate—a point when assessment is more practical and useful. We can survey students getting ready to graduate about their leisure reading choices, their Internet surfing habits, the television shows they watch, and their postgraduate education plans—all clues to their propensity to be passionate lifelong learners. And we can ask them to reflect in writing on the development and breadth of their interests. Student reflection and student behaviors, discussed in Chapter Twelve, can thus serve as proxy measures that give some worthwhile clues on how those students may think and feel later in their lives. These strategies aren't ideal or definitive, but they still give useful insight.

Former Students Who Leave Before Graduating

Former students who leave before graduating are a tempting source of assessment information, especially on factors affecting student retention. Researchers have found, however, that the point of departure or afterward can be the worst time to try to collect information on reasons for student attrition. Because many departing students are disenfranchised from their college by the time they decide to leave, they will say they are leaving because of "financial difficulties" or "personal reasons"—socially acceptable answers that, if true, are often only symptoms of underlying problems. Students who have already left can be difficult to track down, resulting in a poor participation rate.

You'll get far better information if you survey appropriate cohorts of currently enrolled students (such as first-year students or high-risk groups). Hold the results for a term or year, find out who is still enrolled and who has left, and compare the two groups for differences in responses.

Field Experience Supervisors

Supervisors of students in field experiences can be a fountain of information on how well students are demonstrating key goals, including knowledge, skills, attitudes, and dispositions such as conscientiousness and openness to new ideas. A carefully constructed evaluation form—with a rating scale (Chapters Nine and Twelve), comments, or both—can provide direct and compelling evidence of how well students have achieved program goals. Exhibit 9.5 is an example of a rating scale for field experience supervisors.

Employers

Current and prospective employers of alumni can provide valuable information about employer needs and how well a program or college prepares students for careers in their businesses. Because of liability issues, employers will generally refuse to give information about individual employees, so ask them instead for general perceptions of a program or college and its graduates ("How well does Jamesville College prepare students in terms of leadership skills?").

Faculty

Many faculty continually observe and reflect on student learning, including harder-to-assess traits like effort and original thought. Their observations on more ineffable traits can be documented with tools like structured observations (Chapter Nine) and rating scales (Chapter Twelve).

Work Out the Logistics

Once faculty and staff understand the parameters for what they are to do, they can get down to the business of working out the details. Table 7.2 lists some of the logistical questions that may need to be answered for each key learning goal in a program or curriculum.

Table 7.2 lists too many questions to be answered by any one person at one time, so you may want to begin by asking three things about each question:

- Do we have an answer to this?
- If not, who has lead responsibility for getting this question answered?
- What is the deadline for doing so?

Table 7.2. Logistical Questions to Address When Planning a Systematic Assessment of Student Work

---

Who identifies and decides how to assess this learning goal? While faculty within each academic program obviously assume this responsibility for their courses and programs, the line of responsibility isn't clear in some other instances. Exactly who will decide on the learning goals and assessment strategies for the social sciences requirement of a general education curriculum, for example, when students can fulfill that requirement by taking any one of twenty courses offered by eight departments?

Who has lead responsibility for making sure that this assessment gets done? Consider asking each department or program to name a faculty assessment coordinator to handle this responsibility.

What assessment strategy or strategies will be used to assess this learning goal? Chapter Two provides an overview of the many assessment strategies from which you can choose, with the chapters in Part Three providing more details.

In which courses will faculty use this assessment strategy? If this assessment strategy will not be embedded into course work, how will you implement it?

From which sections will you collect examples of student work, if the courses have multiple sections?

How and when will you contact faculty teaching those sections, explain what you're asking them to do, and seek their cooperation?

What assignments or test questions will you be reviewing? If they are not already in place, who will write them and distribute them to the faculty?

How many examples of student work will be examined? (Chapter Three)

How will you choose the samples, if you are looking at samples of student work (Chapter Three)? Will faculty submit copies of all their students' work, with someone else choosing a sample, or will you ask faculty to submit only a sample? If so, how will they choose the sample?

What steps will you take to ensure that identifiable information such as student name is kept confidential? (Chapter Three)

When and how should faculty submit copies of student work? To whom should they send the copies? Should the work be submitted as paper copies, on disk or flash drive, as e-mail attachments, into an assessment management system, or otherwise?

Where and how will student work samples be housed? Who will have access to them?

Who will evaluate the student work? When?

How will the student work be evaluated? If you will use a rubric, who will develop it?

What are your standards for deciding whether student performance is acceptable (Chapter Fifteen)? What will you consider minimally acceptable work? What level of work will you consider unacceptable for a graduate of your program?

Who will summarize and, if necessary, analyze the completed rubrics or other evaluations of student work? (Chapter Sixteen)

How and with whom will the results of the assessment be shared? (Chapters Four, Seventeen, and Nineteen)

How do you expect to use the results? What questions will the results help answer? What decisions will the results help you and others make? (Chapters Four and Eighteen)

How will this all be communicated to the faculty and staff working on this assessment?

As you work out these details, keep in mind two principles from Chapter Five: ownership and flexibility. Involve faculty, staff, and students in deciding these details, and be willing to be flexible. A single time line for everyone across campus probably won't work, for example.

As you plan assessment logistics, aim not just to get things going but to keep the momentum going. Periodic reporting, review, and fine-tuning of the assessment process are essential to ensuring ongoing engagement by faculty and staff. Chapter Nineteen discusses this.

Special Challenges

Four situations may have additional considerations: general education core curricula, interdisciplinary and independently designed programs, adjunct faculty, and a curriculum that's about to change.

General Education Core Curricula

In most respects, organizing to assess a general education core curriculum is not much different from organizing an assessment of an academic program. It is more difficult, however. While assessment activities are now underway in academic programs at many colleges, relatively few general education curricula have fully developed assessment programs in place. Why is it so hard to assess general education (Bresciani, 2007)?

- General education curricula often suffer from lack of ownership. The courses are increasingly taught by part-time adjuncts rather than full-time faculty. Those full-time faculty who do teach general education courses are often more interested in their own academic programs. Sometimes relatively few faculty, if any, have a strong interest in improving general education.
- Some colleges and universities do not have clear definitions of their general education curriculum and its components.
- Some general education curricula have no overall planning, review, or coordination.
- Some general education curricula are ineffective—outdated, politically driven, or both.
- Because general education curricula can be complex and decentralized, they can be particularly difficult and time-consuming to assess and improve.

To overcome these obstacles and organize an assessment of general education, it is especially important to follow the principles, guidelines, and suggestions in Chapter Five for fostering a culture of assessment. In particular, be sure to do the following:

- Provide adequate support for general education activities.
- Identify someone to coordinate general education assessment.
- Charge a faculty committee to set general education assessment policies and review assessment efforts.
- Invite faculty teaching general education courses—both full time and adjuncts—to participate in discussions on general education goals, curriculum structure, and assessments.
- Recognize and reward efforts to assess general education in tangible ways.
- Use general education assessment results to inform important decisions on important goals.

Chapter One describes approaches to assessing general education core curricula.

Interdisciplinary and Self-Designed Programs

Increasing numbers of colleges and universities are developing interdisciplinary programs along with traditional academic majors. While some interdisciplinary programs are carefully designed and taught by a core of committed faculty, many are simply collections of courses in existing academic programs from which students may choose.

Similarly, when students opt for self-designed programs of study, some colleges require them to design a coherent, purposeful program, while others let students take an unstructured collection of courses.

Pick-from-a-list programs that are simply collections of courses are inexpensive to offer, but their lack of curricular coherence and faculty ownership makes student learning assessment a challenge. The lack of common curricular experiences (such as a required capstone course) makes it difficult to find opportunities to collect assessment information at appropriate points in the program. The lack of faculty ownership makes it difficult to get assessments planned, undertaken, reviewed, and used.

But the real problem with these programs is that they are not designed purposefully. They lack clearly articulated student learning goals, and the curricula are not designed to help students achieve those goals. In order to fix the assessment "problem," faculty must first fix the bigger problem of program incoherence.

Begin assessment in interdisciplinary programs by asking faculty affiliated with the program to articulate its key learning outcomes (Chapter Eight). Then ask them to review the curriculum to make sure that it has enough structure to ensure that every student will achieve those goals before graduating. Often this means, at a minimum, providing an entry-level course that introduces students to the program of study plus a capstone experience in which students integrate what they have learned throughout their studies.

Some interdisciplinary programs have so few students that it isn't cost-effective to include a course or seminar as the capstone experience. In these situations, a field experience, an independent study, or a course of directed readings may be an appropriate capstone experience—*if* it emphasizes and reinforces the program's key learning outcomes.

A similar approach can be used for self-designed programs. Begin by having the students, under faculty supervision, articulate their own learning outcomes: what they would like to learn through their studies. Students can always modify these goals as they move through the program and discover new interests. Then, still under faculty supervision, have the student design a program of study—again subject to modification—to achieve those goals.

When interdisciplinary and self-designed programs have clearly articulated learning goals and purposeful, coherent curricula, assessment can be accomplished through a capstone project or experience or a portfolio compiled throughout the program. Students in self-designed programs can plan how they will document achievement of their goals as part of their program planning process.

Adjunct Faculty

Today only the rare college does not include part-time adjuncts among its faculty, especially to teach general education courses. How can assessment be planned and implemented when adjuncts, whose time with and responsibilities to the college are limited, do much of the teaching? While answers depend on campus culture, adjunct contracts, and other factors, here are some ideas:

- Provide common core materials for adjuncts, such as a core syllabus, core learning goals, and core assignments and test questions on which they can build.

- Require participation in assessment activities within adjuncts' contractual responsibilities. Adjuncts might be required to include certain questions in their tests, use a common end-of-course assignment, use a department rubric to evaluate student papers, or participate in workshops or meetings related to assessment.

- Invite adjuncts to professional development opportunities, including those on teaching, learning, and assessment. Schedule these events at times when adjuncts are most able to attend.

- Assign full-time faculty as coordinators for courses and programs that are especially adjunct heavy. Consider offering them a stipend, reduced teaching load, or other compensation for taking on these responsibilities.

- Assign full-time faculty (again with some kind of compensation) as mentors to adjunct faculty in their departments.

A Curriculum in Flux

Colleges and universities are rarely static. There's always some curriculum that's undergoing a review and revision. If a different curriculum is going to be put in place shortly, does it make any sense to start assessment now?

The answer depends on the kinds of changes envisioned. Sometimes the learning goals of a curriculum aren't changing; the only modifications are curricular ones to help students better achieve those goals. In this case, it makes sense to start the assessment now to see if the modified curriculum does indeed lead to improved learning.

In other cases, some learning goals of the curriculum are changing, but others are remaining. It's the rare general education curriculum, old or new, that doesn't have a writing component, for example. In these cases, it usually makes sense to start assessing the learning goals that will continue.

But if faculty will spend the next year completely rewriting a curriculum, it may not make sense to require them to begin now to assess a curriculum that is soon to be obsolete, and a brief postponement may be reasonable.

Time to Think, Discuss, and Practice _____

1. Share your experiences with assessment—either as a faculty or staff member or as a student.

   - What was positive about those experiences, and what was negative, if anything?

   - What did you learn from those experiences—good or bad—that you can use today?

2. Brainstorm a list of information on student learning that your department or program might already have on hand, either in its own files or from another office on campus.

Recommended Readings _____

The following readings are recommended along with the references cited in this chapter.

Council for the Advancement of Standards in Higher Education. (1998). *Outcomes assessment and program evaluation: Standards and guidelines.* Washington, DC: Author.

Maki, P. (2002). Developing an assessment plan to learn about student learning. *Journal of Academic Librarianship, 28*(1–2), 8–13.

Schuh, J. H., & Upcraft, M. L. (2000). Assessment politics. *About Campus, 5*(4), 14–21.

CHAPTER 8

Developing Learning Goals

Some Valuable Ideas You'll Find in This Chapter

- While Bloom's taxonomy is the best-known framework for articulating learning goals, other taxonomies fill in some voids.
- While basic knowledge and conceptual understanding are important, they are less imperative today than thinking skills that use that knowledge and understanding.
- Employers, policymakers, and other higher education audiences increasingly value three skills: communication, information literacy (research and problem solving), and interpersonal skills.
- The most important question to ask when articulating learning goals is, "Why?"
- Well-expressed learning goals minimize fuzzy terms.
- It's okay to have goals that are a bit broad and nebulous, as long as everyone has a common understanding of what they mean.

Assessment begins not with creating or implementing tests, assignments, or other assessment tools but by deciding on your goals: what you want students to learn and why. This chapter discusses why goals are important; the meaning of terms such as *goals, objectives, competencies,* and *outcomes;* and how to develop and express learning goals.

Why Are Goals Important?

Imagine that an English professor teaching nineteenth-century poetry asks his students to keep journals in which they reflect on what they've learned as the course progresses. Without clear goals for the journal, his assignment may be something like, "After every class, jot down your thoughts about what you're learning." With such a vague assignment, his students won't know what to do, and, lacking focus, many won't learn much from the journaling experience. The journal won't be as effective as it would have been with explicit goals that lead to a more purposeful assignment.

Furthermore, with such a vague assignment, it isn't clear how the professor should evaluate the journals. He could evaluate them for writing qualities such as organization, clarity, grammar, or accuracy in reflecting class lectures and discussions. Or he could look for signs that students are developing an increased appreciation of nineteenth-century poetry. Or he could evaluate them in terms of how well students appraise scholarly interpretations of nineteenth-century poetry. Or he could look at how students relate nineteenth-century poetry to other literature, culture, and events of the times. Which of these is the correct way to evaluate the journals? There is no way to tell, because we don't know what the professor wants the students to learn from the journal-keeping experience.

As this example shows, without clear goals, both our students' learning experiences and our assessment of them are ambiguous and unsatisfactory. Our students don't know what to learn, and we don't know what to assess.

The Vocabulary of Goals

Goals, objectives, competencies, learning outcomes, and *proficiencies* all describe what we want students to learn, but educators don't yet use them consistently. Some of the more common uses of these terms are described here, along with some other terms that people confuse with *goals.*

Goals state what you, your colleagues, or your college aim to achieve. They can describe aims outside the teaching and learning process as well as within it. Within the undergraduate teaching and learning process, an astronomy professor might have a goal that her students learn about our solar system, your colleagues may have a goal to offer a high-quality educational program, and your college may have a goal to encourage students to engage in community service. Outside the undergraduate teaching and learning process, you may have a goal to complete some research this year, your department may have a goal to sponsor a regional scholarly conference, and your college may have a goal to raise $8 million in alumni gifts.

Outcomes are goals that refer to a destination rather than the path taken to get there—the end rather than the means, the outcome rather than the process. A goal that truly describes an outcome explains *why* we do what we do. A faculty member's real goal is not that students write a term paper but that they write effectively in their future studies and work. A student activities director's real goal is not to offer a student leadership development program but for students to lead student organizations effectively. A true institutional goal is not to raise $8 million but to increase educational opportunities for deserving students through additional scholarships.

Learning outcomes or *learning goals* are goals that describe how students will be different because of a learning experience. More specifically, learning outcomes are the knowledge, skills, attitudes, and habits of mind that students take with them from a learning experience.

Objectives can describe detailed aspects of goals. Within the broad goal of understanding our solar system, for example, an astronomy professor might have an objective that her students will know basic facts about each planet. Objectives can also describe the tasks to be accomplished to achieve the goal—the means to the end, the process leading to the outcome. If a goal of the astronomy professor is for students to explain science concepts in writing, her objectives might be for them to write essays, critique drafts of their peers, and maintain a journal in which they reflect on their growth as science writers.

Competencies and *proficiencies* are terms sometimes used to describe learning outcomes or objectives. Typically they are used to describe skills rather than knowledge, values, or attitudes.

Performance indicators are quantitative measures of overall student performance or other aspects of college performance. If a learning goal is that students write effectively, for example, the performance indicator might be the percentage of students who earn at least a minimally acceptable score on a rubric or test. Performance indicators are discussed in Chapter One.

Standards and *benchmarks* are the specific targets against which we gauge success in achieving an outcome. For a learning goal that students will write effectively, we might set a standard that 95 percent of our students earn at least a minimally acceptable score on a rating scale or rubric. Or we might set a benchmark that our students score, on average, above the average of students at peer institutions on a published writing test. Chapter Fifteen discusses standards and benchmarks.

Frameworks for Learning Goals

The task of identifying learning goals can seem overwhelming, particularly when establishing goals for a broad program, a general education curriculum, or a college. Faculty and staff who have never before considered or collaborated on articulating learning goals may find the process especially daunting. Understanding some frameworks for learning goals that group them into a few broad categories may be a helpful starting point.

The best-known framework, popularly known as Bloom's taxonomy (Bloom, 1956), has three domains of learning: cognitive, affective (attitudinal), and psychomotor (physical). The cognitive domain has six progressive levels of knowledge and intellectual skills: knowledge, comprehension, application, analysis, synthesis, and evaluation. A recent update of Bloom's taxonomy (Anderson & Krathwohl, 2001) reverses the synthesis and evaluation categories and changes "synthesize" to "create."

While Bloom's taxonomy is the best-known framework, others have filled in some voids and brought to the forefront some important goals not emphasized in Bloom's. Arthur Costa and Bena Kallick (2000) promote "habits of mind" such as persisting, thinking flexibly, and striving for accuracy. Robert Marzano, Debra Pickering, and Jay McTighe (1993) emphasize additional thinking skills such as organizing skills. The learning goals in various frameworks may be summarized into three categories, each discussed below:

- Knowledge and conceptual understanding
- Thinking and other skills
- Attitudes, values, dispositions, and habits of mind

Knowledge and Conceptual Understanding

Knowledge and *conceptual understanding* include remembering, replicating a simple procedure, and defining, summarizing, and explaining concepts or phenomena.

Examples

Explain how to access the Internet from computers in campus labs.

Summarize the distinctive characteristics of a particular novelist.

Understand each component of the scientific method.

Knowledge and conceptual understanding are important outcomes of many courses and programs, but today they are less important than they were a generation or two ago. One reason is that the amount of knowledge available to us has exploded.

We know, for example, far more about the building blocks of matter than we did a generation ago. There is more history to understand than when our parents went to school, and in the United States, the study of history has broadened from a Eurocentric model to a global one. The number of scholarly journals in almost every field has grown exponentially. Today there are so many important concepts that we can't expect students to remember them all.

Coupled with the explosion of knowledge is our increasingly easy access to it through libraries, bookstores, newsstands, and, most significant, the Web. Is it so important to remember a formula, date, or vital statistic when it can be looked up effortlessly? With today's easily accessible information, educators increasingly believe that we should change our focus from remembering facts and concepts to learning how to find them, analyze them, use them appropriately, and appreciate their meaning and value.

Furthermore, our knowledge base will continue to expand and evolve. Today's students will someday need information that hasn't yet been conceived and insight that hasn't yet been drawn, rendering obsolete some of the information we now teach. Should we focus on having students remember material that may soon be outdated or irrelevant? Or should we focus on developing the thinking skills they'll need to master new concepts on their own, after they've left college?

Finally, as we understand better how people learn, we are realizing that much of what students memorize is committed to short-term memory and quickly forgotten. Imagine how your students would do if you popped their final exam on them just a few months later. How much would they remember from the first time they studied for it? Probably not much. So is it worth spending time teaching material that's so quickly lost? Or should we focus instead on developing skills and attitudes that will last a lifetime, such as the ability to write well, analyze the difference between two theories, or appreciate American folk music?

Because of all these factors, educators are increasingly emphasizing thinking and other skills more than knowledge and simple understanding. Does this mean that students shouldn't memorize anything anymore? Absolutely not! We wouldn't want to fly in a jet whose pilot has to look up the meaning of that flashing light as the plane goes into a nosedive. We wouldn't want to be operated on by a surgeon who has to pause to read up on how to stop that excessive bleeding. Students will always need to remember and understand certain fundamental concepts. But today we expect college students to *use* facts and concepts as well as understand them.

Thinking and Other Skills

Many kinds of thinking skills are discussed in this section. As you review them, keep in mind that they are not discrete. It would be hard, for example, to think of someone engaged in sound evaluation who does not bring analysis skills into play.

Application

Application is the capacity to use knowledge and understanding in a new context. It includes the abilities to understand cause-and-effect relationships, understand the meaning of logical propositions, criticize literary works, and apply scientific principles to research problems *when* these relationships, propositions, works, and problems are new to the student. Many mathematics word problems require application skill.

Examples

Locate online resources on a particular topic or issue.

Apply scientific or economic principles to everyday life.

Analysis

Analysis is the capacity to break a complex concept apart to understand the relationships of its components. Students who can analyze can identify the elements, relationships, and underlying principles of a complex process. Analysis is not merely understanding the relationships of components of a process or concept explained in class; that would be simple comprehension. Students who can analyze can understand the structure of things *they haven't seen before.* They can think holistically, make a case, discover the underlying principles of a relationship, and understand organizational structure. They can integrate their learning, relating what they are learning to what they already know.

Examples

Explain chemical reactions not explicitly introduced in prior study.

Explain the impact of the Korean War on U.S.–East Asian relations today.

Analyze errors.

Compare and contrast perspectives and values.

Explain why a particular research paper is structured the way it is.

Evaluation, Problem-Solving, and Decision-Making Skills

These terms have more in common than not. They all refer to skill in making informed judgments about the merits of something the student hasn't seen before. They include the abilities to conduct research, make appropriate choices, solve problems with no single correct answer, and make and justify persuasive arguments. They are not merely understanding and reflecting arguments that have been presented in course work; that would be simple comprehension.

Examples

Judge the effectiveness of the use of color in a work of art.

Evaluate the validity of information on a particular Web site.

Research, identify, and justify potential careers.

Choose the appropriate mathematical procedure for a given problem.

Identify an audit problem in a financial statement, and recommend ways to address it.

Synthesis and Creativity

Synthesis is the capacity to put together what one has learned in a new, original way. It includes the abilities to theorize, generalize, reflect, construct hypotheses, generate new ideas and new ways of viewing a situation, invent, and suggest alternatives.

Examples

Write a poem that uses imagery and structure typical of early-nineteenth-century American poets.

Theorize what is likely to happen when two chemicals are combined, and justify the theory.

Design and conduct a research study.

Design a community service project.

Creativity is a concept whose meaning lacks popular consensus. Jonathan Plucker, Ronald Beghetto, and Gayle Dow (2004) have defined creativity as "the interaction among aptitude, process, and environment" by which someone produces "a perceptible product that is both novel and useful as defined within a social context" (p. 90). It's likely that many people think of creativity as including not only the ability to synthesize but also the abilities to be flexible, take intellectual risks, and be open-minded to new ideas.

Examples

Conceive of original, unorthodox solutions to a problem.

Recognize that one's vision can appropriately exceed one's capacity.

Recognize and celebrate not knowing.

Critical Thinking

Critical thinking is another widely used term whose meaning lacks popular consensus. Critical thinking skills can include many of the thinking skills described in this chapter, including analysis, synthesis, evaluation, problem solving, and some of the habits of mind discussed below. Critical thinking may also include the capacities to seek truth, clarity, and accuracy; distinguish facts from opinions; and have a healthy skepticism about arguments and claims. If critical thinking emerges as a potential learning goal, spell out the kinds of thinking skills it encompasses in your particular situation.

Information Literacy

Information literacy (Association of College and Research Libraries, 2000) is often erroneously thought of as library research skills. It is a much broader set of skills (Table 8.1), reflecting today's reality that much research takes place outside the traditional college library. Information literacy includes many of the (critical) thinking skills discussed in this chapter, and some might consider it synonymous with research or problem-solving skills.

Table 8.1. What Is Information Literacy?

Information literacy includes the capacity to:

Recognize the need for information to answer a question or solve a problem.

Identify what information is needed to answer the question or solve the problem.

Find that information, whether through traditional library research, online sources, professional manuals, colleagues, original research, or other appropriate sources.

Evaluate the information critically for credibility and relevance to the question or problem.

Use the information to answer the question or solve the problem

Use the information *legally and ethically*, citing and acknowledging the work of others accurately.

Other Skills

Performance skills are physical skills such as the abilities to operate equipment, manipulate a tool, wield a paintbrush, hit a softball, or dance gracefully.

Examples

Hold and play a violin in proper position.

Use fitness equipment safely, minimizing the risk of injury.

Interpersonal skills include the abilities to listen, work with people from diverse backgrounds, lead a group, and participate as an effective team member.

Examples

Lead a group to a consensus on a plan of action.

Paraphrase accurately the ideas that others express.

Listen and reflect empathetically to a client.

Attitudes, Values, Dispositions, and Habits of Mind _____

Attitudinal goals include appreciation, integrity, character, enjoying and valuing learning, and becoming more aware of one's values, attitudes, and opinions and their evolution. Richard Shavelson (2007) has used the phrase "personal and social responsibility (PSR) skills" to characterize many of these traits. Chapter Twelve discusses assessing attitudes, values, dispositions, and habits of mind.

Examples

Be intellectually curious.

Appreciate the merits and value of a subject or discipline.

Appreciate the perspective of people from backgrounds different from your own.

Choose ethical courses of action.

Metacognition

Metacognition is learning how to learn and how to manage your own learning by understanding how you learn, thereby preparing for a lifetime of learning. Metacognition includes the traits in Table 8.2.

Because knowledge is growing at an exponential pace, there is increasing recognition that we must prepare students for a lifetime of learning, often on their own, making metacognition an increasingly valued skill.

Table 8.2. What Is Metacognition?

Use efficient learning techniques.
Discuss and evaluate your own problem-solving strategies.
Critically examine and evaluate the bases for your arguments.
Correct or revise your reasoning or arguments when self-examination so warrants.
Form efficient plans for completing work.
Evaluate the effectiveness of your actions.

Examples

> Develop a personal study strategy that makes the most of your learning style.
>
> Identify the strengths and weaknesses of your completed work.

Productive Dispositions or Habits of Mind

Habits of mind (Costa & Kallick, 2000) can include the capacities to work independently, set personal goals, persevere, organize, be clear and accurate, visualize, and be curious.

Examples

> Develop and use effective time management skills.
>
> Follow directions correctly.
>
> Appreciate negatives and failures as opportunities to learn and discover choices.

Which Learning Goals Are Most Important and Valued Today?

While every course, program, and college can and should have unique goals, faculty, administrators, employers, policymakers, and other higher education audiences increasingly agree that

Table 8.3. Learning Goals That Are Important and Valued Today

Communication skills, especially in writing	Virtually everyone needs to be able to express himself or herself clearly in writing and speech.
Information literacy (research and problem-solving) skills	Because virtually everyone needs to continue to learn independently after graduation, both to stay current in their field and for personal enrichment, everyone needs to know how to find information and evaluate its merits and worth in order to solve problems and make decisions.
Interpersonal skills	Many careers require the ability to work with and lead others.

today's college graduates, regardless of major, should have the three capabilities described in Table 8.3.

While general education curricula often address these skills, students need to develop them from a disciplinary perspective as well. A first-year composition course, for example, won't teach biology, psychology, or business students how to write in their discipline; faculty in the discipline need to do that.

Integrated Learning Goals Across Venues and Levels

Colleges, programs, and courses always fit into a larger context. A course is part of a program or general education curriculum, the program is part of a college or university, and the college or university is part of a global society in which its students will live, work, and perhaps continue their studies. Chapter One notes the importance of integrating goals among venues and levels of student learning opportunities so that students can benefit from integrated, collaborative learning experiences.

Table 8.4 gives examples of goals at various venues and levels that address research and problem-solving skills. In this example, the learning goals for a student development program,

Table 8.4. Examples of Interrelationships of Goals Among Venues and Levels

Venue or Level	Learning Goal: Research and Problem-Solving Skills	Assessment Strategy
Institutional	Students will use and analyze a variety of resources to make decisions and solve problems.	A senior capstone research project (Chapter One), assessed using a rubric
Student development program: Greek life	Students will locate and use community resources to address human needs.	Journals (Chapter Twelve) in which students record their service work that helps area residents locate and use community resources
General education	Students will use and analyze a variety of resources to make decisions and solve problems.	Group research projects in courses in the social science component of the general education curriculum, assessed using a rubric
Academic program: English	Students will conduct research on issues in the study of English literature.	Research papers, assessed using a rubric
Course: Shakespeare's Tragedies	Students will analyze scholarly views of the motivations of one of Shakespeare's characters.	Research papers, assessed using a rubric

the general education curriculum, and an academic program all support the institutional goal. In fact, in this example, the institutional and general education learning goals are identical, as they often are at colleges and universities. Also, in this example, the course goal supports both the academic program and general education curriculum goals.

Although interrelated goals are an important way to ensure curricular coherence, it is not practical to expect absolutely lockstep relationships among goals at every level and in every venue. An institutional goal of understanding diverse cultures could be supported by goals in many areas but perhaps not by the mathematics program. A program goal to write effectively in the discipline might be supported by goals in several but not all courses in the program. Exhibit 7.1 includes examples of goals that are not addressed in every component of a program.

Identifying Potential Learning Goals

Because learning goals should be integrated as appropriate across venues and levels, they should be developed not in isolation but as the result of research, reflection, and informed collaborative discussion.

Research

Rather than start with a blank slate, it makes sense to collect information on potential learning goals from internal and external resources (Table 8.5).

Table 8.5. Internal and External Resources for Identifying Potential Learning Goals

---

Internal Resources
Your college's mission statement, vision statement, and strategic goals
Syllabi of current courses, especially capstone experiences (Chapter Seven)
Transcripts of recent graduates (Chapter Seven)

External Resources
Goals or standards espoused by relevant disciplinary associations and accreditors
Surveys or interviews of prospective employers of graduates of your college or program
Admissions criteria for academic programs your students pursue after program completion
Greater Expectations: A New Vision for Learning as a Nation Goes to College
    (Association of American Colleges and Universities, 2002)
Learning Outcomes for the Twenty-First Century (Wilson, Miles, Baker, & Schoenberger, 2000)
Equipped for the Future Content Standards (Stein, 2001)

Reflection

Teaching is fundamentally a personal process, so faculty and staff should have time to reflect on their own goals as well as research what others are doing. Faculty and staff often have an implicit sense of what they want students to learn. Asking them to complete the Teaching Goals Inventory (Angelo & Cross, 1993) may help them verbalize the main things they aim to accomplish in each course or program they teach. Chapter Nine offers some additional suggestions to help faculty and staff who struggle to articulate their goals and grading criteria.

Collaboration

Students learn more effectively when their learning experiences are purposeful, coherent, and integrated (Chapter One). This can happen only when faculty and staff collaborate to articulate key student learning outcomes.

Conversations on learning goals may be difficult, especially when faculty are used to working independently. But these conversations can also be one of the most invigorating and rewarding aspects of an assessment effort, because they address the heart of faculty and staff work: teaching and learning. Chapter Five notes the importance of emphasizing and respecting the many things that faculty and staff already do. Focus these conversations, then, on identifying existing common ground.

Begin by compiling and sharing the results of any research or reflection on learning goals on a handout or large chart for all to see. With this information in hand, faculty and staff can discuss questions such as those in Table 8.6.

Consensus

What if faculty and staff cannot agree on key learning goals for a course, program, or general education requirement? There's no law that 100 percent agreement is needed in order to move forward, and several techniques can help gauge consensus, make decisions, and proceed. One is simply to vote, let the majority rule, and move on. Another is to break the faculty and staff into small groups and ask each group to identify perhaps three goals that everyone in the group agrees are important. The groups can then share their goals and identify common goals across groups. A third technique, shown in Table 8.7, is the Delphi method (Hsu & Sandford, 2007).

Table 8.6. Examples of Discussion Topics Regarding Learning Goals

What is this course or discipline all about? What do we value about our discipline? What are the most important things students learn in this course or program? Why are those things important?

What does our disciplinary association (or major authorities in our discipline) think students should learn?

Why do we offer or require this course, program, or general education requirement? Why is it important that students study this? How do we want this experience to prepare them for or enrich whatever they do after graduation?

What do we expect of students in this course, program, or general education requirement?

What do we want all students to get out of this program or general education requirement, regardless of the particular course, track, or professor they elect?

How does this course relate to other courses in this program or general education curriculum? How does this program or general education requirement relate to other disciplines that students may be studying?

What do we want students who successfully complete this course, program, or general education requirement to know or be able to do five or ten years after graduating?

What do our students do after they graduate? What are the most important things they need for success in those pursuits?

What makes our graduates successful? What makes them attractive to potential employers, graduate programs, and the like?

If our program prepares students for careers, what knowledge, skills, and attitudes do employers look for?

Table 8.7. The Delphi Method for Achieving Consensus

1. Create a list of all identified potential learning goals for a course or program.
2. Distribute the list to faculty and staff members, and ask each to check off those goals that he or she thinks should be one of the key goals of the course or program. Sometimes it is agreed that everyone will vote for no more than a certain number of goals, such as six or eight.
3. Collect the lists, tally the checkmarks, and share the results with faculty and staff.
4. Strike goals with no votes. (The group may also agree to strike goals with just one or two votes.)
5. Sometimes a few goals will clearly emerge as the top vote getters, and the group will agree to focus on them, ending the process.
6. If consensus cannot be reached after the first round, redistribute the (possibly abbreviated) list with the initial results noted, and ask faculty and staff to vote again. Sometimes it is again agreed that everyone will vote for no more than a certain number of goals.
7. Again collect, tally, and share the lists. Human nature is such that few people will persist in voting for a goal supported by few others, so consensus on a few manageable goals is usually reached by this point. If not, the cycle is repeated until consensus is achieved.

Good Ways to Express Learning Goals

Writing effective goals is an art that comes easily to some people and remains a struggle for others. Goals are also more easily crafted for some courses and programs than for others. As with all other aspects of assessment, consider learning goals a work in progress. Be prepared to refine them after you implement them and see how well they work. The following suggestions will help you get started.

Focus on the End, Not the Means, by Asking *Why*

Effective learning goals refer to a destination rather than the path taken to get there—the end rather than the means. Ask yourself what students should be able to do *after* they have successfully completed your course or program, not the tasks they are to do while in your course or program.

If faculty or staff find it hard to make the leap from articulating processes to articulating outcomes, encourage them to ask, "Why? *Why* do we ask students to write a research paper? *Why* do we require five lab reports?" The answers, which are the true goals, can vary considerably. Faculty might ask students to write a research paper, for example, to improve their skill in:

- Conducting original research in the discipline
- Conducting library research in the discipline
- Understanding and interpreting the published research of others
- Writing in the discipline
- Critical thinking and analysis

Understanding the true goal of the assignment helps create a more effective assignment and evaluate it more fairly and appropriately. A faculty member who wants students to learn how to conduct library research, for example, might ask them to prepare an annotated bibliography rather than a full-blown research paper and evaluate it more in terms of library research skills than writing quality. A faculty member who wants students to learn how to write in the discipline might ask students to write a research proposal rather than a full-blown research paper and evaluate it more in terms of writing skills.

Clarify Fuzzy Terms

Learning goals are sometimes phrased using broad, nebulous terms such as these:

- Students will learn . . .
- Students will know . . .
- Students will understand . . .
- Students will become aware of . . .
- Students will appreciate . . .

- Students will think critically.
- Students will write proficiently.
- Students will demonstrate knowledge, skill, proficiency, or understanding of . . .

Vaguely stated learning goals like these can lead to confusion. Consider a goal that students will "understand basic concepts about our solar system." Astronomy professors may have differing opinions about what constitutes basic concepts. Are we talking about basic facts about each planet or also theories about how the solar system was created? The faculty may also have differing opinions about what it means to "understand" those basic concepts. Does this mean memorizing basic facts? Or does it mean using information about our solar system to speculate about the characteristics of other solar systems?

If a learning goal isn't clear to us, it certainly won't be clear to students. They'll have difficulty figuring out what and how to learn, and we'll have difficulty coming up with an appropriate assessment. Clarifying fuzzy terms gives faculty, staff, and students a clearer common understanding of what to teach, what to learn, and what to assess. Restating, "Think critically," as "Analyze and evaluate arguments," for example, helps everyone understand what they are to do.

Learning goals are developed for more than one audience, of course. Sometimes they have a public relations purpose as well as a role in the teaching and learning process. "Think critically" and "communicate effectively" are the kinds of statements that parents and other public audiences want to see in mission statements, brochures, and Web sites, even if they are not clear. If you need a fuzzy statement for these purposes, it's fine to "translate" it into clearer terms for teaching, learning, and assessment purposes.

Aim for Goals That Are Neither Too Broad Nor Too Specific

While fuzzy goals are problematic, so are goals that are too specific, because "the price of precision is the narrowness of scope" (Shulman, 2007, p. 24). The best learning goals thus fall between these two extremes:

Too vague: Students will demonstrate information literacy skills.
Too specific: Students will be able to use the college's online services to retrieve information.
Better: Students will locate information and evaluate it critically for its validity and appropriateness.

There is a wide continuum of acceptable specificity. Some faculty and staff find that relatively broad statements of learning goals work best for them, while others find that relatively specific statements are more useful.

Use Concrete Action Words When Possible

Fuzzy, vague goals can be avoided by stating outcomes using concrete action words that describe in explicit, observable terms what students can do after they've learned the material. After completing the astronomy professor's solar system unit, for example, perhaps her students will be able to *describe* the key characteristics of each planet. Perhaps they will be able to *create a scale model* of the solar system. Perhaps they will be able to *explain* why each planet except Earth cannot support human life.

Concrete action words help students understand what we want them to learn. They also make assessment easier, as they practically dictate what the assessment will be (Table 8.8).

But occasionally concrete action words make learning goals too specific. Translating "communicate effectively in writing" into action words would result in a long list of the many characteristics of effective writing—a list so long as to be unwieldy. With so much detail, the forest—the major learning goal—may be lost among the trees of specific action-word outcomes. In this kind of situation, it may be more useful to express a learning goal in relatively vague terms such as "know," "understand," "become aware of," or "appreciate" rather than action words. Then clarify the goal by developing an accompanying rating scale or rubric (Chapter Nine) that lists, say, the key characteristics of effective writing.

Table 8.9 provides examples of effectively expressed learning goals that use action words and are neither too broad nor too specific.

Table 8.8. Examples of Action-Word Goals and Corresponding Assessments

Action-word goal: Describe the key characteristics of each planet.
Assessment: Write short descriptions of the key characteristics of each planet.

Action-word goal: Create a scale model of the solar system.
Assessment: Create a scale model of the solar system.

Action-word goal: Explain why each planet except Earth cannot support human life.
Assessment: Write a short explanation of why each planet except Earth cannot support human life.

Table 8.9. Examples of Effectively Expressed Learning Goals

Biology	Make appropriate references and deductions from biological information.
Business Management	Develop graphic, spreadsheet, and financial analysis support for positions taken.
Chemistry	Design an experiment to test a chemical hypothesis or theory
Communication Studies	Systematically analyze and solve problems, advocate and defend one's views, and refute opposing views.
Earth Science	Analyze the surface and subsurface (three-dimensional and four-dimensional) geological characteristics of landforms.
English	Present original interpretations of literary works in the context of existing research on these works.
Environmental Science	Critically evaluate the effectiveness of agencies, organizations, and programs addressing environmental problems.
Health Care Management	Apply basic problem-solving skills along with health care financial management knowledge to develop recommendations related to the financial issues confronted by a health care organization.
Medieval and Renaissance Studies	Write with clarity, unity, coherence, and correctness.
Metropolitan Studies	Conduct and present sound research on metropolitan issues.
Speech-Language Pathology/Audiology	Use appropriate interpersonal qualities and professional characteristics of responsibility, empathy, and openness to self-exploration during interactions with peers, academic and clinical faculty and staff, and clients.
Theater	Use voice, movement, and understanding of dramatic character and situation to affect an audience.
Women's Studies	Use gender as an analytical category to critique cultural and social institutions.

Time to Think, Discuss, and Practice

1. A professor has asked his students to write a paper in which they are to "discuss" an historical event. Under what circumstances would this assignment assess only simple understanding of the event? Under what circumstances would this assignment assess a thinking skill? What thinking skills might it assess?

2. The Landisville College faculty have agreed that they would like to include the following aims, taken from the Teaching Goals Inventory (Angelo & Cross, 1993) as goals of their general education curriculum. Restate these aims so that they meet the characteristics of well-expressed goals discussed in this chapter:

   • Develop analytical skills.

   • Prepare for transfer or graduate study.

   • Develop aesthetic appreciation.

3. Dover College faculty are designing a first-year seminar to help students develop the skills and dispositions they need to succeed in college. They have decided that students need to develop critical thinking skills, but they are not sure what this means, how to teach it, or how to assess it.

   • What critical thinking skills do you think students most need to succeed in today's colleges? Try to identify two or three such skills.

   • For each critical thinking skill you've identified, come up with one suggestion for an assignment that students in the seminar might complete to help them develop that skill.

4. Write a learning goal for students in a program in which you teach or are enrolled that would focus on developing evaluation, problem-solving, or decision-making skills.

Recommended Readings

The following readings are recommended along with the references cited in this chapter.

Angelo, T. A. (1991). Ten easy pieces: Assessing higher learning in four dimensions. In T. A. Angelo (Ed.), *Classroom research: Early lessons from success* (pp. 17–31). New Directions for Teaching and Learning, no. 46. San Francisco: Jossey-Bass.

Association of American Colleges and Universities. (2002). *Liberal education outcomes for the 21st century*. Washington, DC: Author.

Association of American Colleges and Universities. (2005). *Liberal education outcomes: A preliminary report on student achievement in college*. Washington, DC: Author.

Biggs, J. (2001). Assessing for quality in learning. In L. Suskie (Ed.), *Assessment to promote deep learning*. Sterling, VA: Stylus.

Facione, P. A. (2007). *2007 update: Critical thinking: What it is and why it counts*. Retrieved September 16, 2008, from www.insightassessment.com/pdf_files/what&why2007.pdf.

Gaff, J. (2004). What is a generally educated person? *Peer Review*, 7(1), 4–7.

Gronlund, N. E. (1999). *How to write and use instructional objectives* (6th ed.). Upper Saddle River, NJ: Prentice Hall.

Jones, E. A. (1997). Problem-solving and critical reading outcomes expected by faculty, employers, and policymakers. *Assessment Update*, 9(6), 8–10.

Jones, E. A., & Voorhees, R., with Paulson, K. (2002). *Defining and assessing learning: Exploring competency-based initiatives* (NCES 2002–159). Washington, DC: U.S. Department of Education, National Center for Education Statistics.

Marzano, R. J., & Kendall, J. S. (2006). *The new taxonomy of educational objectives* (2nd ed.). Thousand Oaks, CA: Corwin Press.

National Leadership Council for Liberal Education and America's Promise. (2007). *College learning for the new global century*. Washington, DC: Association of American Colleges and Universities.

North Central Regional Educational Laboratory. (2004). *Skills and competencies needed to succeed in today's workplace*. Retrieved September 16, 2008, from www.ncrel.org/sdrs/areas/issues/methods/assment/as7scans.htm.

Smith, D. K. (1999). *Make success measurable! A mindbook–workbook for setting goals and taking action*. Hoboken, NJ: Wiley.

Wick, M. R., & Phillips, A. T. (2008). A liberal education scorecard. *Liberal Education, 94*(1), 22–29.

PART THREE

The Assessment Toolbox

CHAPTER 9

Using a Scoring Guide or Rubric to Plan and Evaluate an Assignment

---

Some Valuable Ideas You'll Find in This Chapter

- Rubrics are terrific tools for student learning as well as for assessment.
- Rubrics can speed up the grading process.
- Rubrics come in many formats, and no one format is best for every situation.
- Use a rubric as a tool to plan your assignment: write the rubric before you write the assignment that it will evaluate.

Educators are increasingly recognizing the value of performance assessments (Chapter Two): papers, projects, field experiences, performances, and other assignments that ask students to perform or demonstrate their skills. This chapter and Chapter Ten explain how to plan, create, and evaluate these kinds of assessments.

What Is a Rubric?

A *rubric* is a scoring guide: a list or chart that describes the criteria that you and perhaps your colleagues will use to evaluate or grade completed student assignments. At a minimum, a rubric lists the things you're looking for when you evaluate assignments. The list is often accompanied by guidelines for evaluating each of those things.

One of the great things about rubrics is that they have no rules. There is no single correct way to write or format rubrics. Any format that you're comfortable with is fine, so long as you fulfill the rubric's purposes, articulated in Table 9.1. This chapter discusses just four of the many ways to format rubrics: checklists, rating scales, descriptive rubrics, and holistic scoring guides. It also discusses structured observation guides—qualitative assessment tools that are somewhat related to rubrics.

Some faculty and staff are put off by the jargony nature of the word *rubric.* If this is the case, simply substitute in your discussions a term such as *scoring guide* or *grading criteria.*

Why Use a Rubric?

Using a rubric to grade student assignments makes your life easier and improves student learning in the ways shown in Table 9.1.

Checklist Rubrics

A checklist rubric is a simple list indicating the presence of the things you're looking for in a completed assignment. Exhibit 9.1 is an example.

Checklist rubrics are used most often in primary grades (Did you write your name on your paper? Did you show all your work?). In higher education, expectations are more sophisticated (Did you summarize very well or merely adequately?), so checklist rubrics are used less often. Faculty might choose them when they observe student performance in laboratory or studio settings (Did the student wear goggles? Follow safe practices? Clean up at the end of the lab?). Students might use them to self-assess their work before they turn it in (Have I proofread my paper? Does my bibliography use proper formatting conventions? Did I include at least eight references?).

Rating Scale Rubrics

A rating scale rubric is a checklist with a rating scale added to show the degree to which the things you're looking for are present in completed assignments. Exhibits 9.2 and 9.3 are examples of rating

Table 9.1. Advantages of Rubrics

Rubrics help clarify vague, fuzzy goals. A goal such as, "Demonstrate effective writing skills" is admittedly vague—what *are* effective writing skills?—but difficult to clarify succinctly (Chapter Eight). A rubric can provide this clarification.

Rubrics help students understand your expectations. If you distribute a rubric with an assignment, students will understand better what you want them to do and where they should focus their energies. You'll have fewer questions from students, and they may find the assignment a richer, more rewarding experience.

Rubrics can help students self-improve. If you encourage students to use the rubric to self-evaluate their work before turning it in, in order to make sure the assignment is complete and up to acceptable standards, you are helping them develop the important lifelong skill of metacognition (Chapter Eight): understanding how they learn by reflecting on how they learn.

Rubrics can inspire better student performance. Rubrics show students exactly what you value and what you'll be looking for when you evaluate their assignments. Knowing what you expect will motivate some (not all!) to aim for the targets you've identified.

Rubrics make scoring easier and faster. While it may seem that using a scoring guide adds an extra burden to the grading process, rubrics actually make the grading process faster because they remind you of what you're looking for. You also won't need to write as many comments on papers.

Rubrics make scoring more accurate, unbiased, and consistent. Rubrics ensure that every paper is evaluated using the same criteria.

Rubrics improve feedback to students. Marked rubrics give students a clearer picture of their strengths and weaknesses than a few comments scrawled on their papers.

Rubrics reduce arguments with students. By making evaluation criteria explicit, rubrics stop student arguments ("Why did he get a B− when I got a C+?") cold. You can focus your conversations with students on how they can improve their performance rather than defending your grading practices.

Rubrics improve feedback to faculty and staff. If a number of students aren't demonstrating understanding of a particular concept or skill, rubrics bring this to your attention. The consistency of rubrics can help track changes in student performance as you refine your teaching. Rubrics can help determine, for example, whether introducing collaborative learning activities into classes has improved students' analysis skills.

Exhibit 9.1. A Checklist Rubric for a Web Site

- ☐ The purpose of the site is obvious.
- ☐ The site's structure is clear and intuitive.
- ☐ Titles are meaningful.
- ☐ Each page loads quickly.
- ☐ The text is easy to read.
- ☐ Graphics and multimedia help convey the site's main points.
- ☐ The design is clean, uncluttered, and engaging.
- ☐ Spelling, punctuation, and grammar are correct.
- ☐ Contact information for the author or sponsor is given.
- ☐ The date each page was last updated is provided.

Exhibit 9.2. A Rating Scale Rubric for an Oral Presentation

The presenter . . .	Strongly Agree	Agree	Disagree	Strongly Disagree
Clearly stated the purpose of the presentation	☐	☐	☐	☐
Was well organized	☐	☐	☐	☐
Was knowledgeable about the subject	☐	☐	☐	☐
Answered questions authoritatively	☐	☐	☐	☐
Spoke clearly and loudly	☐	☐	☐	☐
Maintained eye contact with the audience	☐	☐	☐	☐
Appeared confident	☐	☐	☐	☐
Adhered to time constraints	☐	☐	☐	☐
Had main points that were appropriate to the central topic	☐	☐	☐	☐
Accomplished the stated objectives	☐	☐	☐	☐

Source: Adapted with permission from Sharon B. Buchbinder and Donna M. Cox from a rubric used by faculty in the Health Care Management Program, Towson University.

scale rubrics for assignments. Exhibit 9.4 is one used by students to evaluate their peers, and Exhibit 9.5 is one used by field experience supervisors. (Chapter Seven has more information on obtaining assessment information from field experience supervisors and student peers.) Exhibit 13.4 is a rating scale rubric to evaluate portfolios, and Exhibit 19.3 is one to evaluate assessment reports.

The major shortcoming of rating scale rubrics is that performance levels are not clearly described. In the rubric in Exhibit 9.3, the difference between "outstanding" and "very good" articulation of information and ideas isn't clear. The vague nature of rating scale rubrics can lead to several problems:

- *Faculty and staff may be inconsistent in how they rate performance.* One faculty member might rate a paper "outstanding" in its articulation of information and ideas, while another faculty member might rate the same paper "very good" in this respect.

- *Students don't receive thorough feedback.* Yes, students can learn from a completed rating scale rubric that their paper's organization was relatively weak and their grammar was relatively strong, but from the scored rubric alone, they won't learn exactly how their organization was weak or how it might be improved.

- *Rating scale rubrics can lack credibility with some audiences.* Some might look skeptically on the faculty rating 85 percent of

Exhibit 9.3. Rating Scale Rubric for an Information Literacy Assignment

Indicate the student's skill in each of the following respects, as evidenced by this assignment, by checking the appropriate box. If this assignment is not intended to elicit a particular skill, check the Not Applicable box.

	Outstanding (A)	Very Good (B)	Adequate (C)	Marginally Adequate (D)	Inadequate (F)	Not Applicable
1. Identify, locate, and access sources of information.	☐	☐	☐	☐	☐	☐
2. Critically evaluate information, including its legitimacy, validity, and appropriateness.	☐	☐	☐	☐	☐	☐
3. Organize information to present a sound central idea supported by relevant material in a logical order.	☐	☐	☐	☐	☐	☐
4. Use information to answer questions and solve problems.	☐	☐	☐	☐	☐	☐
5. Clearly articulate information and ideas.	☐	☐	☐	☐	☐	☐
6. Use information technologies to communicate, manage, and process information.	☐	☐	☐	☐	☐	☐
7. Use information technologies to solve problems.	☐	☐	☐	☐	☐	☐
8. Use the work of others accurately and ethically.	☐	☐	☐	☐	☐	☐
9. What grade are you awarding this assignment?	☐	☐	☐	☐	☐	
10. If you had to assign a final course grade for this student today, what would it be?	☐	☐	☐	☐	☐	

Exhibit 9.4. A Rating Scale Rubric for Evaluating Fellow Group Members

Your name:
Name of the group member you're evaluating:

This group member...	Almost Always	Often	Sometimes	Rarely
1. Did his or her fair share of the work.	☐	☐	☐	☐
2. Participated actively in the group's activities.	☐	☐	☐	☐
3. Contributed useful ideas, suggestions, and comments.	☐	☐	☐	☐
4. Listened carefully.	☐	☐	☐	☐
5. Was considerate of others and appreciated their ideas.	☐	☐	☐	☐
6. Asked others to clarify their ideas if necessary.	☐	☐	☐	☐
7. Expressed disagreements respectfully.	☐	☐	☐	☐
8. Did not dominate the conversation or interrupt others.	☐	☐	☐	☐
9. Tried to help the group reach consensus.	☐	☐	☐	☐
10. Helped the group stay on the topic.	☐	☐	☐	☐
11. Helped the group not waste time.	☐	☐	☐	☐
12. Helped me learn more than if I had worked alone.	☐	☐	☐	☐

student essays "excellent" and the rest "very good." (Using external raters such as prospective employers would make the ratings more credible.)

Rating scale rubrics are quick and easy to create and use, however, so they do have an important place in many assessment programs, especially for relatively minor assignments.

Descriptive Rubrics

Descriptive rubrics replace the checkboxes of rating scale rubrics with brief descriptions of the performances that merit each possible rating. Exhibit 9.6 is an example of a descriptive rubric, as is Exhibit 15.1. Other examples are in Appendix C of *Effective Grading* (Walvoord & Anderson, 1998), *Learning Centered Assessment on College Campuses* (Huba & Freed, 2000), and *Introduction to Rubrics* (Stevens & Levi, 2004).

Descriptive rubrics are increasingly popular because they explicitly document faculty and staff standards for student

---

Exhibit 9.5. A Rating Scale Rubric for Health Education Field Experience Supervisors

Evaluate the student under your supervision using the following scale:

5 = Superior for an entry-level health educator
4 = Slightly better than an entry-level health educator
3 = Acceptable for an entry-level health educator
2 = Slightly less than an entry level-health educator
1 = Seriously deficient
N/O = Not sufficient observation for evaluation

	5	4	3	2	1	N/O
1. Access, use, and evaluate current, reliable health knowledge.	☐	☐	☐	☐	☐	☐
2. Demonstrate word processing skills.	☐	☐	☐	☐	☐	☐
3. Read, interpret, and use research information.	☐	☐	☐	☐	☐	☐
4. Demonstrate problem-solving skills.	☐	☐	☐	☐	☐	☐
5. Develop appropriate educational materials.	☐	☐	☐	☐	☐	☐
6. Use audiovisual equipment skillfully and appropriately.	☐	☐	☐	☐	☐	☐
7. Demonstrate teaching skills.	☐	☐	☐	☐	☐	☐
8. Demonstrate promotional or publicity skills.	☐	☐	☐	☐	☐	☐
9. Use knowledge of learning styles in development of presentations.	☐	☐	☐	☐	☐	☐
10. Sensitive to individual differences.	☐	☐	☐	☐	☐	☐
11. Know how and where to refer clients or students for further help and information within organizational guidelines.	☐	☐	☐	☐	☐	☐
12. Develop a professional network.	☐	☐	☐	☐	☐	☐
13. Show positive work attitude and ethic.	☐	☐	☐	☐	☐	☐
14. Demonstrate willingness to work beyond minimum expectations.	☐	☐	☐	☐	☐	☐
15. Display professional appearance appropriate to the organization.	☐	☐	☐	☐	☐	☐

Source: Adapted with permission from a rubric used by faculty in the Department of Health Science, Towson University.

performance (what Chapter Fifteen calls *local standards*). Students, faculty, accreditors, and other audiences all clearly understand exactly what an "outstanding" or "inadequate" rating means.

But coming up with succinct, explicit descriptions of every performance level for everything you're looking for in completed assignments is not easy! This process can require negotiation, try-outs, and revisions and can therefore be time-consuming.

Exhibit 9.6. Descriptive Rubric for a Slide Presentation on Findings from Research Sources

	Well Done (5)	Satisfactory (4–3)	Needs Improvement (2–1)	Incomplete (0)
Organization	Clearly, concisely written. Logical, intuitive progression of ideas and supporting information. Clear and direct cues to all information.	Logical progression of ideas and supporting information. Most cues to information are clear and direct.	Vague in conveying viewpoint and purpose. Some logical progression of ideas and supporting information, but cues are confusing or flawed.	Lacks a clear point of view and logical sequence of information. Cues to information are not evident.
Persuasiveness	Motivating questions and advance organizers convey main idea. Information is accurate.	Includes persuasive information.	Includes persuasive information with few facts.	Information is incomplete, out of date, or incorrect.
Introduction	Presents overall topic. Draws in audience with compelling questions or relating to audience's interests or goals.	Clear, coherent, and related to topic.	Some structure but does not create a sense of what follows. May be overly detailed or incomplete. Somewhat appealing.	Does not orient audience to what will follow.
Clarity	Readable, well-sized fonts. Italics, boldface, and indentations enhance readability. Text is appropriate length. Background and colors enhance readability.	Sometimes fonts are readable, but in a few places fonts, italics, boldface, long paragraphs, color, or background detract.	Overall readability is difficult, with lengthy paragraphs, too many fonts, dark or busy background, overuse of boldface, or lack of appropriate indentations.	Text is very difficult to read. Long blocks of text, small fonts, inappropriate colors, or poor use of headings, indentations, or boldface.
Layout	Aesthetically pleasing. Contributes to message with appropriate use of headings and white space.	Uses white space appropriately.	Shows some structure but is cluttered, busy, or distracting.	Cluttered and confusing. Spacing and headings do not enhance readability.

Source: Adopted with permission from a rubric developed by Patrica Ryan, lecturer, Department of Reading, Special Education, and Instructional Technology, Towson University.

Thus, while descriptive rubrics might be considered the gold standard of rubrics, don't feel that you need to develop them for every assignment. Descriptive rubrics are a good choice under the following circumstances:

- You are undertaking important assessments whose results may contribute to major decisions such as accreditation, funding, or program continuance.
- Several faculty and staff are collectively assessing student work, because descriptive rubrics' clear descriptions make scoring more consistent across faculty and staff.
- It is important to give students clear, detailed feedback on their strengths and weaknesses.
- Skeptical audiences will be examining the rubric scores with a critical eye.

Holistic Scoring Guides

Sometimes assessment projects are so massive that faculty and staff don't have time to complete a rating scale rubric or descriptive rubric for every assignment. Perhaps they must read and score 1,500 entering students' essays to decide who should enroll in a developmental writing course. Perhaps they must review 150 senior portfolios to get an overall sense of the writing skills of graduates. The major purpose of such summative assessments is not to give feedback to individual students but to make decisions within a tight time frame.

In these situations, holistic scoring guides may be a good choice. They do not have a list of the things you're looking for in completed assignments. Instead, they have short narrative descriptions of the characteristics of outstanding work, acceptable work, and unacceptable work. Exhibit 9.7 is an example of a holistic scoring guide. Exhibit 13.1 includes another brief example, as does Figure 5.2 of *Developing Outcomes-Based Assessment for Learner-Centered Education* (Driscoll & Wood, 2007).

Holistic scoring guides have two major shortcomings. First, it can be difficult for faculty and staff to assign scores consistently, because few student works will meet any one description precisely. Second, holistic scoring guides do not yield feedback on students' strengths and weaknesses.

Structured Observation Guides

Some faculty and staff find it difficult to come up with a rubric or holistic scoring guide to evaluate student work. Some may simply be uncomfortable with the idea of quantifying their evaluations

Exhibit 9.7. A Holistic Scoring Guide for Students in a Ballet Program

A: Active learner – Enthusiastic – Very energetic – Fully engaged in every class – Able to accept corrections – Able to make and synthesize corrections – Able to maintain corrections – Able to self-assess – Shows continuous improvement in major problem areas – Connects movement sequences well – Demonstrates strong dynamic phrasing – Very musical – Continuously demonstrates correct epaulment – Demonstrates advanced understanding and applies correct alignment, fully extended classical line, full use of rotation, and use of classical terminology – Daily demonstrates commitment to the art form and addresses areas of weaknesses without instructor input

B: Active learner – Enthusiastic – Energetic – Engaged in every class – Able to accept most corrections – Able to make and synthesize most corrections – Able to maintain most corrections – Able to self-assess – Shows improvement in major problem areas – Connects movement sequences relatively well – Demonstrates adequate dynamic phrasing – Generally musical – Generally demonstrates correct epaulment – Demonstrates understanding and generally applies correct alignment, classical line, and use of classical terminology – Continues to address areas of weakness and shows general improvement

C: Active learner but not fully physically/mentally engaged in class – Able to accept most corrections – Not quite able to make and synthesize corrections – Not yet able to maintain corrections – Unable to fully self-assess – Shows some improvement in major problem areas – Connects some movement sequences – Demonstrates limited dynamic phrasing – Almost musical – Working toward correct epaulment – Working on understanding and applying correct alignment, continuing to find classical line, unable to fully execute artistry and use classical terminology – Continues to address areas of weakness but unable to demonstrate consistent visible improvement

D: Not an active learner/lacks sufficient energy – Not physically or mentally engaged in class – Unable to accept/understand most corrections – Unable to make and synthesize corrections – Unable to maintain corrections – Unable to self-assess – Shows very little improvement in major problem areas – Seldom connects movement sequences well – Demonstrates marginal dynamic phrasing – Seldom musical – Unable to demonstrate correct epaulment – Unable to apply correct alignment, demonstrate classical line, execute artistry, or use classical terminology – Seldom addresses areas of weakness – Unable to demonstrate visible improvement in most areas of weakness – Lacks self-motivation

Source: Adapted with permission from a holistic scoring guide used by the faculty of the Department of Dance, Towson University.

and prefer a qualitative approach. Some may never have thought about what they expect and value in student work. Yes, these faculty have been awarding grades (they "know an A when they see it"), but they have done so more on instinct than anything else. These faculty may prefer a structured observation guide: a rubric without a rating scale. Structured observation guides are subjective, qualitative—but nonetheless direct and valid—assessments of student learning (Chapter Two).

To develop a structured observation guide, take informal notes the next time you grade an assignment. What made you decide to give one paper an A? Why did you give another a C? After all the

Exhibit 9.8. A Structured Observation Guide for a One-Act Play

*The effectiveness of each of the
following in conveying the
production's meaning or theme:*   *Notes*

Pace and rhythm

Characterizations

Stage presence and business

Stagecraft: Costume, lighting, set,
and sound designs

Creative vision and risk taking

"Sparkle" and audience engagement

Total integrated production effect

assignments are graded, look through your notes for any common patterns or themes. You may identify some factors you noted repeatedly. These may represent your implicit goals and expectations for your students and can become the factors of a structured observation guide (Exhibit 9.8).

Structured observation guides can be helpful in several ways:

- They can help faculty articulate learning goals (Chapter Eight).
- They can help faculty articulate the criteria for rating scale rubrics or descriptive rubrics.

- They can help faculty assess ineffable goals like attitudes and values (Chapter Twelve).
- They can be used by students to evaluate the work of their peers.

Creating Effective Rubrics

It may strike you as curious that this chapter, on creating a rubric or scoring guide for an assignment, comes before the chapter on creating the assignment itself. Shouldn't we first create the assignment and then the scoring guide? But think of planning a road trip. When we use a map to plot a route, we first locate our destination and then chart the most appropriate route to get there. When we teach, we are taking our students on a journey. Our assignments are more effective if we first clarify what we want students to learn from the assignment (the destination) and then design an assignment that will help them achieve those ends (the route to get there). Creating assignments thus begins not by writing the assignment itself but by writing the criteria or standards that will be used to evaluate it.

If this process differs from your experience and therefore seems daunting ("How can I possibly create grading criteria when I don't know what I'm asking students to do?"), use an iterative process to create an assignment. First, list your learning goals: the most important things you want students to learn by completing the assignment. Then draft the assignment itself. Next, use the drafted assignment to refine your learning goals into more complete evaluation criteria. Once you've spelled out the evaluation criteria, revise the assignment so it will elicit the work described in the criteria.

Rubrics are not difficult to create, although descriptive rubrics can be time-consuming. The suggestions that follow may be helpful.

Look for Models

Rubrics are increasingly widespread assessment tools, so it makes sense to begin creating a rubric by looking for models that you can adapt to your circumstances. (If you use or adapt someone else's rubric, ask for permission and acknowledge the work of the original author.)

Start with a simple online search, as many colleges, programs, and faculty post rubrics there. If you subscribe to a discussion list on teaching in your discipline, post a query asking for examples of rubrics. Rubrics are far more common in basic (K–12) education than in higher education, so if you search for, say, science lab report rubrics, you may find more examples from high school than college. Don't despair; high school rubrics can still give you good ideas.

A number of Web sites offer free templates and other simple software for creating and saving rubrics; use search terms like *rubric generator, rubric builder,* or *create rubrics* to find them.

List the Things You're Looking For

Start creating a rubric by listing the traits or criteria you want students to demonstrate in the completed assignment. Chapter Eight and the questions in Table 9.2 may be helpful.

Discussing these questions collaboratively with other faculty and staff can be immensely helpful. Even if you are developing a rubric for a course that you alone teach, it can be helpful to discuss these questions with other faculty in your discipline or in related disciplines.

If the initial list you generate is long, it probably needs to be pruned. A long rubric makes assignments more time-consuming to score and makes it harder for your students to understand the chief skills that they are to focus on as they complete the assignment. Effective rubrics can have as few as three criteria and generally have no more than eight or so. Lengthy rubrics may be more appropriate when the assignment is a holistic, culminating experience such as a senior thesis or field experience in which students are expected to demonstrate a broad range of learning outcomes.

So review your list and reduce it to the most significant tasks, skills, or abilities that you'd like students to demonstrate. Discard anything that isn't a high-priority goal or observable in this particular assignment. (Enthusiasm for science might not be observable in a lab report, for example.) Perhaps a group of similar skills can be combined into one category.

Now edit the list so that each criterion is expressed in explicit, concrete terms, preferably action verbs or clear adjectives, as discussed in Chapter Eight. "Writing quality" tells students and colleagues little about what you're looking for; "organization and structure" tells them far more. Think twice about terms like "adequate organization," "appropriate vocabulary," or "acceptable grammar" that don't tell students or colleagues what kind of organization, vocabulary, or grammar is acceptable.

Table 9.2. Questions to Help Identify What You're Looking for in Student Work

Why are we giving students this assignment? What are its key learning goals? What do we want students to learn by completing it?

What are the skills we want students to demonstrate in this assignment?

What are the characteristics of good student work? What are the characteristics of good writing, a good presentation, a good lab report, or good student teaching?

What specific characteristics do we want to see in completed assignments?

Leave Room for the Ineffables and the Unexpected

Some faculty and staff have found that students who are given rubrics along with an assignment do exactly what the rubric tells them to do but no more. The result is solid but somewhat flat and uninspired products. To encourage originality, creativity, effort, and that unexpected but delightful something extra, build these qualities into the rubric. You might tell students, for example, that 10 percent of the assignment score will be based on effort, originality, or insight.

Create the Rating Scale

If you are creating a rubric other than a checklist, once you have listed the things you're looking for, the next step is defining the levels that make up the rating scale. Faculty and staff who have never articulated their learning goals or evaluation criteria before may find it helpful to first develop and use the qualitative structured observation guide described earlier.

Create at least three levels. At a minimum, you will need to include performance levels for adequate and inadequate performance, plus an exemplary level to motivate students to do better than merely adequate work. You may want to add a category between exemplary and adequate, and you may wish to add an "almost adequate" category. Usually no more than five levels are needed. If faced with too many levels, faculty and staff may have a hard time distinguishing consistently between, say, 6 and 7 on a 10-point scale.

Label each level with names, not just numbers. Don't ask, for example, for a rating of 1 through 5, with 1 being Best and 5 being Worst. People will have different conceptions of 2, 3, and 4 unless you spell them out. There is no hard and fast rule on how to label each performance level. Use descriptors that are clear and relevant to you, your colleagues, and your students. Labels that work well for one assignment or discipline may not work for another. Examples of possible performance levels are:

- Exceeds standard, meets standard, approaching standard, below standard
- Complete evidence, partial evidence, minimal evidence, no evidence
- Excellent, very good, adequate, needs attention
- Letter grades (A, B, C, D, F)

Whatever labels you choose, make sure that they make clear which category represents minimally acceptable performance. If you use letter grades, for example, does C or D represent minimally acceptable performance?

If you are developing a descriptive rubric, fill in its boxes.   In other words, create brief descriptors for each trait at each performance level. (If you are creating a holistic scoring guide, once you have defined the performance levels, your next step is to create a written description for each performance level.) What exactly do you want to see in an exemplary assignment? An adequate assignment? What kind of work merits a failing grade?

This task can be easier if you look at a few samples of student work. Choose a range of student work—good, bad, and mediocre—and consider the following questions:

- Which samples represent exemplary work? Why? Would it be realistic to establish these as the targets we aim for in all students?
- Which samples are unacceptably inadequate? Why?
- What kinds of student performance represent minimally acceptable work for a graduate of our program or college?
- How do the exemplary, acceptable, and inadequate samples differ?

Setting standards is discussed further in Chapter Fifteen.

If the work of creating a descriptive rubric seems overwhelming or contentious, start by creating a rating scale rubric. Once faculty use it, they may come to realize that they need a rubric with greater clarity and may be ready to invest the time and effort to develop a descriptive rubric.

Try Out the Rubric

Use the rubric to score some actual samples of student work, including some of your students' best and worst work. Are your standards appropriate, unrealistically high, or insufficiently challenging? Revise the rubric if necessary to improve its clarity and value. Chapter Three discusses ways to avoid biases and inconsistencies as you use a rubric.

Keeping the Scoring Burden Manageable _____

One of the reasons that traditional multiple-choice tests continue to be popular is that they can be scored quickly. Finding time to evaluate performance assessments can be a challenge, especially for faculty who are teaching courses with high enrollments. Chapter Six offers a number of suggestions for minimizing the burden of assessment. Here are some more:

- *Don't waste your time scoring assignments with obviously inadequate effort.* Establish what Barbara Walvoord and Virginia Anderson (1998) call gateway criteria, and give them to students, in writing, with the assignment. Then return or fail assignments that don't meet those minimum standards.

- *Try Richard Haswell's (1983) minimal marking strategy.* Instead of correcting student writing errors, put a check in the margin on the line of the error, and have the student figure out what's wrong on that line and what the correction should be.

- *Investigate software designed to score essays.* The latest software is based on artificial intelligence and is a promising means of scoring writing samples. Chapter Six offers suggestions on investigating assessment technologies.

Time to Think, Discuss, and Practice _____

One of Belleville College's general education goals is, "Students will be able to write effectively." The faculty has decided to assess this by asking all graduating students to write a one-page review and analysis of arguments for and against making community service a college graduation requirement. Create a descriptive rubric to assess these papers, following the three steps suggested in Chapter Five of *Effective Grading* (Walvoord & Anderson, 1998):

1. Begin by brainstorming descriptions of a perfect paper, an unexceptional but acceptable paper, and an unacceptable paper. (Faculty are assessing only the finished paper, not the writing process.)

2. Use your brainstormed descriptions to make a list of the criteria or traits that will count in the evaluation.

3. For each trait, construct a three-point scale, where 3 = exemplary, 2 = acceptable but unexceptional, and 1 = unacceptable. These are descriptive statements.

4. Exhibit 9.9 is a student submission for this assignment. Use your rubric to evaluate this paper. Compare your completed rubrics. Are you all in reasonable agreement? Does the rubric appear to work the way you intended, or does it need refinement?

Exhibit 9.9. A Student Essay on Making Community Service a Graduation Requirement

Of all the requirements for graduation, community service is not usually one of them. However, some colleges are considering adding this as a prerequisite to receiving a diploma. This idea has caused disputes between some students, who do not wish to volunteer, and faculty, who feel that volunteering should not be required in order to graduate from an institute of higher learning.

One opinion is that as a graduating college student, you should not only be well educated, but also well rounded in general, and community service is one aspect that will help you to become a more well rounded person in general. This is the opinion of the people who advocate for community service. By requiring students to perform so many mandated hours of community service, they feel that the students will become enriched in ways that a classroom cannot provide.

Another opinion of faculty is that students do not have to volunteer in order to get a good education, which is the primary function of a university, and therefore, required community service should not be necessary in order to receive a diploma. Some students share this opinion also. They feel that community service should be a personal opinion based on personal interests and reasons for wishing to volunteer. They believe that if students are forced to volunteer in order to receive the diploma they have worked so hard for, since the community service work is not coming from their hearts, they will not be giving their all, simply going through the motions to satisfy the requirement.

If students are required to provide a certain number of community service hours, this may also detract from their attention to their school work, causing grades to suffer. Some faculty have taken this into consideration. They are not sure if creating mandatory community service hours is worth the possible decline in students' GPAs because they are so concerned with finding places to conduct community service and finding the time to perform their mandated hours.

Another question that is concerning the faculty of universities is whether or not there are enough locations in which students could perform community service. For some colleges that are not located around a large city, the number of places that needs volunteer work may not be sufficient enough to accommodate all the students that are attending the school. If there are not enough open spaces in volunteer organizations outside of the school, should the university be obligated to create situations in which volunteers are needed in the school so that students can perform their needed hours of community service?

All of these questions and concerns need to be adequately addressed before a decision is made at any university or postsecondary school. They should be addressed not only with faculty and staff of the school, but also students, in order to hear their points of view.

Recommended Readings

The following readings are recommended along with the references cited in this chapter.

Andrade, H. G. (2000). Using rubrics to promote thinking and learning. *Educational Leadership, 57*(5), 13–18.

Arter, J., & McTighe, J. (2001). *Scoring rubrics in the classroom: Using performance criteria for assessing and improving student performance.* Thousand Oaks, CA: Sage.

Butler, S. M., & McMunn, N. D. (2006). *A teacher's guide to classroom assessment: Understanding and using assessment to improve student learning.* San Francisco: Jossey-Bass.

Chicago Board of Education. (2000). *How to create a rubric from scratch: A guide for rugged individualists.* Retrieved September 16, 2008, from http://intranet. cps.k12.il.us/Assessments/Ideas_and_Rubrics/Create_Rubric/create_ rubric.html.

Dodge, B. (2001). *Creating a rubric for a given task.* Retrieved September 16, 2008, from http://webquest.sdsu.edu/rubrics/rubrics.html.

Mertler, C. A. (2001). Designing scoring rubrics for your classroom. *Practical Assessment, Research and Evaluation, 7*(25). Retrieved September 16, 2008, from http://PAREonline.net/getvn.asp?v=7&n=25.

Moskal, B. M. (2000). Scoring rubrics: What, when and how? *Practical Assessment, Research and Evaluation, 7*(3). Retrieved September 16, 2008, from http:// PAREonline.net/getvn.asp?v=7&n=3.

Moskal, B. M. (2003). Recommendations for developing classroom performance assessments and scoring rubrics. *Practical Assessment, Research and Evaluation, 8*(14). Retrieved September 16, 2008, from http://PAREonline. net/getvn.asp?v=8&n=14.

Moskal, B. M., & Leydens, J. A. (2000). Scoring rubric development: Validity and reliability. *Practical Assessment, Research and Evaluation, 7*(10). Retrieved September 16, 2008, from http://PAREonline.net/getvn.asp?v=7&n=10.

Pickett, N., & Dodge, B. (2007). *Rubrics for web lessons.* Retrieved September 16, 2008, from http://webquest.sdsu.edu/rubrics/weblessons.htm.

TeacherVision. (2000–2008). *Creating rubrics.* Retrieved September 16, 2008, from www.teachervision.fen.com/teaching-methods-and-management/ rubrics/4521.html.

Tierney, R., & Simon, M. (2004). What's still wrong with rubrics: Focusing on the consistency of performance criteria across scale levels. *Practical Assessment, Research and Evaluation, 9*(2). Retrieved September 16, 2008, from http:// PAREonline.net/getvn.asp?v=9&n=2.

CHAPTER 10

Creating an Effective Assignment

> **Some Valuable Ideas You'll Find in This Chapter**
>
> - Every assignment should help students achieve important learning goals.
> - Give students a variety of assignments, not just traditional essays and research papers.
> - Ask yourself if students will learn significantly more from a thirty-page assignment than a five-page assignment—enough to justify the time that they and you will spend on it.
> - Break apart large assignments into pieces that are due at various times.
> - Address plagiarism consistently and collaboratively across campus through education as well as consequences.

When we ask students to write an essay, complete a research project, create a work of art, use laboratory materials, or give a speech, providing clear instructions and guidance on what students are to do and why will help them learn what we value. This is where prompts—the subject of this chapter—come in.

What Is a Prompt?

A prompt is simply an assignment: the statement or question (usually written) that tells students what they are to do in a performance assessment (Chapter Two), essay test question, and virtually everything else we ask students to do except to complete objective tests and rating forms.

There are two basic kinds of prompts. *Restricted response* prompts ask everyone to provide pretty much the same response, just in his or her own words. An example is giving all students the same chart and asking them to write a paragraph summarizing its major points. Many mathematics problems and science laboratory assignments are restricted response prompts.

Extended response prompts give students latitude in deciding how to complete the assignment. Their completed assignments may vary considerably in organization, style, and content. Suppose that students are asked to speculate, with appropriate justification, on how our daily lives might be different today if the United States had never engaged in space exploration. The visions and supporting evidence in equally outstanding papers might vary a great deal.

Why Are Good Prompts Important?

Carefully crafted prompts are critical parts of the teaching-learning process because, regardless of what we state in syllabi or say in class, the assignments we give students are the most powerful way we communicate our expectations to them. A good prompt inspires students to give the assignment their best effort and thereby achieve the assignment's learning goals. With a poorly written prompt, students may complete an assignment without learning what we want them to learn.

Suppose that history faculty want students to be able to analyze the impact of a noteworthy individual on the outcome of World War II. They ask students simply to write a term paper on "a person involved with World War II," with no further guidance or direction. Some students might complete the assignment by summarizing the life history of an individual, doing nothing to develop—or demonstrate—their analysis skills. When faculty review the papers for assessment purposes, they may find little evidence of analysis skill, not because students are poor at analysis but because this assignment never explicitly asked the students to analyze.

Identifying Specific, Important Learning Goals for the Assignment

Begin creating a good prompt by deciding what you want students to learn from the assignment. The assignment should focus students on the skills and conceptual understandings that you consider most important. For a writing assignment, identify the specific kinds of writing skills that you most want students to strengthen. The best way to identify the learning goals you want students to achieve by completing the assignment is to develop a rubric (Chapter Nine).

A good assignment sets challenging but realistic expectations. Often when students know exactly what they need to do to achieve a high score, they will rise to meet that standard, even if it means accomplishing things to which they never thought they could aspire. Ask students to demonstrate not just simple understanding but also thinking skills such as analysis, evaluation, and creativity. Focusing on these kinds of skills makes the assignment more challenging, worthwhile, and interesting and promotes deeper learning. If you give students a copy of the rubric you will use to evaluate their completed assignments, as suggested in Chapter Nine, make sure that it states clearly what you consider outstanding work.

Creating a Meaningful Task or Problem Corresponding to Those Goals

Once you have clarified the key learning goals of an assignment, identify a task that corresponds to those goals and will help your students achieve them. (A writing assignment would obviously be a poor way to learn presentation skills!) Chapter Three discussed the importance of giving students a variety of ways to demonstrate their learning. Table 10.1 lists examples of assignments beyond the usual term paper or essay. Most of these assignments are performance assessments (Chapter Two) that ask students to demonstrate skills—often in realistic settings—rather than simply describe or explain those skills.

Textbooks and other curricular materials may give you some ideas for assignments, but a better approach is to think of a real-life task. Such assignments engage students and help them see that they are learning something worthwhile. Try "you are there" scenarios: "You are an expert chemist [statistician, teacher, anthropologist, or whatever] asked to help with the following situation . . ." Such role playing need not be realistic: "You are one of President Andrew Jackson's closest advisors . . ."; "You are a member of the first space team traveling to Mars . . ."

Exhibits 10.1 and 10.2 are examples of prompts that abide by most of the suggestions that follow. More examples are in *Effective Grading* (Walvoord & Anderson, 1998) and *Learning-Centered Assessment on College Campuses* (Huba & Freed, 2000).

Table 10.1. Examples of Assignments Beyond Essays, Term Papers, and Research Reports

Abstract or executive summary
Advertisement or commercial
Annotated bibliography
Autobiography or realistic fictional diary from a historical period
Briefing paper
Brochure or pamphlet
Campaign speech
Case study or analysis
Client report
Collaborative group activity
Database
Debate or discussion (plan, participation, or leadership)
Debriefing interview preparation
Dramatization of an event or scenario, in writing or a presentation
Editing and revising a poorly written paper
Evaluation of opposing points of view or the pros and cons of alternative solutions to a problem
Experiment or other laboratory experience
Field notes
Game invention
Graph, chart, diagram, flowchart, or other visual aid
Graphic organizer, taxonomy, or classification scheme
Handbook or instructional manual
Journal or log (Chapter Twelve)
Letter to an editor or business
Model, simulation, or illustration
Narrative
Newspaper story or news report on a concept or from a historical period
Oral history recording of an event
Plan to research and solve a problem
Plan to conduct a project or provide a service
Portfolio (Chapter Thirteen)
Poster, display, or exhibit
Presentation, demonstration, or slide show
Process description
Proposal for and justification of a solution to a problem
Reflection on what and how one has learned (Chapter Twelve)
Review and critique of one's own work, that of a peer, a performance, an exhibit, a work of art, a writer's arguments, or how something could have been done better
Selected portions of an essay or term paper (for example, only the problem statement and the review of literature)
Survey, including an analysis of the results
Teaching a concept to a peer or child
Video or audio recording
Web site

Exhibit 10.1. A Prompt for a First-Year Composition Essay Assignment

In *The Color Purple*, by Alice Walker, Celie and her husband Albert, known simply as Mr. _____, have a heated exchange in which Celie reveals to him that she is leaving him to move to Memphis to start her own business. Afterward, he retorts with the following remarks: "Look at you, you black, you pore, you ugly, you a woman . . . You nothing at all."

Some men who have engaged in physical and mental abuse of women have been asked to attend a program on abuse. As part of the program, they will be asked to read an essay in which you persuade them not to engage in the kind of behavior that Mr. _____ displays.

Write this essay. Keep in mind that most of the men will be unfriendly or hostile to your ideas, so you must really convince them with your arguments.

Your essay will be graded in terms of content, organization, style/expression, and grammar/mechanics.

Source: Adapted with permission from a prompt by Lena Ampadu, associate professor of English, Towson University.

Choose an Assignment That's a Worthwhile Use of Learning Time

Consider carefully whether the time students put into your assignment will yield an appropriate payoff in terms of their learning. Will they learn twice as much from an assignment that takes twenty hours of out-of-class time as from one that takes ten hours? Will students learn significantly more from a thirty-page paper than from a five-page paper (which may take you one-sixth the time to evaluate)? Sometimes your learning goals may not demand a traditional term paper or research project. Students may achieve learning goals just as effectively by completing a research proposal or a relatively short annotated bibliography.

Aim Students at the Desired Outcome

Give your students clear, written directions and scaffolding on which they can successfully create their best work. Begin the prompt with an introductory sentence that's an overview of what you want them to do, and then answer the questions in Table 10.2.

While good prompts are often generous in the guidance they give to students, some faculty like to give purposefully vague assignments because they want students to learn how to figure out the assignment on their own. This practice can be fine, but only if:

- One of the learning goals of the assignment is to learn how to choose, define, or clarify a problem or issue; *and*

Exhibit 10.2. A Prompt for an Educational Research Problem Statement

To help you be an intelligent consumer of educational research, your major task in this course will be to write a proposal to conduct an educational research project. You won't actually conduct the research, but by writing a proposal you will demonstrate that you understand what good-quality research is. You will also be able to learn more about a topic in education that interests you.

The first part of the research proposal is a statement of the problem to be investigated and will constitute 15 percent of your final grade. If you submit the statement before the due date, I will critique your work and give you a tentative grade. If you're satisfied with that grade, you may stop work, and if you'd like to improve your grade, you may submit a revision by the due date.

The statement of the problem should:

- Be no longer than two pages

- Include a statement of the research problem to be investigated, the reasons you chose this topic, and what you hypothesize would be the results of your research

- Include definitions of any key terms relevant to your topic, woven into the discussion rather than listed separately

- Be accompanied by a completed reflection page that shows evidence of serious thought.

An *outstanding (A)* paper has the following characteristics:

- It meets all the *content requirements* of the assignment, as described above.

- It is *error free:* For example, it has no erroneous conclusions or misunderstandings of research concepts.

- It uses *appropriate language.* Sentence and paragraph structure and vocabulary are all simple ("because" instead of "due to the fact that"). Unemotional, professional terms and phrasings are used (*not* "I was amazed to find . . ."). There are no contractions.

- It is *well written.* It is clear, understandable, and well organized, with an appropriate flow and headings. There are sound rationales for conclusions and decisions, evidence of serious thought, and no inconsistencies in what is said.

A *good (B)* paper is well done, but with some significant flaws not in an A paper (such as some errors or unclear statements).

An *adequate (C)* paper meets the content requirements, and its major points can be understood, but it has several significant flaws not in an A paper (for example, the content is not uniformly clear or consistent, or the paper has minimal discussion.).

An *inadequate (F)* paper seriously fails to meet most of the characteristics of an A paper. Most critically, it does not meet the content requirements and/or is so poorly written that its major points cannot be understood.

- Students have opportunities to learn and practice these skills before tackling the assignment; *and*

- This learning goal is reflected in the rubric (Chapter Nine) used to evaluate the assignment.

Good prompts for major assignments such as portfolios or term projects can run a page or more. Brevity is important,

Table 10.2. Questions to Address in a Prompt for an Assignment

---

Why are you giving students this assignment?

What is its purpose?

What do you expect students to learn by completing it? For example, are students simply to summarize information or use the information to persuade? Barbara Walvoord and Virginia Anderson (1998) point out that the title of an assignment is a powerful way to convey to students what you want them to do. They suggest using terms like *argumentative essay, original research project,* or *sociological analysis,* which make the assignment clearer than the usual *term paper.*

What should the completed assignment look like?

Who is the (perhaps hypothetical) audience for the assignment: academicians, people working in a particular setting, or the general public?

What skills and knowledge do you want students to demonstrate?

Explain terms that may be fuzzy to your students even if they are clear to you, such as *compare, evaluate,* and *discuss.*

What should be included in the completed assignment?

How should students format the completed assignment?

How are students to complete the assignment? How do you expect them to devote their time and energy?

How much time do you expect them to spend on this assignment? If this is a class assignment, how much will it count toward their final course grade?

If the assignment is to write something, what is an optimal length for the paper?

What readings, reference materials, and technologies are they expected to use?

Can they collaborate with others? If so, to what extent?

What assistance can you provide while they are working on the assignment? (Are you willing to critique drafts, for example?)

How will you score or grade the assignment? The best way to communicate this is to give students a copy of the rubric that you will use to evaluate completed assignments.

---

however, when you are asking for very short responses such as minute papers (Chapter Twelve) or when you are giving timed in-class assignments such as an essay exam. In these situations, every minute counts, and time spent reading your prompt is time that can't be spent thinking or responding.

Break Apart Large Assignments

Rather than distribute a major assignment on the first day of class and collect the papers on the last day, break the assignment into pieces that are handed in or checked at various points during the course. You might ask students to submit an outline of a research paper first and then an annotated bibliography. This kind of approach helps students manage their time and, more important, gets those heading in a wrong direction back on track before it's too late for them to salvage their project. Breaking an assignment into pieces can also discourage plagiarism, as discussed below, and it makes your job of evaluating the completed assignments more manageable.

Depending on your students' needs, your goals, and your time constraints, at these checkpoints you might:

- Simply check off that this portion of the project is complete or in progress
- Review and comment on this portion of the project
- Have student peers evaluate this portion of the project using a rubric that you provide
- Give this portion of the project a tentative grade (pending subsequent revisions) or a final grade

Encourage Students to Reflect on Their Work

Reflection can promote deep, lasting learning, so consider asking students to submit written reflections with at least some of their assignments. Chapter Twelve discusses this further.

Countering Plagiarism

The work of others is so readily available today that student plagiarism is a growing concern. Although there is no way to eliminate plagiarism, the strategies in Table 10.3 (Carroll, 2004) may help.

Time to Think, Discuss, and Practice

1. Choose one of the following (poorly written!) prompts:
   - Compare the writing styles of F. Scott Fitzgerald and Ernest Hemingway.
   - Compare the Republican and Democratic parties.
   - Describe the operation of a microscope.
   - Research the demographics of various ethnic groups in the United States.
   - Compare the strengths, weaknesses, and uses of quantitative and qualitative assessment.
2. Choose one person in your group to play the role of the faculty member who wrote the prompt. That person will answer your group's questions about the course or program for which the prompt was written and the learning goals that the prompt is intended to assess.

Table 10.3. Strategies to Counter Plagiarism

Use detection judiciously.

After papers are turned in, ask students to summarize them.

Use online tools such as Google to search for similar passages.

Interview students or ask them to write reflectively about the process they used to write the paper.

Review papers for out-of-character work; abrupt changes in language, referencing systems, or vocabulary; fully finished works with no evidence of research and writing processes; and anachronisms or only dated references

Explicitly teach and model academic rules, values, and conventions.

Provide plenty of instruction and assignments that help students understand exactly what plagiarism is. Focus on what students should do rather than what they should not do. Test their understanding through realistic test questions and assignments on plagiarism.

Model academic integrity in your own examples, lectures, and discussions by citing the sources to which you refer.

Provide opportunities to practice and receive feedback on academic integrity.

Provide opportunities for students to learn, practice, and get feedback on research and writing skills.

Teach research and writing skills as they apply to your discipline.

Use fair assessment practices (Chapter Three).

Give clearly articulated assignments that are plainly linked to key learning outcomes (Chapter Eight).

Vary the kinds of assignments you give.

Give creative assignments that don't lend themselves to plagiarism. Assign oral or visual presentations rather than written papers; break large assignments into small pieces; or give assignments that ask students to relate concepts learned to personal or local experiences.

Work with your colleagues to make a concerted and consistent effort to address plagiarism.

Develop and implement appropriate and consistent policies for all students and programs.

Be consistent in how plagiarism policies are explained, applied, and enforced.

Provide timely, transparent, and defensible penalties.

3. Identify what makes the prompt ineffective.

4. With input from the role-playing group member, rewrite the prompt so it meets the criteria of good prompts.

Recommended Readings

The following readings are recommended along with the references cited in this chapter.

Cashin, W. E. (1987). *Improving essay tests* (IDEA Paper No. 17). Manhattan: Kansas State University, Center for Faculty Evaluation and Development.

Chicago Board of Education. (2000). *Performance assessment tasks.* Retrieved September 16, 2008, from http://intranet.cps.k12.il.us/Assessments/Ideas_and_Rubrics/Assessment_Tasks/assessment_tasks.html.

Cizek, G. J. (2003). *Detecting and preventing classroom cheating: Promoting integrity in assessment.* Thousand Oaks, CA: Sage.

Coalition of Essential Schools. (1998). How to analyze a curriculum unit or project and provide the scaffolding students need to succeed. *Horace, 15*(2). Retrieved September 16, 2008, from www.essentialschools.org/cs/resources/view/ces_res/85.

Coalition of Essential Schools. (1998). *Overview of alternative assessment approaches.* Retrieved September 16, 2008, from www.essentialschools.org/cs/resources/view/ces_res/127.

Council of Writing Program Administrators. (2003). *Defining and avoiding plagiarism: The WPA statement on best practices.* Retrieved September 16, 2008, from http://wpacouncil.org/files/WPAplagiarism.pdf.

Keenan, J. (1983, September 28). A professor's guide to perpetuating poor writing among students. *Chronicle of Higher Education*, p. 64.

Moskal, B. M. (2003). Recommendations for developing classroom performance assessments and scoring rubrics. *Practical Assessment, Research and Evaluation, 8*(14). Retrieved September 16, 2008, from http://PAREonline.net/getvn.asp?v=8&n=14.

Testa, A., Schechter, E., & Eder, D. (2002). Web corner: Authenticating student work in the digital age. *Assessment Update, 14*(2), 11.

Writing a Traditional Test

While performance assessments (Chapter Two) are growing in popularity, multiple-choice and other objective tests often still have a place in the assessment toolbox. This chapter discusses how to plan an objective test, how to write effective multiple-choice questions and other objective test items, and how objective tests can be used to assess some thinking skills. Essay test questions follow the principles for prompts (assignments) that are discussed in Chapter Ten.

What Is an Objective Test?

Objective tests might be defined as those that can be scored by a competent eight year old armed with an answer key, while subjective tests and assignments require professional judgment to score.

The most common kind of objective test item is the multiple-choice item. It consists of two parts. The *stem* asks the question; it may be phrased as a question or an incomplete sentence. The remainder of the test item is a set of *responses* or *options* from which the student chooses one answer. The incorrect options are called *distracters* or *foils* because their purpose is to distract or foil students who don't know the correct answer from choosing it.

Other kinds of objective test items are simply variations on the multiple-choice theme. A *true-false* item is a multiple-choice item with only two options. *Matching* items are a set of multiple-choice items with identical options. And a *completion* or *fill-in-the-blank* item is a multiple-choice item with no options.

Why Use an Objective Test?

Despite years of often-justified criticisms, objective tests remain widely used for the reasons noted in Table 2.8. They are especially good for assessing fundamental knowledge and understanding. They can also assess some important thinking skills, such as the ability to identify correct applications, examples, functions, causes, or effects. Interpretive exercises, a special kind of objective item discussed later in this chapter, can assess application, problem-solving, and analysis skills.

Well-constructed multiple-choice tests can also help diagnose problem areas. Consider this simple example:

What is $2 \times .10$?

A. 20
B. 2.10
C. 0.2
D. 0.02

Each distracter gives a clue as to where the student's thinking goes wrong. Choosing B, for example, indicates that the student confuses multiplication and addition signs. Choosing A indicates that the student confuses multiplication with division, and choosing D indicates a problem with decimal place value. Faculty and staff can thus use the results of well-written multiple-choice tests to identify areas of difficulty and help their students accordingly.

Objective tests are not always an appropriate assessment choice, however, for the reasons noted in Table 2.7. They cannot measure many important thinking skills and do not measure real-world performance as well as performance assessments (Chapter Two) do. They have other shortcomings as well:

- As you will learn in this chapter, writing good, clear items with good distracters can be difficult and time-consuming.

- Most objective tests require significant reading ability, so students who fail, say, a multiple-choice science test might truly understand the tested scientific concepts but fail because they read unusually slowly. While reading skill is essential for success in academic efforts, if we are assessing understanding of science concepts, we want an assessment tool that assesses just that.

- It's possible to guess the correct answer to most objective items through plain luck or through skill in being test-wise. While a well-constructed test minimizes test-wise students' advantage, there is always the possibility that a student who doesn't know the material will do well on a test through chance.

Planning an Objective Test with a Test Blueprint

Effective assignments are planned by developing a rubric: a list of the learning goals that students are to demonstrate in the completed assignment (Chapter Nine). Effective tests are similarly planned by developing a *test blueprint*: an outline of the test that lists the learning goals that students are to demonstrate on the test. Test blueprints are critical to creating effective tests for several reasons:

Test blueprints help ensure that the test focuses on the learning goals you think are most important.   Suppose that you are writing a test for units 8, 9, and 10 of a particular course. While you consider unit 10 the most important of the three, you may find that it's much easier to think of test questions for unit 8. If you write your test without a blueprint, you can easily end up with too many questions on unit 8 and too few on unit 10. Students taking such a test may be able to do fairly well without having mastered important concepts of unit 10.

Test blueprints help ensure that a test gives appropriate emphasis to thinking skills.   Faculty writing test questions without a blueprint often find that questions asking for simple conceptual knowledge are easier to write than those asking students to interpret, infer, analyze, or think in other ways. Tests written without blueprints can thus become tests of trivia rather than of thinking skills. Students who do well on such tests may not have mastered important skills, and students who have truly learned those important skills may earn low scores.

Test blueprints make writing test questions much easier. Armed with a test blueprint, you'll know exactly what must be covered on the test (one question on concept A, two on skill B, and so on), and you'll spend less time pondering what questions to write.

Test blueprints help document that students have achieved major learning goals. Test scores or grades alone give little direct information on exactly what students have learned (Chapter One). But if those scores or grades are accompanied by test blueprints that describe the learning goals covered on the tests, you'll have direct evidence of exactly what students who did well on the tests have learned. This makes test blueprints an important part of an assessment program. Exhibit 16.3 shows how test results can be mapped back to the test blueprint.

Begin creating a test blueprint by using syllabi, lecture notes, readings, and other curricular materials to list the major areas that the test will cover. A midterm exam, for example, might cover the first five chapters in the textbook. A comprehensive exam for graduating seniors might cover the six courses required of all majors.

Next, allocate fractions of the test to each of those areas, in proportion to the relative importance of each area, by assigning points or a number of test questions to each area (perhaps twenty points or four questions to unit 1, thirty points or six questions to unit 2, and so on).

Next, within each area, list the learning goals you want to assess. To make clear to both yourself and your students exactly what you want them to demonstrate on the test, phrase the learning goals using action verbs that describe what students should be able to think and do (Chapter Eight). Instead of simply listing "Hemingway" in a test blueprint on twentieth-century American literature, state the knowledge and skills you want students to demonstrate regarding Hemingway ("Identify works written by Hemingway," "Distinguish Hemingway's writing style from those of his peers").

Finally, spread the points or test questions within each area among the learning goals within that area, again in proportion to their importance. For example, if you have allocated four questions to unit 1 and list four learning goals within that chapter, you may decide to have one question on each learning goal. But perhaps one of the learning goals is especially important. In that case, you may decide to have two questions on that goal, and you will need to eliminate one of the other unit 1 learning goals from the test.

Exhibit 11.1 is an example of a test blueprint. It has one test question on each topic unless otherwise indicated.

Exhibit 11.1. A Test Blueprint for an Examination in an Educational Research Methods Course

Sampling

- Understand the difference between a sample and a population.
- Understand how each type of sample is selected.
- Understand how to choose an appropriate sample size.

Instrumentation and Survey Research

- Understand the relative merits and limitations of published and locally developed instruments.
- Recognize examples of each of the four frames of reference for interpreting scores.
- Understand appropriate uses of each item format (such as multiple choice and Likert scale).
- Understand the characteristics of a good instrument item, including how to avoid biased questions.

Descriptive Statistics

- Select the most appropriate descriptive statistic for a given research situation.
- Use percentage guidelines to interpret standard deviations.
- Identify the direction and strength of r and/or a scatter plot.

Validity and Reliability

- Identify the type of reliability or validity evidence provided by given information on an instrument. (two questions)
- Understand the meaning and implications of measurement error.
- Recognize examples of measurement error in a given situation.
- Understand the general principles for ensuring validity.

Inferential Statistics

- Select the most appropriate inferential statistic (t, F, or χ^2) for a given research situation. (two questions)
- Know the most common cutoff points that statisticians use in deciding whether two means differ statistically significantly from one another.
- Interpret the results of t-tests as presented in research articles.

Experimental Research

- Interpret the symbolic representations of experimental designs.
- Identify the appropriate research design for a given research situation.

Correlational Research

- Understand what r^2, R, and R^2, and partial correlations are and what they tell us. (two questions)
- Understand what multiple regression analysis is used for and what it tells us.

Once you have finalized the test blueprint, give copies to your students to help them focus their studies on the learning goals that you think are most important.

Writing Good Multiple-Choice Items

As with any other assessment, multiple-choice tests should yield fair and truthful information on what students have learned (Chapter Three). There are just two basic precepts to writing fair and truthful multiple-choice items.

- *Remove all the barriers that will keep a knowledgeable student from answering the item correctly.* Students who have truly learned the concept or skill that a particular item tests should choose the correct answer.

- *Remove all clues that will help a less-than-knowledgeable student answer the item correctly.* Students who truly haven't learned the concept or skill that a particular item tests should answer the item incorrectly.

The suggestions in Table 11.1 follow these two precepts. Exhibit 11.2 gives some examples of multiple-choice items that follow most of these suggestions and assess thinking skills as well as conceptual understanding.

Writing good multiple-choice items can be difficult. Test publishers write, try out, and discard many, many items for each one that ends up in a published test. Even the examples in Exhibit 11.2 don't

Table 11.1. Tips for Writing Good Multiple-Choice Questions

General Tips

Keep each item as concise as possible. Short, straightforward items are usually easier to understand than complex statements. Avoid irrelevant material, digressions, and qualifying information unless you are specifically assessing the skill of identifying needed information. Don't repeat the same words over and over in the options; put them in the stem.

Define all terms carefully. If you ask, "Which of the following birds is largest?" make clear whether you mean largest in terms of wingspan or weight. What do you mean by "sometimes," "usually," or "regularly"?

Don't make the vocabulary unnecessarily difficult. Except for terms you are specifically assessing, keep the vocabulary simple—perhaps high school level. Otherwise you may unfairly penalize students who know the material but don't have a strong general vocabulary.

Watch out for "interlocking" items: items in which a student can discern the answer to one question from the content of another. Review carefully all items that share similar options. In a similar vein, don't ask students to use their answer to one question to answer another. If they get the first question wrong, they will automatically get the other question wrong as well, even if they understand the concept tested in the second question.

Writing a Good Stem

The stem should ask a complete question. The student shouldn't have to read the options to discern the question. To check this, ask yourself if students would be able to answer the question posed in the stem correctly if no options were provided.

Avoid "Which of the following" items. They require students to read every option and can penalize slow readers in a timed-testing situation.

Don't ask questions that can be answered from common knowledge. Someone who hasn't studied the material shouldn't be able to answer the questions correctly.

Avoid negative items. In a stressful testing situation, students can miss the word *not* or *no*. If you must have negative items, underline, capitalize, or boldface words like NOT or EXCEPT.

Avoid grammatical clues to the correct answer. Test-wise students know that grammatically incorrect options are wrong. Use expressions like "a/an," "is/are," or "cause(s)."

Writing Good Options

You needn't have the same number of options for every question. Four options are fine. A good fifth option is often hard to come up with, takes extra reading time, and reduces the chances of guessing the correct answer only from 25 to 20 percent. Some questions may have only three plausible options (for example, "Increases," "Decreases," and "Remains unchanged").

Order responses logically. Order responses numerically if they are numbers and alphabetically if they are single words. This helps students who know the answer find it quickly. If the options have no intuitive order, insert the correct answer into the responses randomly.

Line up responses vertically rather than horizontally. It's much easier—and less confusing—to scan down a column than across a line to find the correct answer. If you are using a paper test and your options are so short that this seems to waste paper, arrange the test in two columns.

Make all options roughly the same length. Test-wise students know that the longest option is often the properly qualified, correct one. (For this reason, a relatively long option can make a good distracter!)

Avoid repeating words between the stem and the correct response. Test-wise students will pick up this clue. (On the other hand, verbal associations between the stem and a distracter can create an effective distracter.)

Avoid using "None of the above." A student may correctly recognize wrong answers without knowing the right answer. Use this option only when it is important that the student know what *not* to do. If you use "none of these," use it in more than one question, both as a correct answer and an incorrect answer.

Avoid using "All of the above." This option requires students to read every option, penalizing those in a timed testing situation who know the material but are slow readers. Students who recognize option A as correct and choose it without reading further are also penalized. "All of the above" also gives full credit for incomplete understanding; some students may recognize options A and B as correct and therefore correctly choose "All of the above" even though they don't recognize option C as correct.

Writing Good Distracters

The best distracters help diagnose where each student went wrong in his or her thinking. Identify each mental task that students need to do to answer a question correctly, and create a distracter for the answer students would arrive at if they completed each step incorrectly.

Use intrinsically true or at least plausible statements. Test-wise students recognize ridiculous statements as wrong. To see if your test has such statements, ask a friend who has never studied the subject to take the test. His or her score should be roughly what would be earned from guessing randomly on every item (25 percent for a four-option multiple-choice test).

Exhibit 11.2. Multiple-Choice Questions on Assessment Concepts

Correct answers are in italics.

1. Which statement refers to measurement as opposed to evaluation?
   A. *Emily got 90 percent correct on the math test.*
   B. Lin's test scores have increased satisfactorily this year.
   C. Justin's score of 20 on this test indicates that his study habits are ineffective.
   D. Keesha got straight A's in her history courses this year.

2. Alyssa took a test on Tuesday after a big fight with her parents Monday night. She scored a 72. Her professor let her retake the same test on Thursday when things cooled off. She scored 75. The difference in her scores may be attributed to:
   A. chance or luck.
   B. lack of discrimination.
   C. lack of validity.
   D. *measurement error.*

3. People who score high on the Meyers Musical Aptitude Scale usually score low on the Briggs Biologists Aptitude Test. People who score low on the Meyers usually score high on the Briggs. Which of the figures below *most likely* represents the correlation between the two tests?
   A. .80
   B. .00
   C. −.10
   D. *−.60*

4. Choose the *most likely* correct answer to this nonsense question, based on what you know about informed guessing on tests. A drabble will coagulate under what circumstances?
   A. Only when pics increase
   B. Only when pics change color
   C. By drawing itself into a circle
   D. *Usually when pics increase, but occasionally when pics decrease*

---

completely follow the suggestions in Table 11.1. So don't expect to be able to follow all these suggestions all the time, and don't expect your test questions to work perfectly the first time you use them. Analyze the results (Chapter Sixteen), revise the test accordingly, and within just a few cycles you will have a truly good test.

Avoiding Trick Questions

Many tests aim to include a few difficult questions to challenge the very best students. Unfortunately, writing difficult multiple-choice questions is, well, difficult. It's very hard to come up with meaningful distracters that will foil all but the best students.

Table 11.2. Tips for Writing Challenging Rather Than Trick Questions

Use a test blueprint. It ensures that each item assesses an important concept or skill.

Make your tests open-book, open-note. Tell students they can bring to the test anything they like except a friend or the means to communicate with one. Using open-book, open-note tests forces you to eliminate items assessing simple knowledge that students can look up. Your test will include only items that assess deeper comprehension and thinking skills.

Build items around common misconceptions. Many people, for example, think that plants get nutrients only from soil and water, not air; this misconception can become the basis of an effective botany test question.

Create interpretive exercises (discussed below). They assess thinking skills such as application and analysis.

Evaluate your test results using the tools in Chapter Sixteen. Revise any misleading or unnecessarily difficult items before including them in another test.

Too often, difficult questions are trick questions that focus on trivia or some finely nuanced point rather than an important concept. Follow the suggestions in Table 11.2 to write meaningful, challenging multiple-choice questions that assess important learning goals rather than trick questions.

Some faculty pride themselves on writing complex multiple-choice questions that require well-developed analytical reasoning skills to understand and answer correctly. These kinds of question can be fine *if*:

- One of the learning goals of the course is to develop these skills; *and*

- Students have opportunities to learn and practice these skills before taking the test; *and*

- This learning goal is reflected in the test blueprint.

Interpretive Exercises

Interpretive exercises, sometimes referred to as context-dependent or enhanced multiple-choice items or scenario testing, consist of a stimulus, such as a reading passage or a chart, that students haven't seen before, followed by a set of objective items. Many published aptitude and achievement tests include interpretive exercises.

Interpretive exercises have three defining characteristics:

- *The stimulus material must be new to the students*; they must never have seen it before. This requires students to apply what they have learned to a new situation, making interpretive exercises a good way to assess application skills.

- *Students must read or examine the material in order to answer the objective items that follow.* They should not be able to answer any of the items simply from their general understanding of what they've learned in the course or program. Again, this defining characteristic makes an interpretive exercise an assessment of application skill rather than simple conceptual understanding.

- *The items must be objective, with one and only one correct answer for each item.* If you ask students to write or otherwise create something in response to the stimulus, you have a performance assessment (Chapter Two), not an interpretive exercise.

While all interpretive exercises by definition assess skill in applying knowledge and skills to new situations, interpretive exercises can also assess skill in generalizing, inferring, concluding, problem solving, and analysis. Performance assessments can assess these skills as well, but interpretive exercises are more efficient. Given the same amount of work time, students will give you information on a broader range of skills through interpretive exercises than they can through performance assessments, and you can score interpretive exercises more quickly.

Interpretive exercises are not always appropriate, however. As with other objective items, they can be difficult and time-consuming to write. If the stimuli are reading passages, interpretive exercises may unfairly penalize students who have the knowledge and skills being assessed but are slow readers. And although interpretive exercises are good for assessing some thinking skills, they cannot assess some other thinking skills such as organizing, defining problems, and creating.

Table 11.3. Tips for Writing Good Interpretive Exercises

Keep the size of the stimulus in proportion to the questions asked. Having students read a full page of text in order to answer only three questions is hardly an efficient use of their time. Generally aim to ask at least three questions about any stimulus, and ask more about longer stimuli.

Be on the lookout for interlocking items. They seem to crop up more often in this format.

Give students realistic scenarios. Possibilities include:

A chart, diagram, map, or drawing with real or hypothetical information

A brief statement written by a scholar, researcher, or other significant individual

A passage from a novel, short story, or poem

A description of a real or imaginary scenario, such as a scientific experiment or a business situation

For foreign language courses and programs, any of the above written in the language

Be creative! Remember that the stimulus need not be a reading passage; it can be a diagram, or picture, or chart, as shown in Exhibit 11.3.

The key to writing good interpretive exercises is to keep in mind the three defining characteristics listed above. Table 11.3 offers other suggestions for creating effective interpretive exercises.

Exhibit 11.3 is an example of an interpretive exercise that follows most of these suggestions. (Correct answers are in italics. Item analysis—the concept assessed by these items—is discussed in Chapter Sixteen.)

Exhibit 11.3. An Example of an Interpretive Exercise

Items 1 to 5 refer to the item analysis information given below. The correct options are marked with an asterisk.

Item 1	A	B*	C	D
Top third			10	
Bottom third	1	4	3	2

Item 2	A*	B	C	D
Top third	8		2	
Bottom third		7	3	

Item 3	A	B	C*	D
Top third	5		1	4
Bottom third	2		4	4

Item 4	A*	B	C	D
Top third	10			
Bottom third	9	1		

Write the item number (1, 2, 3, or 4) in the space provided.

1. _4_ Which item is easiest?
2. _3_ Which item shows negative (*very* bad) discrimination?
3. _2_ Which item discriminates *best* between high and low scores?

For the remaining items, write the option letter (A, B, C, or D) in the space provided.

4. _B_ In item 2, which distracter is most effective?
5. _B_ In item 3, which distracter *must* be changed?

Matching Items _____

Matching items are a set of multiple-choice items with a common set of responses. If, as you write a multiple-choice test, you find yourself writing several items with similar options, consider converting them into a matching set.

Matching items are even more efficient than multiple-choice questions. Because students need to read only one set of options to answer several items, they can often answer five well-written matching items more quickly than five multiple-choice items, giving you more assessment information in a given amount of testing time. They are also faster to write because you don't have to come up with a fresh set of distracters for each item.

Matching items are a good way to assess certain kinds of basic knowledge. Students can match terms and definitions, causes and effects, authors and titles of their works, people and their achievements, foreign words and their English translations, or tools and their uses. Matching items need not be entirely verbal; students can match symbols with the concepts they represent, pictures of objects with their names, or labeled parts of a pictured entity (say, a microscope or a cell) with their functions.

Matching items can also assess some thinking skills, especially the ability to apply what students have learned to new situations and the ability to analyze interrelationships. Students can match concepts with new examples of them, causes with likely effects, and hypothetical problems with the tools, concepts, or approaches needed to solve them.

Table 11.4 offers suggestions for creating good sets of matching items—possibly quite different from matching items you may have used or seen in the past.

Exhibit 11.4 gives an example of a matching set that follows these suggestions and assesses application skill as well as conceptual understanding.

True-False Items _____

True-false items are multiple-choice items with only two options. Their most common use is simple knowledge: Is a given statement correct or not? But they can also be used in other situations with just two possible answers: Is a statement fact or opinion? Is it an example of qualitative or quantitative assessment evidence? Does A cause B?

True-false items have no particular advantages beyond those of any other objective format. Because they have the following serious shortcomings, they should be used rarely, if at all:

Table 11.4. Tips for Writing Good Matching Items

A matching set should consist of homogeneous items. Every option in the answer key should be a plausible answer for every item or question. Otherwise test-wise students will quickly eliminate implausible answers, and students who are not test-wise will read and consider the full set of responses over and over.

Make an imperfect match between the two columns. Allow students to use each option more than once or not at all. A perfect match (in which each option is the answer for exactly one item) gives an unfair advantage to test-wise students, who will cross out each option as it's chosen and then guess among the remaining options. A perfect match also gives an unfair disadvantage to students who misunderstand one item but truly know all the other answers; if they choose one incorrect answer, they must, by process of elimination, choose a second incorrect answer, because it's the only option left.

Make it easy for students who know the material to find the correct answer. Make the longer statements the "questions," and limit the answer key to single words or short phrases. For example, list definitions as the questions and the terms they define as the options. Or list accomplishments as the questions and the people achieving them as the options. Otherwise students will need to keep scanning through a list of lengthy options to find the correct answers. This penalizes those who have learned the material but are slow readers. Limit the number of matching items in a set to no more than ten or so, and keep the entire exercise on one page. Arrange the options in a logical order (usually alphabetically).

Give clear directions. In an introductory sentence, explain how the two columns are related—for example, "Match each theory with the person who conceived it." Point out that options may be used more than once or not at all; your students may never have seen this kind of matching set before. Give each column an explanatory title (for example, "Theory" and "Originator") if that would be helpful.

Be inventive! The answer key need not be words or phrases in a column; it can be lettered parts of a diagram, drawing, map, or chart.

Exhibit 11.4. Matching Items from a Nursing Research Methods Test

In this set of matching items, some options may be used more than once or not at all. Correct answers are in italics.

Match each measurement with its level of measurement.

A. Interval
B. Ordinal
C. Nominal
D. Ratio

D 1. Fluid intake, in ounces, of a postsurgical patient

C 2. Religious affiliation

D 3. Medication dosage

C 4. Type of adjuvant therapy (chemotherapy, hormonal therapy, or radiation therapy)

B 5. Level of patient advocate support for a patient (very supportive, moderately supportive, somewhat supportive, not supportive)

Source: Adapted with permission from test questions written by Christina Barrick, associate professor of Nursing, Towson University.

Table 11.5. Tips for Writing Good True-False Items

Keep them simple. Avoid lengthy qualifiers and broad generalizations, which can be confusing and hard to make plausible as true or false statements.

Use them only to assess important learning goals. It's easy for true-false items to descend into trivia.

Avoid negative and double-negative statements. These are confusing in a true-false format.

Keep the proportion of true statements close to but not exactly 50 percent. Test-wise students will scan the number of true statements they've marked and use that to decide how to guess on the items they don't know.

- Students who haven't learned the material have a high probability (50 percent) of guessing the correct answer.
- Unlike multiple-choice and matching items, true-false items give no clues about where students who answered incorrectly went wrong in their thinking.
- It's difficult to write true-false items assessing thinking skills, although they can be used in interpretive exercises.
- For classic true-false items—those giving true or false statements—it can be very difficult to write unambiguous, unqualified statements that are either definitely true or definitely false.
- Students may correctly recognize a false statement without knowing its true counterpart.

If true-false items appear to be appropriate for your situation, the suggestions in Table 11.5 will help make the best of them.

Completion or Fill-in-the-Blank Items

Completion items are multiple-choice items with no options provided. They pose questions that students answer with a word, number, or symbol. A fill-in-the-blank item is a completion item posed as a sentence with a missing word, number, or symbol.

To be true objective items, completion items should have only one correct answer. Recall the definition of an objective test given at the beginning of this chapter: a test is objective if a reasonably competent eight year old armed with an answer key can score it accurately. True completion items can be scored in this fashion. Many short-answer items are really subjective, with a number of acceptable answers that require professional judgment to score. While such subjective items may be an appropriate part of an assessment program, considering the time they take to score and the limited information they provide, performance assessments (Chapter Two)

Table 11.6. Tips for Writing Good Completion or Fill-in-the-Blank Items

Keep all blanks or spaces for recording answers of uniform length. Blanks or spaces of varying length give test-wise students clues. To facilitate scoring, have students record all their answers in a column on one side of the page. If you are using fill-in-the-blank items, make the blanks in the sentences very short placeholders, and have students write their answers in a column of longer blanks.

If you are using fill-in-the-blank items, structure sentences so the blanks are toward the ends of the sentences. Sentences will be easier for your students to understand than if the blanks are at the beginning.

Avoid lifting sentences out of a textbook. Too often the resulting items are ambiguous or focus on trivia.

may be a better choice, as they assess thinking skills and give students more opportunities to acquire and demonstrate deep, lasting learning.

Completion items are a good choice for assessing those essential facts that must be memorized and should not be guessed from multiple-choice items. They are also appropriate when the correct answer would be easy for students to recognize in a multiple-choice format. Completion items are widely used in mathematics, for example, when a test-wise student might deduce the correct multiple-choice answer by working backward from each option. They can be a good way to develop multiple-choice distracters for future tests: simply choose the most common incorrect answers as foils.

Truly objective completion items rarely assess thinking skills except in mathematics. Because scoring is difficult to automate, this format is not a good choice for large-scale assessment programs.

The key to writing truly objective completion items is to design them so that one specific word, number, or symbol is the only correct answer. Table 11.6 offers other suggestions.

Pulling an Objective Test Together

Before assembling items into a test, review them in terms of these questions:

- *Do the items follow the test blueprint?* Does each assess an important learning outcome, or are any of them trick questions that ask about trivia? Are the formats and content appropriate for the learning goals you are assessing?

- *Are the items at an appropriate reading level?* Other than vocabulary terms that you are specifically assessing, are the items simple, clear, and straightforward? Are they free of excessive verbiage?

- *Would experts agree on the answers?*
- *Are the items of appropriate difficulty?* Ideally, there should be a few easy items on fundamental concepts that virtually everyone answers correctly. Perhaps there are also a few items designed to challenge the top students. An excessively difficult test, no matter how you curve the scores, is frustrating and demoralizing for students. See Chapter Sixteen for further discussion of item difficulty.
- *Are there any interlocking items* or items with any other clues for test-wise students?

Next, order the items. The first ones should be the easiest, to reassure the test anxious, and quickly answered, to help those who aren't test-wise. The last items should be the most difficult and the most complex (requiring the most thinking time). Interpretive exercises often go toward the end.

Then write directions that explain:

- The purpose of the test
- How the answers will be scored
- How to answer (Can they choose more than one answer? Should they choose the one best answer? Is guessing encouraged?)
- How to record answers
- Any time limits (if the test is lengthy and timed—a two-hour final exam, for example—you may want to suggest time limits for each section)

Finally, let the test sit for twenty-four hours after you have completed it, and then proofread it one last time. Prepare the scoring key before the test is duplicated or posted online, as the process of preparing the key can identify typos and unclear items missed in earlier readings.

Should Students Explain Their Answers to Objective Items?

A major concern with objective items, especially true-false items, is the possibility that students who haven't learned the material can still guess the correct answer. One way to solve this problem is to ask students to write brief explanations of why they chose their answer. For true-false items, students can be asked to correct any statements they mark as false.

While this does eliminate the possibility of students' blind guessing the correct answer, it also removes one of the fundamental advantages of objective items: their efficiency. Students won't be able to answer as many questions in a given amount of testing time, so the test will assess a narrower range of goals. And rather than having a scanner or a competent eight year old score the tests, you must read every answer and use your professional judgment to decide which are correct and which are not, which takes far more of your time and energy.

If you want students to explain their answers, consider instead giving them an assignment or essay question (Chapter Ten) for which they must compose a more complete written response. This will elicit deeper thought, give you richer assessment information, and give your students a better learning experience.

Should Students Be Encouraged to Guess?

In a word, yes. The "correction for guessing" used on some published tests aims to equate the scores of students who answer questions randomly with those who leave questions blank. Test-wise students readily guess on items of which they're unsure. They know that if they can eliminate even one option as implausible, they raise their odds of guessing correctly beyond random chance. If students who aren't test-wise aren't encouraged to guess, they're being unfairly penalized for not being sufficiently test-savvy.

Time to Think, Discuss, and Practice _____

Write each of the following for a unit or concept that you teach or have studied, following as many of the guidelines in this chapter as you can. Share your drafts with group members for comments and suggestions.

1. Six multiple-choice items
2. A set of matching items
3. An interpretive exercise

Recommended Readings _____

The following readings are recommended along with the references cited in this chapter.

Berk, R. (1998). A humorous account of 10 multiple-choice test item flaws that clue testwise students. *Journal on Excellence in College Teaching, 9*(2), 93–117.

Clegg, V. L., & Cashin, W. E. (1995). *Improving multiple choice tests* (IDEA Paper No. 16). Manhattan: Kansas State University, Center for Faculty Evaluation and Development.

Frary, R. B. (1995). More multiple-choice item writing do's and don'ts. *Practical Assessment, Research and Evaluation, 4*(11). Retrieved September 16, 2008, from http://PAREonline.net/getvn.asp?v=4&n=11.

Gronlund, N. E. (2005). *Assessment of student achievement* (8th ed.). Needham Heights, MA: Allyn & Bacon.

Haladyna, T. M. (1997). *Writing test items to evaluate higher order thinking.* Needham Heights, MA: Allyn & Bacon.

Haladyna, T. M. (2004). *Developing and validating multiple-choice test items* (3rd ed.). Needham Heights, MA: Allyn & Bacon.

Kehoe, J. (1995). Writing multiple-choice items. *Practical Assessment, Research and Evaluation, 4*(9). Retrieved September 16, 2008, from http://PAREonline.net/getvn.asp?v=4&n=9.

Kubiszyn, T., & Borich, G. D. (2002). *Educational testing and measurement: Classroom application and management* (7th ed.). San Francisco: Jossey-Bass.

Linn, R. L., & Gronlund, N. E. (2000). *Measurement and assessment in teaching* (8th ed.). New York: Macmillan.

CHAPTER 12

Assessing Attitudes, Values, Dispositions, and Habits of Mind

Some Valuable Ideas You'll Find in This Chapter

- Some traits are not teachable. Don't hold faculty accountable for things they cannot teach.
- Reflective writing is valuable as a learning strategy as well as an assessment strategy.
- Phrase questions about attitudes and values so that there are no obviously socially acceptable answers.
- Ecosystem rating scales are a good way to assess the attainment of attitudinal goals.

It's relatively easy to figure out how to assess knowledge, understanding, thinking skills, and performance skills. We can assess writing skills by examining student papers, for example, and interpersonal skills by observing students interacting with one another. But what about the "ineffables": traits that are not as easily observable? How can we assess appreciation of a subject or discipline, spiritual development, valuing diverse points of view, a lifelong interest in a subject, an openness to new ideas, integrity, commitment to serving others, or self-understanding?

Can These Goals Be Assessed? _____

Assessing these traits is admittedly more difficult and less precise than assessing thinking and performance skills. Direct evidence (Chapter Two) such as graded tests or assignments is usually inappropriate, because students are more likely to give the answers they think we want to hear than their true thoughts and feelings. Students might say on a test or indicate on a rating scale that they have grown spiritually, for example, even if they haven't truly done so.

These traits can also be difficult to assess because they are often ill defined. What does "appreciate" really mean, after all? If you ask a variety of faculty and staff, you'll likely get a variety of answers. As I note throughout this book, an ill-defined goal is very difficult, if not impossible, to assess meaningfully.

Some of these kinds of goals are not just difficult but virtually impossible to assess—because they are not teachable. Consider the goal that students will "have a lasting curiosity about other places, people, and cultural experiences." Faculty and staff certainly hope that they will instill this trait in students by modeling this behavior, encouraging the expressions of curiosity, and so on, but it is hard to think of assignments and class work that will actively help students develop this trait.

One way to figure out if a learning goal is assessable is thus to ask faculty and staff to share how they help students achieve it. What tasks, assignments, and classwork do they give students to help them achieve the goal? If the faculty and staff can name specific assignments or classwork, the goal is assessable. Indeed, the assignments or classwork can probably serve as the assessment strategy. But if the question draws blank stares and comments such as, "Well, I think they pick it up by osmosis," the goal may not be teachable—or assessable. These kinds of goals should be acknowledged as important, but they are not the kind to which we should hold ourselves accountable. As Peter Ewell (2002) has noted, "Don't hold people accountable for things they cannot do" (p. 16).

What about goals that appear difficult—but not impossible— to assess? That's not an excuse to abandon the assessment of them. As Richard Shavelson (2007) has noted, if we do not measure these kinds of traits, "they will drop from sight as accountability pressures force campuses to focus on a more restricted set of learning outputs that can be more easily and less expensively measured" (p. 1). Acknowledge and celebrate difficult-to-assess goals as important, and perhaps put them on a back burner for now in terms of assessment, but don't neglect them altogether.

Two Windows: Reflections and Behaviors _____

The two primary windows into attitudes, values, and the like are *reflection* and *behaviors*. If we collect information on these carefully and with a variety of measures, we can often infer from reflection and behaviors whether students have achieved our goals.

Some believe that these kinds of goals should be assessed by contacting alumni and seeing how they are living their lives. But as I explained in Chapter Seven, there are limitations to this approach, and it may be more meaningful and useful to get proxy measures from students about to graduate.

Encouraging Reflection

An intriguing development in education has been the increasing value placed on reflection: encouraging students to reflect on what, how, and why they have learned. Students can be asked to reflect on who they are, their growth and development, their experiences, and their satisfaction.

Reflections can be obtained in a variety of ways, all discussed in this chapter. If some of the strategies sound like the informal assessments that faculty and staff have always used to evaluate student performance, the difference is that strategies for assessment through reflection are structured, systematic, and consistent rather than sporadic or anecdotal. Hearing a few students exclaim about the insight they gained from a class is exciting and rewarding, but it is not a truly useful and meaningful assessment unless you ask all your students, or a representative sample of them, about insight on a regular basis.

Reflection offers a number of benefits beyond the capacity to assess values, attitudes, and the like:

Reflection helps students learn. The best assessments are learning experiences for students as well as opportunities for us to see what they have learned, and this is where reflection shines as an assessment strategy. Reflection helps students learn by encouraging two increasingly important skills: metacognition and synthesis (Chapter Eight). Metacognition is learning how to learn and how to manage that learning by reflecting on how you learn best, thereby preparing for a lifetime of learning. Synthesis is the ability to put together what you have learned and see the big picture. Asking students to reflect at the end of a course or program on the major lessons that they have learned throughout the curriculum, the strategies they used, and how the pieces fit together can help them develop metacognition and synthesis skills.

Reflection balances quantitative assessments with qualitative information.   Most reflection is a form of qualitative research: collecting information using flexible, naturalistic methods. Qualitative assessments (Chapter Two) give us fresh insight, allow us to explore possibilities that we haven't previously considered, and help us discover problems and solutions that we wouldn't find through quantitative assessments alone.

Reflection can yield useful information quickly and easily.   You can use minute papers and the other short questions discussed in this chapter literally in your next class. If you ask students for very brief reflections, analyzing the results can also be easy: read through the responses (or, if you have hundreds, a sample of them) for a quick sense of the most common themes. You can then address any areas of concern in your next class.

Can and should student reflections be scored or graded? Opinions on this are decidedly mixed. On one hand, one of the purposes of reflection is to elicit honest, truthful thoughts from students. Scoring student reflections may stifle that honesty, encouraging students to write only what they think we want to hear instead of what they truly think and feel. Indeed, asking students to put their names on their reflections, even if the reflections aren't graded, may dissuade them from providing honest, and therefore trustworthy, information.

On the other hand, reflection is an opportunity to develop skill in analysis and synthesis, and we can certainly evaluate how well students are demonstrating these skills in their reflective writing. Scores and grades can also be important incentives for students to give careful thought to their reflections.

Both of these positions have merit, and the best approach depends on your students and what you are asking them to do. Some students may be more comfortable reflecting anonymously until they develop increased confidence in their ability to reflect. Other students may need the incentive of credit toward a final grade to complete a thoughtful journal.

Looking at Behaviors

Suppose that one of your college's goals is for students to be "passionate, lifelong learners" and that you run into two alumni from your college. As you talk with them, it becomes clear that Jasmine is a passionate, lifelong learner, and Carly is not. How might you discern this? You might learn that Jasmine:

- Reads more than Carly.
- Reads about a broader array of topics from a broader array of sources than Carly.
- Watches more educational programs on television and visits more educational Web sites than Carly.
- Attends a variety of cultural events, while Carly has attended virtually none.
- Furthers her education, perhaps by enrolling in a graduate program, taking courses, or even taking noncredit classes, while Carly has not.
- Expresses curiosity about things outside her experience and areas of knowledge, while Carly does not.
- Travels more, and to a broader variety of places, than Carly.

Of course Carly might not do any of these particular things and still be a passionate lifelong learner. Similarly, Jasmine could do these things and still not be a truly passionate lifelong learner. (Maybe she simply goes along with friends who do these things.) But the more evidence we have of these kinds of behaviors and the greater the variety of evidence, the more confidently we can infer that alumni have indeed developed these traits.

One of the reasons that asking about behaviors is an appealing assessment strategy is that it is easier for people to describe concrete actions accurately than to make accurate generalizations, especially about their feelings or opinions. Questions such as, "Do you consider yourself a hard-working student?" tempt students to tell you what they think you want to hear, even if you collect their responses anonymously. Asking, "How many hours per day do you usually study?" will elicit more honest answers.

To keep information on behaviors as accurate as possible, avoid making significant memory demands. Asking, "How many hours did you study yesterday?" will elicit more accurate information than asking, "How many hours per day do you usually study?" Along the same vein, avoid asking for very precise responses. Questions asking for annual salary to the exact dollar or grade point average to two decimal places will probably not be answered accurately. Rather than asking for precise amounts, consider using a multiple-choice format that asks participants to choose from ranges of responses, such as salaries in $10,000 or $20,000 ranges.

Another Use of Reflection and Behaviors: Understanding *Why*

Reflection and behaviors can serve another important role beyond assessing the ineffables. Collecting direct evidence of student learning outcomes (Chapter Two) from assignments and tests can give an incomplete picture of student learning. Such evidence helps us learn *what* students have or haven't learned, but it may not reveal *why* students are or aren't successful. To understand better how we are helping students learn and how we might improve what we do, we need to understand learning inputs and processes. The assessment tools and strategies discussed in this chapter can help illuminate student backgrounds, experiences, and attitudes and thereby draw a richer picture of the learning experience.

Getting Honest, Accurate Information

Assessment evidence from reflection and behaviors is indirect evidence (Chapter Two) that calls for a greater inferential leap than direct measures such as tests and papers. It's therefore especially important that these assessments follow the suggestions in Chapter Three for ensuring good-quality, fair, and unbiased assessments. If you are using a survey or reflective writing, consider these additional tips:

Ask about both the pros and cons of an issue. Don't ask anyone to make criticisms without giving them a chance to praise as well. Don't ask them if they favor extending the hours that an office is open (who wouldn't?) without noting the costs and other drawbacks.

Avoid questions that people are uncomfortable answering honestly. People are generally comfortable agreeing with the status quo and providing a socially acceptable answer. They are usually uncomfortable admitting inferiority or wrongdoing and may deceive themselves about their inclinations in sensitive areas, even if you are asking for information anonymously. Researchers have found that many people will not answer honestly when asked if they smoke, watch TV, go to art museums or religious services, or vote. Many will also not report accurately their salary, age, job, grade point average, or whether they failed a particular course.

Phrase questions so that you elicit thoughtful replies. If your goal is that students appreciate modern art, asking, "What is your attitude toward modern art?" may elicit responses such as,

"I like it" or "I've learned a lot about it." Questions such as, "Which work of art studied in this course or program would you most like to display in your home if you could? Why?" are far likelier to elicit thoughtful responses and tell you more about your students' true attitudes toward modern art.

If appropriate, let people admit that they don't know or can't remember. Forcing an opinion from people who don't have one or a memory from people who can't remember one is tantamount to forcing them to lie.

———————

Even with these precautions, self-reported assessment information is notoriously unreliable. People are known to misrepresent their experiences and views. The more sensitive the information—grade point averages, salaries, and alcoholic beverage consumption—the more inaccurate the information is likely to be. Self-reported information should thus be corroborated by supporting information from other sources when possible.

While people do sometimes purposely or inadvertently misrepresent themselves, there is usually no reason to believe that your students are any more likely to misrepresent themselves than other students, including students from a few years ago or students at other colleges. So comparing self-reported results against internal or external peers or historical trends, all discussed in Chapter Fifteen, may be more meaningful than comparing results against a standard.

Minute Papers

The easiest, fastest way to encourage reflection is to give students a couple of thought-provoking questions and ask them to write no more than a sentence in response to each. The minute paper (Angelo & Cross, 1993; Weaver & Cotrell, 1985) is one of the best ways to do this. It's called a minute paper because students take no more than a minute or two to complete it, usually answering just two questions:

- What was the most important thing you learned during this class/course/program?
- What important question remains unanswered?

These questions can be modified, of course. The first question could be stated, for example, as, "What was the most useful or meaningful thing you learned . . .?" and the second could stated, "What question remains uppermost in your mind as we end this . . . ?" Chapter Sixteen discusses how to interpret answers to these kinds of questions.

To encourage honest feedback, faculty and staff often ask students to complete minute papers anonymously. But consider giving students the option of adding their name if they would like a response from you. This lets you provide individual assistance to students and makes minute papers a stronger learning opportunity.

Other Short Questions and Prompts

The minute paper concept—asking students for very brief reflections on what they have learned—can be modified to ask students about other aspects of their learning process or their developing attitudes and values. Table 12.1 presents a host of questions and prompts you might ask students to reflect on. To preserve one of the minute paper's strengths—its brevity—ask no more than three questions at one time.

The questions in Table 12.1 are not an exhaustive list; use them as inspiration for developing your own. If you do, take care to phrase your questions so that there are no obviously right or wrong answers.

Short questions and prompts can be incorporated into surveys as well as posed on their own. If they are part of a survey, keep in mind that they are usually not very popular with survey recipients because they lengthen the time required to complete the survey and require more mental energy to respond. Often survey respondents simply leave them blank. These kinds of open-ended items are therefore best used sparingly in surveys. Use them only when your question is interesting enough that people will want to answer it, when a rating scale might bias responses by steering participants in a particular direction, and when your question can be answered in no more than one sentence.

Before-and-After Reflection

Asking students to reflect at both the beginning and end of a course or program and comparing their responses can give a sense of their growth and development. You might ask students to rate their skills and attitudes, define a key concept ("What is poetry?")

Table 12.1. Examples of Prompts for Self-Reflection on an Assignment, Course, or Program

---

How do you feel about writing/teaching/biology/sociology/whatever?

What makes a person a good writer/teacher/biologist/sociologist/whatever?

How do you feel about yourself as a writer/teacher/biologist/sociologist/whatever?

What are your strengths as a writer/teacher/biologist/sociologist/whatever? Your weaknesses?

Describe something major that you've learned about yourself from this assignment/course/program.

What was your favorite part of this course/program? Why?

If you have a chance to speak to your friends and family, what might you say about this course/program?

What suggestions would you give other students on ways to get the most out of this course/program?

What was the one most useful or meaningful thing you learned in this assignment/course/program?

What did you learn about writing/research/other skill from this assignment/course/program?

What was your biggest achievement in this course/program?

What one assignment for this course/program was your best work? What makes it your best work? What did you learn by creating it? What does it say about you as a writer/teacher/biologist/sociologist/whatever?

If you could change any one of the assignments you did for this course/program, which one would it be? What would you change about it?

What goals did you set for yourself in this assignment/course/program? How well did you accomplish them?

What strategies did you use to learn the material in this assignment/course/program? Which were most effective? Why?

What risks did you take in this assignment/course/program?

If you were to start this assignment/course/program over, what would you do differently next time?

What problems did you encounter in this assignment/course/program? How did you solve them?

In what ways have you improved as a writer/teacher/biologist/sociologist/whatever?

List three ways you think you have grown or developed because of this assignment/course/program.

What have you learned in this assignment/course/program that will help you continue to grow as a writer/teacher/biologist/sociologist/whatever?

What did you learn from this assignment/course/program that is not reflected in your work?

What would you like to learn further about this subject/discipline? Why?

In what area would you like to continue to strengthen your knowledge or skills?

Write one goal for next semester/year and tell how you plan to reach it.

---

or explain why a subject or discipline is important. Table 12.2 gives examples of student definitions of leadership before and after participating in a leadership development program. The pairs of responses powerfully convey what students learned in the program.

Table 12.2. Student Definitions of Leadership Before and After Participating in a Leadership Development Program

Initial Definition of Leadership	Later Definition of Leadership
The ability to give and take orders and being able to take charge of a large group of people.	I have learned that leadership is not a one-man/woman show. To be a good leader, you must have the respect from your committee, and you must be able to communicate.
The presence of a strong, task-oriented, and social-oriented yet compromising force or person	Leadership isn't as easy as it looks! Leadership takes a lot of hard work, and there are ups and downs to the position of a leader. My definition has changed to include the importance of diverse people.
Leadership is a responsibility or a skill/trait one possesses that makes a person stand out above everyone else.	Leadership is a collective process. You need leaders and followers to make an event or organization successful.
Leadership involves taking control in an organizational way. A leader must know how to dictate responsibility as well as work with others to achieve a goal.	Leadership has a lot to do with confidence. Most of the confidence lies within yourself, but you also have to have confidence in the people you're working with. My definition of leadership has changed in the sense that I feel like it is more delegating and following up with your delegations than actually taking a lot of work upon yourself.
Leadership is an important element of life that can only be fulfilled by individuals possessing the motivation, insight, and communication skills to fulfill the mission, goals, and objectives of an organization.	Leadership is ever changing. Now I think leadership is defined by the people being led.

Source: Adapted with permission from responses to prompts by Tess Shier, coordinator for campus programs, Office of Student Activities, Towson University.

Longer Self-Reflection Assignments

While short questions and prompts for reflective writing are excellent ways to gain quick and easy insight into student learning, longer assignments reflecting on learning experiences throughout a course or program can help students synthesize what they've learned and clarify their attitudes, values, and learning strategies.

These kinds of assignments require clear, specific instructions (prompts) to students. Exhibit 12.1 is an example of such a prompt. Chapter Ten provides more information on creating effective prompts.

Exhibit 12.1. A Prompt for a Reflective Paper on an Internship

Write a reflective paper on your internship experience. The purpose of this assignment is for you to develop and demonstrate the ability to:

- Set explicit goals for your own work
- Monitor your progress toward meeting goals
- Seek out and use feedback from others
- Evaluate your learning and performance
- Assess personal strengths and weaknesses
- Communicate clearly and professionally through writing

Your reflective paper should be five pages, double-spaced, ten- or twelve-point font with one-inch margins. Use the objectives listed above as a basis for your reflection, and answer the following questions:

- How valuable was the internship experience to you?
- What specific experiences do you think made you stretch and grow as a professional?
- What could you have done differently during your internship to improve the learning experience?
- Would you recommend this placement to others? Why or why not?

Source: Adapted with permission from a prompt created by Sharon B. Buchbinder and Donna M. Cox, Health Care Management Program, Towson University.

Journals

Journals are documents into which students make repeated entries during a course or program. They can be used for reflection, to record behaviors, and to help students develop any of the following:

A skill through repeated practice. One of the most effective ways to learn is through time on task (see Table 18.3), and journals can help ensure that students routinely practice important skills such as writing, critical thinking, and problem solving. Students in a first-year composition course might be asked to write a paragraph each day in a journal, while students in a literature course might be asked to write short critical analyses of each reading assignment.

Study skills. Students might be asked to make weekly journal entries on their work on a major project such as a term paper to ensure that they are staying on track toward its timely completion.

Conceptual understanding.   Faculty can periodically review journals of brief summaries of lessons or readings to ensure that students are grasping key points correctly.

Metacognitive and synthesis skills.   Students might be asked to journal what they learned from each assignment, how they solved each problem, their reactions to each reading, or how each assignment or reading has affected their attitude toward the subject. After making routine entries on a regular basis, students might be asked to look back through their journals and reflect on how their skill or attitude has developed.

As with any other assignment or assessment, journals are worthwhile only if they are carefully planned. Effective journals require, first and foremost, a *clear learning goal* (Chapter Eight). Students should understand the journal's purpose and what they will learn by creating it. Effective journals also require *clear instructions or prompts* (Chapter Ten). Students should understand exactly what they should write in the journal and how often. Finally, effective journals require *useful feedback* from faculty and staff on how well students are achieving the journal's goals. If the journal's purpose is to strengthen writing, critical thinking, or other skills, students should receive feedback on the quality of those skills. A simple rubric (Chapter Nine) can provide this.

If the journal's purpose is to encourage metacognition or the development of attitudes or values, providing constructive feedback is more of a challenge, as we want to encourage honest reflection that won't be marked right or wrong. But faculty and staff can offer feedback on whether the journal includes the underlying elements necessary for valid statements on attitudes, values, and insight. Faculty and staff can note, for example, whether the student has:

- Made an adequate effort to complete the journal assignment
- Demonstrated sufficient understanding of the lesson or reading passage to be able to reflect on it meaningfully
- Included meaningful personal responses and opinions in the journal entry
- Connected his or her opinions to what he or she has learned in class

Journals can be time-consuming to read and evaluate. If you don't have time to read and comment on every journal entry, try asking students to read and comment on each other's journals, following your guidelines, or you can read and offer feedback on random excerpts.

Interviews and Focus Groups

Interviews usually consist of open-ended questions asked by an interviewer over the telephone or in person. People can be asked to complete simple rating scales in these settings as well. *Focus groups* are in-person interviews of small, often homogeneous groups of people. Both can be used to ask participants to reflect on themselves and their experiences and also to collect information on their behaviors. Because interview and focus group responses can be wide ranging and generally do not yield numerical results, qualitative summaries (Chapter Sixteen) are typically used to look for response patterns and themes.

Interviews and focus groups are generally time-consuming and therefore not the best choice for making inferences about a large group of students. Nonetheless, they can have an important role in an assessment program by helping with these aspects of the assessment process:

- Planning an assessment by identifying goals, issues, and questions that your assessment efforts should address.

- Corroborating the results of quantitative assessments. If a questionnaire survey or test yields a finding that your audience is likely to dispute, corroborating the finding with some focus groups strengthens the credibility of your results.

- Understanding the results of quantitative assessments. If your students' academic performance is disappointing, for example, some focus groups can help you understand why your students did not meet your expectations.

Table 12.3 (Suskie, 1996) offers suggestions for conducting effective focus groups and interviews.

A major drawback of interviews and focus groups is that they are usually add-on assessments (Chapter Two). Motivating people to participate—and to take the interview or focus group seriously, providing thoughtful responses—is a significant challenge. Chapter Two offers suggestions for motivating participation in optional add-on assessments and information on determining an appropriate participation rate.

Rating Scales

Rating scales can provide information on many topics from many kinds of people. Students can rate their knowledge, skills, values, attitudes, and other traits. They can rate their opinions about an

Table 12.3. Tips for Focus Groups and Interviews

Plan focus group sessions and interviews as carefully as you would any other assessment. Have a clear purpose for the sessions and know how you will use the results. Don't let them turn into unfocused gripe sessions.

Plan on conducting several focus groups, not just one or two, because of the possibility that one opinion driver may dominate participants' comments in any one group. Professionals continue conducting focus groups until they begin to hear the same themes expressed repeatedly across groups.

Select a site in a conducive environment that participants find comfortable.

Make sure participants are a representative sample of the group whose thoughts you seek.

Offer an inducement to attend. Only rarely will the topic alone be a sufficient enticement to participate. You may need to offer a meal or a gift certificate, reimburse participants for travel expenses, or pay them outright.

Select and train interviewers and focus group moderators carefully. Focusing questions is an art. Focus group moderators must be trained to elicit responses from all participants and keep the talkative few from dominating the session. Write out the moderators' introduction and questions beforehand so sessions stay on track, and arrange to have participants' comments recorded in some way.

Plan questions carefully. They should be broad enough to elicit discussion yet focused enough to make replies useful. Here are some examples:

"What did you think was the best part of this program?"

"Tell me one way you would improve this program."

"How has Bellefonte College helped you to be successful here?"

"What do you think will be the biggest barrier to your finishing your degree?"

---

experience or how frequently they engage in an activity or use a service. Faculty and staff, field experience supervisors, and fellow students can use rating scales to record how often students engage in a particular behavior. (If they rate the quality of the student's behavior, the rating scales may be considered rubrics, discussed in Chapter Nine.)

Rating scales are popular assessment tools because they are efficient (a great deal of information can be obtained quickly and compactly), the results can be easily tallied and summarized, and they permit comparisons among answers within the rating scale. The main disadvantage of rating scales is that they are transparent: "right" and "wrong" answers are self-evident, and students may be tempted to give the answers they think you want to hear rather than their honest appraisals. Because of this, information on behaviors and reflections provided using rating scales should be viewed with caution and used only in conjunction with other assessment evidence.

Rating scales can use any descriptors that span a spectrum, such as Excellent to Poor, Frequently to Never, Very Positive to Very Negative, Very Comfortable to Very Uncomfortable, Strongly Approve to Strongly Disapprove, and Much Better to Much Worse.

Letter grades (A, B, C, D, and E or F) can be a good choice when asking for evaluations because they are so widely understood. For more tips on constructing an effective rating scale, follow the suggestions for rubrics in Chapter Nine.

Likert Rating Scales

Likert (pronounced *Lick*-ert) rating scales, probably the best-known rating scales, ask respondents to indicate their level of agreement or disagreement with a series of statements. Exhibit 12.2 is an example of a Likert scale for graduating students.

If you use a Likert scale, include some statements presenting a negative or opposing view. This will help prevent the "yeasayer/naysayer" effect, in which some people with generally positive feelings toward your topic may check all the Strongly Agree responses without reading each item and those with generally negative feelings may do the opposite.

A frequent question is whether a Likert scale should include a Neutral or Neither Agree nor Disagree column in the center. Include it if it is inappropriate to force your participants to agree or disagree. It could be argued, for example, that students might be truly neutral on whether "The library facilities are conducive to study." But if you are asking students whether "The instructor spoke clearly," it could be argued that the instructor either spoke clearly or didn't, and every student should be able to agree or disagree with this statement.

Ecosystem Rating Scales

Ecosystem rating scales (also known as goal attainment scaling or gap analysis) ask for two ratings, with the second rating giving information on the environment in which the first rating is made and thus helping to interpret the first rating. In Exhibit 12.3, students are asked to rate each goal first in terms of their skill level and second on how much library sessions have helped them develop each skill.

Ecosystems can be a good way to evaluate the attainment of goals, as responses in the second column greatly improve interpretation of the first. Chapter Seventeen discusses how to summarize and understand ecosystem results.

Ecosystems can ask for many kinds of information. A popular use of an ecosystem is to ask first for the participant's satisfaction with various aspects of a program and second for the relative importance of each aspect. Ecosystems might also ask first for satisfaction with various aspects of a program and second on how much the participant participated in each aspect.

Exhibit 12.2. An Exit Survey for Students Completing a B.S. Degree in Computer Information Systems

Please tell us how well each CIS program learning goal was met for you personally. For each objective, please check the one response that best reflects your feelings, opinions, and/or experiences.

SA = Strongly agree
A = Agree
U = Unsure
D = Disagree
SD = Strongly disagree

This objective was met for me: Graduates will:	*SA*	*A*	*U*	*D*	*SD*
1. Have a thorough grounding in key IS principles and practices and the quantitative analysis principles that underpin them.	☐	☐	☐	☐	☐
a. Demonstrate proficiency with IS tools, IS analysis and design, and the role of IS in organizations.	☐	☐	☐	☐	☐
b. Demonstrate proficiency in relevant aspects of quantitative analysis.	☐	☐	☐	☐	☐
2. Understand the quantitative and business principles that underlie IS principles and practices.	☐	☐	☐	☐	☐
a. Understand calculus and statistics.	☐	☐	☐	☐	☐
b. Understand basic principles of accounting and economics.	☐	☐	☐	☐	☐
3. Be informed and involved members of their communities and responsible IS professionals.	☐	☐	☐	☐	☐
a. Be familiar with basic concepts and contemporary issues in the social sciences and humanities.	☐	☐	☐	☐	☐
b. Understand global, social, professional, and ethical considerations related to IS.	☐	☐	☐	☐	☐
4. Have appropriate social and organizational skills.	☐	☐	☐	☐	☐
a. Be able to work effectively in teams.	☐	☐	☐	☐	☐
b. Be able to communicate effectively.	☐	☐	☐	☐	☐
5. Be able to acquire new knowledge in the information systems discipline and engage in lifelong learning.	☐	☐	☐	☐	☐

Source: Adapted with permission from a survey developed by the faculty of the Department of Computer and Information Sciences, Towson University.

Surveys

Surveys are systematic efforts to collect information about people by asking them to respond to specific questions about their backgrounds, experiences, plans, opinions, and attitudes. Surveys can be

---

Exhibit 12.3. A Self-Assessment of Library Skills, with (Fictitious) Students' Responses

For each of the following skills, please make TWO ratings:

1. How strong are your skills in each of the following areas?

2. How much have the library session(s) in this course helped you to develop each of the following skills?

	Your Skill Level					How Much Library Session(s) Have Helped				
	Low				High	Low				High
	1	2	3	4	5	1	2	3	4	5
1. Identify potential sources of information related to this course.	☐	☐	☐	☐	X	☐	☐	☐	☐	X
2. Find information that's appropriate for and relevant to this field of study.	☐	☐	☐	☐	X	X	☐	☐	☐	☐
3. Critically evaluate information that you find, including its accuracy, authority, coverage, objectivity, and currency.	X	☐	☐	☐	☐	☐	☐	☐	☐	X
4. Cite the work of others accurately and ethically.	X	☐	☐	☐	☐	X	☐	☐	☐	☐

Source: Adapted with permission from a rubric developed by the Library faculty of Towson University.

---

a combination of rating scales, requests for factual information, and prompts for reflection. They usually ask for brief, predetermined responses, such as a rating or a number. Participants are rarely asked to provide more than a word or two in response to any one question. Surveys can be a useful assessment tool when you want to learn about the experiences, views, or plans of a large number of people and you want participants to make simple ratings or provide other short responses.

Surveys are increasingly conducted online, although they can also be administered in person (such as in class or at a meeting), by mail, or by telephone. The format you choose may be affected by the following:

- *The completeness and accuracy of participants' contact information.* The mailing addresses you have for students and alumni may be more complete and accurate than e-mail addresses or telephone numbers.

- *The accessibility of your group through each format.* Even if you have telephone numbers for most people in your group, a sizable number may use caller ID or voice mail to screen incoming calls. Questionnaires administered in person to a class may have a higher participation rate than other formats.

- *How comfortable your participants are with each format.* Online surveys might be relatively successful with first-year students but less so with older alumni.

A major drawback of surveys is that they are usually add-on assessments (Chapter Two). Motivating people to participate—and provide thoughtful responses—is a challenge. Chapter Two offers suggestions for motivating participation in optional add-on assessments and information on determining an appropriate participation rate.

A number of published surveys are available on subjects such as first-year students' attitudes, factors affecting student retention, faculty views, alumni satisfaction, and campus climate. Should you participate in these surveys, or conduct your own? Chapter Fourteen discusses the pros and cons of using published assessment instruments, including surveys, and offers advice on how to choose one.

Time to Think, Discuss, and Practice

1. One of Miller College's goals is to prepare students for "success in a diverse, global society." Brainstorm some ways that the college could assess student achievement of this goal.

2. Faculty in your department would like to survey recent alumni to assess their satisfaction with your program and identify areas for improvement. Draft an ecosystem rating scale that could be used in the questionnaire.

3. Think of a course you have taught or taken. Develop a short question or prompt for reflective writing that might provide insight into student achievement of one of the key learning goals of the course.

Recommended Readings

The following readings are recommended along with the references cited in this chapter.

Anderson, J. (1993). Journal writing: The promise and the reality. *Journal of Reading, 36*(4), 304–309.
Boud, D. (1995). *Enhancing learning through self assessment.* London: Kogan Page.

Bradburn, N., Sudman, S., & Wansink, B. (2004). *Asking questions: The definitive guide to questionnaire design—for market research, political polls, and social and health questionnaires.* San Francisco: Jossey-Bass.

Butler, S. M., & McMunn, N. D. (2006). *A teacher's guide to classroom assessment: Understanding and using assessment to improve student learning.* San Francisco: Jossey-Bass.

Chandler, A. (1997). Is this for a grade? A personal look at journals. *English Journal, 86*(1), 45–49.

Costa, A. L., & Kallick, B. (2000). *Assessing and reporting on habits of mind.* Alexandria, VA: Association for Supervision and Curriculum Development.

Costa, A. L., & Kallick, B. (2000). Getting into the habit of reflection. *Educational Leadership, 57*(7), 60–62.

Dillman, D. A. (2006). *Mail and Internet surveys: The tailored design method 2007 update with new Internet, visual, and mixed-mode guide* (2nd ed.). Hoboken, NJ: Wiley.

Fowler, F. J., Jr. (2001). *Survey research methods* (3rd ed.). Thousand Oaks, CA: Sage.

Hoepfl, M. C. (1997). Choosing qualitative research: A primer for technology education researchers. *Journal of Technology Education, 9*(1). Retrieved September 16, 2008, from http://scholar.lib.vt.edu/ejournals/JTE/v9n1/hoepfl.html.

Kaufman, J. C., Plucker, J. A., & Baer, J. (2008). *Essentials of creativity assessment.* Hoboken, NJ: Wiley.

Krueger, R. A., & Casey, M. A. (2000). *Focus groups: A practical guide for applied research* (3rd ed.). Thousand Oaks, CA: Sage.

Porter, S. R. (Ed.). (2004). *Overcoming survey research problems.* New Directions for Institutional Research, no. 121. San Francisco: Jossey-Bass.

Ross, J. A. (2006). The reliability, validity, and utility of self-assessment. *Practical Assessment, Research and Evaluation, 11*(10). Retrieved September 16, 2008, from www.PAREonline.net/pdf/v11n10.pdf.

CHAPTER 13

Assembling Assessment Information into Portfolios

Some Valuable Ideas You'll Find in This Chapter

- Portfolios should have a clear educational purpose as well as a clear assessment purpose.
- Student reflection is an essential component of a portfolio.
- Portfolios are an especially good assessment choice for programs with small numbers of students and self-designed majors.
- Portfolios can take a great deal of time and thus call for careful planning and gradual implementation.

Portfolios may be the most exciting and the most challenging assessment tool that we have. They can be valuable learning opportunities and assessment tools, but they can also take a great deal of time to manage and evaluate. This chapter explains what portfolios are and when and how to use them most effectively.

What Is a Portfolio?

You may remember keeping a folder of your work in one or more of your grade school classes. What are the differences between that folder and portfolios as they are used today?

Clear educational purpose. While many folders simply serve as repositories for student work, portfolios have clear educational purposes and help students learn. Many portfolios are used to assess what students have learned and to identify ways to improve student learning. But these should not be the sole purposes of a portfolio; there are simpler tools, discussed in other chapters, that can assess student learning and provide feedback more quickly and easily.

Student participation in selecting contents using faculty selection criteria. While the contents of folders are specified by the teacher and often include everything students do in a particular class, students participate in choosing what goes in their portfolios, using selection criteria provided by faculty and staff. Students might be asked, for example, to choose and include four assignments: one that best shows their research skills, one that best shows their writing skills, one that best shows their ability to use a particular concept to solve a problem, and one from which they feel they learned the most.

Evaluation criteria. While folders may not be evaluated systematically, portfolios are assessed using evaluation criteria developed by faculty and staff, often in the form of a scoring guide or rubric (Chapter Nine).

Illustration of growth. While folders are often composed only of final products, portfolios can illustrate growth, either by including student work from the beginning as well as the end of a course or program or by including documentation of the process students went through in producing their work, such as notes, drafts, or work logs.

Continual updating. While students add to folders but don't refine them, they can continually update portfolios, substituting one assignment for another. As students' writing skills evolve, for example, students may substitute a different assignment for the one they think best shows their writing skills.

Student reflection. While folders often do not represent a substantive learning opportunity, portfolios include written student reflections on the significance and contribution of each item in the portfolio (Zubizarreta, 2004). In this way, portfolios help students develop skill in synthesizing what they have learned and in metacognition: the ability to learn how to learn by reflecting on what and how they have learned (Chapter Eight).

When Are Portfolios Most Effective and Useful?_____

Faculty and staff can use portfolios to document and evaluate student learning within a course, across multiple courses, throughout an entire academic program, and within another learning opportunity such as a service-learning experience. Table 13.1 summarizes the main reasons to use portfolios.

Portfolios can be used in virtually any learning experience, but they are particularly appropriate in courses and programs with the following characteristics:

Courses and programs that focus on developing thinking skills. The papers and projects typically included in portfolios provide strong evidence of thinking skills such as writing, analysis, and evaluation but do not paint a comprehensive picture of students' knowledge. If your goals are largely to develop broad, comprehensive conceptual understanding (say, to understand the principal figures and events affecting East Asian history), traditional tests (Chapter Eleven) will help you assess those goals more effectively than portfolios.

Courses and programs that focus especially on developing synthesis and metacognition skills. The self-reflection element of portfolios makes them ideal for developing these skills.

Courses and programs with small numbers of students. When only a handful of students graduate each year, assessment measures such as tests, surveys, and capstone projects may not be very useful, because changes and differences in results may be due more to fluctuations in student characteristics than to changes in teaching and learning processes. Portfolios are a better choice in

Table 13.1. Why Use Portfolios?

A portfolio is compelling evidence of what a student has learned.
It assembles in one place evidence of many different kinds of learning and skills.
It encourages students, faculty, and staff to examine student learning holistically—seeing how learning comes together—rather than through compartmentalized skills and knowledge.
It shows not only the outcome of a course or program but also how the student has grown as a learner. It's thus a richer record than test scores, rubrics, and grades alone.

A portfolio is valuable to students, faculty, and staff.
It encourages students to become actively involved in their learning by thinking about and choosing how to document achievement of goals.
It encourages student reflection (Chapter Twelve), which develops skill in synthesis and metacognition (Chapter Eight).
It encourages diversity rather than conformity in student learning activities.
It provides fodder for rich conversations among students, faculty, and staff.
By giving information not only on what students have learned but also how they have learned, portfolios help faculty and staff refine what and how they teach.

---

these situations because they give a more thorough picture of student growth and development.

Self-designed programs. Students pursuing self-designed programs of study (Chapter Seven) typically have unique learning goals and unique collections of assessment evidence. Portfolios are an ideal way to document student learning of one-of-a-kind sets of goals.

Is a Portfolio Appropriate and Feasible for Your Course or Program?

A great deal of thought, time, and effort precede successful portfolio implementation. The biggest problems are time and logistics. Portfolios can take a great deal of time, both for students to compile and for faculty and staff to monitor and assess, so they pose a challenge in large classes and programs. Storing portfolios securely yet accessibly can be another challenge. Electronic portfolios, discussed later in this chapter, solve the storage problem but not the time problem.

The questions in Table 13.2 can help you decide whether a portfolio might be an appropriate element of your assessment program. The balance of this chapter discusses some of these questions in more detail.

Table 13.2. Considering a Portfolio? Questions to Ask Before You Decide

What are the goals of the portfolio? Why are you having students create portfolios? What learning goals should the portfolio demonstrate? What important things will students learn from the process of compiling the portfolio?

Who are the portfolio's audiences: students, faculty, administrators, employers, accreditors, or some other group? What questions does each audience group want answered by the portfolios? What decisions do they need to make?

How and when will students choose what to put in the portfolio? What kinds of student work will answer audience questions? If the portfolio covers an entire academic program, do all students in the program, regardless of the program options they choose, complete these kinds of assignments?

How will student and faculty reflection be ensured in the portfolio process?

How will the portfolios be evaluated? What will be your evaluation criteria? Will the portfolios be graded? If not, what incentives (Chapter Two) will you provide to ensure that students put good effort into assembling and reflecting on their portfolios?

Who will review and evaluate the portfolios? When?

How will the portfolio compilation and evaluation process be kept manageable? How and where will portfolios be stored?

Who "owns" each portfolio? What happens to each portfolio when the student completes the course, graduates, or leaves the program before graduating?

What are the benefits of moving toward portfolio assessment?

What are the areas of concern? Are portfolios a feasible practice in your situation?

Table 13.3. Contents of Typical Portfolios

A table of contents, perhaps a checklist of potential items (Exhibit 13.2)

Examples of student work, which may include, depending on the portfolio's goals:
    Papers and other assignments (see Table 10.1)
    Peer assessments
    Attitude and interest surveys
    Tests or logs of test scores
    Statements of students' goals for their learning and development
    Notes from faculty, staff, and supervisors from observations, conferences, and interviews
    Internship supervisor evaluations

Evidence of learning processes, growth, and improvement such as:
    Work completed early in the course or program (Note that this material may not be available
       for students who transfer into a program after completing early course work elsewhere.)
    Drafts
    Work logs

A reflection page, in which students reflect on the overall contents of the completed portfolio

Faculty's evaluative summary of the portfolio, perhaps in the form of a completed rubric

An introductory statement, if you choose to have the student write one, that will help those
    evaluating the portfolio understand it better. Students might state, for example, why they
    enrolled in this course or program, their learning goals, their background before enrolling,
    their strengths and weaknesses, or their career or life goals.

Reflections on each item in the portfolio. Exhibit 13.3 is an example.

Faculty comments on or evaluation of each item in the portfolio. Because of the volume of materials,
    the rubric or comments may be very brief and simple.

What Can Go into a Portfolio?

Table 13.3 suggests items that might be included in portfolios. While students should choose at least some items for their portfolios, faculty and staff may specify some items, and some may be chosen collaboratively by the student and faculty.

What Guidelines Should Students Receive on Assembling Portfolios?

Because preparing a portfolio may be a new experience for some students, it is important to give clear written guidelines that explain the assignment. Guidelines should answer the questions in Table 13.4.

If students are developing a program portfolio, give them written guidelines as soon as they enter the program. Review the guidelines with them to emphasize the importance of the portfolio and answer any questions they might have. The guidelines should

Table 13.4. Questions to Address in Portfolio Guidelines to Students

---

What are faculty and staff goals for the portfolio? What will students learn by compiling it, beyond what they will learn by completing each individual item?

What will be included in the portfolio? Which items are mandatory, and which do the students choose? When will the choices be made?

When are key deadlines? When do students review and update their portfolios?

How will the portfolio be stored? When and how can students access it? What will happen to it at the end of the course or program or if students leave before the end?

How and when will faculty and staff evaluate each item and the overall portfolio?

---

provide periodic points at which students update their portfolios and review them with a faculty or staff member. Because portfolios may identify the need for additional study in a particular area, the need to develop further a particular skill, or an interest in further study of a particular topic, these reviews can help students plan their studies. Students with inadequate portfolios should have time to make them acceptable without delaying their graduation.

Exhibit 13.1 is an example of an assignment for a course portfolio. Exhibit 13.2 is the checklist that accompanies this assignment, and Exhibit 13.3 is a reflection sheet for individual items in the portfolio.

How Might Students Reflect on Their Portfolios?

One of the defining characteristics of portfolios is the opportunity for students to learn by reflecting holistically on their work. Students can be asked for brief reflections on each item in their portfolio (Exhibit 13.3), a longer reflective essay on the portfolio as a whole, or both. Questions they might reflect on include:

- Which item is your best work? Why?
- Which item is your most important work? Why?
- Which item is your most satisfying work? Why?
- Which item is your most unsatisfying work? Why?
- In which item did you stretch yourself the most, taking the greatest risk in what you tried to do?
- List three things you learned by completing this portfolio.
- What does this portfolio say about you as an emerging professional or scholar in this discipline?
- What are your goals for continuing to learn about this discipline?

Exhibit 13.1. A Portfolio Assignment for a Graduate Course on Assessment Methods

Develop a portfolio of assessment tools that you can use in your classes. My goals for this assignment are for you:

- To become familiar with a broad variety of assessment tools
- To create types of assessment tools that you are not now using
- To create assessment tools that are better quality (more valid) than the tools you are now using
- To create assessment tools that assess thinking skills

Selection Guidelines

Include at least *eight* items in your portfolio, choosing from the list on the "Portfolio Table of Contents" (Exhibit 13.2). Your portfolio must also include the table of contents, a cover sheet for each portfolio item (Exhibit 13.3), and a completed "Reflections on the Course" form, provided separately.

Other Guidelines

- Your portfolio items should be in the order shown on the table of contents, with cover sheets preceding each assessment tool.
- Your portfolio items need not all be tied to the same class topic. You can write a test blueprint for one topic, for example, and a rubric for another.
- You are welcome to submit more than the minimum number of items. Don't expect to include an example of every kind of assessment tool, however, as some may not be appropriate for what you teach.
- The items you submit in your portfolio need not be your "best" work, but they should represent a serious effort to create something you can use in the classes you teach.

Evaluation Criteria

Each item submitted—and the portfolio as a whole—will be evaluated using the following standards.

- *Outstanding:* Meets "good" standards and, in addition, shows extra effort, insight, or creativity
- *Good:* Reflects concepts and guidelines taught in class; shows serious effort, particularly at stretching—using new assessment methods—and at assessing thinking skills
- *Needs Improvement:* Fails to meet "good" standard in at least one respect

Table 12.1 has more examples of questions to stimulate self-reflection. To keep things manageable and encourage students to refine their thinking, limit the number of questions you pose, and stipulate a maximum length for each response. Many reflection questions can be answered effectively in a single sentence.

Exhibit 13.2. A Portfolio Table of Contents Checklist from a Graduate Course on Assessment Methods

Check each item that you are including in your portfolio.

- ☐ This table of contents *(required)*
- ☐ A list of ten learning goals, including at least six for thinking skills
- ☐ A checklist rubric
- ☐ A rating scale rubric
- ☐ A descriptive rubric
- ☐ A holistic scoring guide
- ☐ A prompt for an assignment
- ☐ A prompt for self-reflection
- ☐ A prompt for a portfolio
- ☐ A test blueprint
- ☐ Six multiple-choice items
- ☐ A set of matching items
- ☐ One interpretive exercise with at least three items
- ☐ A prompt for a journal
- ☐ A reflection sheet for each item in the portfolio *(required)*
- ☐ The completed "Reflections on the Course" form *(required)*

Evaluating Portfolios

Your intent for a portfolio assignment should determine how you will evaluate the completed portfolios. Here are four examples:

Assessing student progress in achieving major course or program learning goals. Use a rubric (Chapter Nine) that lists those learning goals and provides criteria for acceptable performance. Exhibit 13.4 is an example of a simple rating scale rubric for assessing program portfolios, and Exhibit 13.1 includes a simple holistic scoring guide for assessing course portfolios. If faculty and staff are collectively reviewing portfolios, use the rubric to score a few portfolios, compare your scores, and discuss and resolve any differences before launching a full-scale review.

Encouraging metacognition. Evaluate the portfolios in terms of the effort students put into self-reflection that helps them learn how to learn (Chapter Eight).

Exhibit 13.3. A Reflection Sheet for Individual Portfolio Items from a Graduate Course on Assessment Methods

1. What type of assessment tool is this?

2. In what course or unit will you use this assessment tool?

3. What learning goals does this tool assess?

4. Why did you choose this item for your portfolio?

5. What does this item show me about you as a teacher?

6. What did you learn by creating this item?

7. Do you have any questions about this item?

My comments to you:

Exhibit 13.4. A Rubric for Assessing Portfolios of Business Administration Majors

Learning Goal	Outstanding	Satisfactory	Inadequate	Insufficient Information to Evaluate
1. Write articulate, persuasive, and grammatically correct business materials.	☐	☐	☐	☐
2. Use critical, flexible, and creative thinking to generate sound conclusions, ideas, and solutions to problems.	☐	☐	☐	☐
3. Use software and networking services to obtain, manage, and share information.	☐	☐	☐	☐
4. Apply understanding of domestic and international diversity concepts and issues to business situations.	☐	☐	☐	☐
5. Recognize ethical challenges and reach ethical business decisions.	☐	☐	☐	☐

Encouraging students to improve their performance. Have students include drafts and early work in their portfolios, and evaluate the portfolios in terms of improvement from beginning to final products.

Encouraging risk taking and creativity. Evaluate the portfolios in terms of reflections that students provide on the risks they took in their work.

Keeping Things Manageable

Imagine a class or program with twenty-five students, each of whom submits a portfolio with ten work examples (plus reflections on each). That's 250 items (plus reflections) to be reviewed—a daunting task. How can you keep the work of creating, managing, and evaluating portfolios from overwhelming both students and faculty?

Chapters Five through Seven offer many suggestions for keeping the assessment burden manageable. Here are some additional ideas:

- Limit the number of items in each portfolio.

- Keep portfolio items short (no more than a few pages each). Consider including only excerpts from lengthier items.

- Start small. Perhaps ask for only one or two items the first time you use portfolios, and then gradually increase the contents for subsequent cohorts of students.

- For program portfolios, ask the faculty member making each assignment to attach a rubric showing his or her evaluation of it. This saves the labor of a second review.

- For program portfolios in programs with many majors, consider reviewing only a sample of portfolios each year (assuming that students have already received feedback on individual items in their portfolios).

Electronic Portfolios

Electronic or digital portfolios, in which students store their work electronically on a secure Web site or shared server, are far easier to store and access than paper portfolios, and unlike paper portfolios they can easily include multimedia projects such as videos, slide shows, and Web sites. John Zubizarreta (2004) has compiled extensive lists on the advantages and disadvantages of electronic portfolios.

A number of commercial software packages support electronic portfolios. Their features and capabilities vary, so before you choose one, have a clear sense of the kinds of student work that will go into your portfolios and how the portfolios will be accessed and used. Table 6.2 offers some questions to consider when you're evaluating assessment technologies.

If you are interesting in learning more about electronic portfolios, attend an assessment conference, speak to colleagues who use electronic portfolios, or do an online search for "electronic portfolios," "e-portfolios," and "digital portfolios."

Time to Think, Discuss, and Practice

1. Do you have any experience with portfolios as a teacher or as a student?

   - If you do, share what you learned from the experience. What was the best part of the experience? What was the least satisfying aspect? If you had the opportunity, what would you improve about the experience?

- If you haven't had any experience with portfolios, share what excites you about portfolios and what makes you skeptical about them.

2. Identify someone in your group teaching a course that doesn't now use a portfolio but for which a portfolio might be a worthwhile learning experience. Help that group member answer the following questions:

- What should be the learning goals of the portfolio? What should students learn through the process of assembling and reflecting on their portfolios?

- What should the portfolio include? (Remember to keep the portfolios small enough to be manageable)

- What might be the criteria for evaluating each completed portfolio?

Recommended Readings _____

The following readings are recommended along with the references cited in this chapter.

Banta, T. W. (Ed.). (2003). *Portfolio assessment uses, cases, scoring, and impact.* San Francisco: Jossey-Bass.

Burke, K., Fogarty, R., & Belgrad, S. (2001). *The portfolio connection: Student work linked to standards.* Thousand Oaks, CA: Corwin Press.

Butler, S. M., & McMunn, N. D. (2006). *A teacher's guide to classroom assessment: Understanding and using assessment to improve student learning.* San Francisco: Jossey-Bass.

Cambridge, B. L., Kahn, S., Tompkins, D. P., & Yancey, K. B. (Eds.). (2001). *Electronic portfolios: Emerging practices in student, faculty, and institutional learning.* Sterling, VA: Stylus.

Cambridge, D., Cambridge, B. L., & Yancey, K. (Eds.). (2008). *Electronic portfolios 2.0: Emergent findings and shared questions.* Sterling, VA: Stylus.

Canada, M. (2002). Assessing e-folios in the on-line class. In R. S. Anderson, J. F. Bauer, & B. W. Speck (Eds.), *Assessment strategies for the on-line class: From theory to practice* (pp. 69–75). New Directions for Teaching and Learning, no. 91. San Francisco: Jossey-Bass.

Hutchings, P. (Ed.). (1998). *The course portfolio: How faculty can examine their teaching to advance practice and improve student learning.* Sterling, VA: Stylus.

Paulson, F. L., Paulson, P. R., & Meyer, C. A. (1991). What makes a portfolio a portfolio? *Educational Leadership, 48*(5), 60–63.

CHAPTER 14

Selecting a Published Test or Survey

Some Valuable Ideas You'll Find in This Chapter

- Use a published instrument only when:

    Your learning goals match those covered by the instrument.

    The results can be readily and easily used to improve teaching and learning and inform planning and budgeting decisions.

    You have enough confidence in the meaning and quality of the results to be able to use them to help make decisions.

- The major challenge with many published instruments is convincing students not only to participate but also to give the instruments serious thought and effort.

Published tests and surveys play a role in many assessment programs. This chapter discusses why published instruments might be useful, how to find potential instruments, and how to evaluate them to determine if they are appropriate for your situation. (Specific instruments mentioned in this book are offered as examples, not endorsements.)

What Kinds of Published Instruments Are Available?

Table 14.1 lists four categories of published instruments that may be useful in higher education assessment. A common misconception is that published instruments consist exclusively of multiple-choice

Table 14.1. Examples of Published Instruments for Higher Education Assessment

Published Instrument	Publisher
Tests Designed to Assess General Knowledge and/or Skills	
Collegiate Assessment of Academic Proficiency (CAAP)	ACT
College-Base Academic Subjects Examination (College BASE or C-BASE)	Academic Resource Center, University of Missouri
Collegiate Learning Assessment (CLA)	Council for Aid to Education (CAE)
iSkills (Information and technology skills)	Educational Testing Service (ETS)
Measures of Academic Proficiency and Progress (MAPP)	Educational Testing Service (ETS)
Praxis I Pre-Professional Skills Test in reading, writing, and mathematics for prospective teachers	Educational Testing Service (ETS)
Tests Designed to Assess the Knowledge and Skills Acquired in Major Fields of Study	
Major Field Tests in a variety of subjects	Educational Testing Service (ETS)
Graduate Record Examinations in a variety of subjects	Educational Testing Service (ETS)
Tests published by disciplinary associations and other organizations to assess or certify student learning in specific fields, such as the National Council Licensure Examination for Registered Nurses (NCLEX-RN), published by the National Council of State Boards of Nursing	
Praxis II Subject Tests in a variety of subjects taught in kindergarten through twelfth grade	Educational Testing Service (ETS)
Surveys of Student Goals, Experiences, Satisfaction, and Plans	
National Survey of Student Engagement (NSSE), Beginning College Survey of Student Engagement (BCSSE), and Law School Survey of Student Engagement (LSSSE)	Indiana University
Community College Survey of Student Engagement (CCSSE)	Community College Leadership Program of the University of Texas at Austin
Student Satisfaction Inventory	Noel-Levitz
Cooperative Institutional Research Program (CIRP) Freshman Survey, College Senior Survey (CSS), and Your First College Year Survey (YFCY)	Higher Education Research Institute (HERI) at the University of California at Los Angeles (UCLA)
Instruments not Specifically Designed for Higher Education That May be Nonetheless Useful	
Tests of basic skills such as the Nelson-Denny Reading Test, published by Riverside	
Instruments to identify learning styles such as the Myers-Briggs Type Indicator, published by Consulting Psychologists	
Career interest inventories such as the Vocational Preference Inventory, published by Psychological Assessment Resources	

or rating-scale questions. While multiple-choice and other bubble formats predominate, some published instruments ask students to provide writing samples that are evaluated by trained scorers or special software.

Standardized instruments are published instruments that are administered and scored under standardized or consistent, comparable conditions. This ensures that scores are comparable across colleges and universities and across time. All students receive exactly the same instructions on how to complete the instrument. If there is a time limit for completing the instrument, it is enforced at all administration sites. If there are writing samples that are scored using rubrics, the scorers are trained so that scoring is consistent.

Why Use a Published Instrument? _____

Chapter Three emphasizes that any assessment effort should include multiple measures of student learning because all assessment tools and strategies, including published instruments, are inherently imperfect. Although published instruments should thus not constitute an entire college or program assessment effort, they can add some important dimensions.

Published instruments get us out of the ivory tower.   Published instruments let us compare our students against those at other colleges, a potentially valuable perspective. Without peer benchmarking, we may think our students are learning a great deal when in fact they are learning less than their peers. Or we may be disappointed by our findings, only to learn that our results are better than those at many peer colleges. The availability of peer information is probably the strongest argument for using a published instrument. But some published instruments do not have good-quality peer information, and even if they do, peer benchmarking is inappropriate in some situations. Chapter Fifteen discusses peer benchmarking along with nine other ways to benchmark student performance.

Published instruments can have greater perceived legitimacy than locally designed assessments.   Board members, legislators, donors, and other external audiences may be more impressed by student performance on a published examination than they are by the results of locally designed tests and rubrics.

Published instruments can have good-quality questions.   Many publishers design questions in consultation with experts in the field and test them extensively before including them in the published instrument. Yes, there have been many publicized examples of poorly written questions on published instruments, but far more could be found on most locally designed instruments.

Published instruments can provide good breadth of coverage.   A published chemistry test, for example, may include a broader range of chemical concepts and skills than we might think to include in our own test.

Published instruments sometimes have evidence of their quality. Some publishers have made serious efforts to evaluate and document instrument quality. Because publishers may have more resources than an individual college to invest in time-consuming and expensive validation studies, their research may be more rigorous and extensive than what we might accomplish locally.

Published instruments sometimes allow us to identify strengths and weaknesses.   Some instruments provide subscores that can be compared against one another. The Measures of Academic Proficiency and Progress (MAPP), for example, provides subscores for reading, writing, critical thinking, and mathematics, making it easy to identify relative strengths and weaknesses in student performance across these areas.

Published instruments require less of our time.   It can take months of hard work by many people to draft, refine, and pretest a locally designed survey or test before it is good enough to use. Once the instrument is developed, campus staff need to handle scoring, processing, and reporting each time it is administered. Published tests and surveys can be researched, adopted, and implemented more quickly and with less work by fewer people. Some publishers also take care of all the work of summarizing and analyzing results.

When Is a Locally Designed Assessment a Better Choice?

While published instruments have value under some circumstances, a locally designed assessment tool may be a more appropriate choice under the following circumstances.

Local goals and aims may not match the goals and content of available published instruments.   If your college defines critical thinking as the ability to think creatively and originally, most published critical thinking tests will not provide the information you are looking for. If your chemistry program focuses on preparing students for entry-level work in medical laboratories, a chemistry test designed to assess preparation for graduate study isn't appropriate. If your college is primarily or exclusively in the distance-learning business, a survey asking students about their satisfaction with parking, residence halls, and other campus facilities won't be helpful. *The degree of congruence between the goals of a college or program and those addressed by any published instrument is the most important consideration in deciding whether to adopt it.*

Trudy Banta (2008) has pointed out that even tests designed to test general skills like writing are never content free. Depending on what students are asked to write or analyze, students in different fields "will react differently; some will be advantaged by their choice of major, others disadvantaged" (p. 4). A test that asks students to use critical thinking skills to, say, design a marketing campaign will give an advantage to students who have studied concepts related to marketing.

Published instruments may not provide results that are detailed enough to be useful. While external audiences interested in accountability want to see a quick snapshot of student learning, we need detailed feedback in order to use the results to improve student learning. Larry Braskamp and Steven Schomberg (2006) have noted that "assessment strategies that have relied heaviest on external standardized measures of achievement have been inadequate to detect with any precision any of the complex learning and developmental goals of higher education [such as] critical thinking, commitment, values." There's no point in investing in a test that doesn't provide the detailed results you need to help decide how to improve student learning. A critical thinking test that provides only a single "critical thinking" score for each student won't help you identify strengths and weaknesses in students' thinking skills nor how to improve them.

Local students may be atypical, so comparing them against other students is not helpful. Suppose that Roslyn College has many students for whom English is a second language and who therefore do relatively poorly on typical writing assessments. Many students at Woodwyn College never studied algebra in high school, leaving them far behind typical college students in quantitative skills. In these cases, a locally designed assessment, interpreted using a value-added or historical trends perspective (Chapter Fifteen), may be more useful. The need for relevant norms against which your students may be compared is discussed later in this chapter.

A published instrument may not be practical. Many published tests and surveys are add-on assessments (Chapter Two), and it can be extraordinarily difficult to motivate students not only to participate in such assessments but to give them serious thought and effort. Published instruments may also not be practical to administer in terms of time and logistical requirements.

The cost of a published instrument may outweigh the benefits or simply be unaffordable. A single administration of some published instruments can cost thousands of dollars. An important question is whether the information gained from the instrument will be worth this investment. Some colleges don't have this kind of hard cash available, but they do have faculty and staff willing to spend the time developing and administering a local instrument.

Identifying Potential Published Instruments

If you think that a published instrument might be a useful component of your assessment effort, collaborate with faculty, staff, and students in the review and decision process to ensure buy-in (Chapter Five). Begin by clarifying the instrument's purpose (Chapter Four). There's no point in surveying students about, say, satisfaction with tutoring services if campus leaders aren't interested in addressing any shortcomings identified by the survey. Questions to consider include the following:

- What learning goals are you trying to assess?
- What information do you need?
- How will you use the results?
- What key decisions will the results inform?
- How might the results be used to improve student learning or the environment for it?

Once purpose is clarified, use the resources in Table 14.2 to identify potential published instruments. Then contact their publishers for more information. Ideally, you should be able to obtain the information in Table 14.3.

Evaluating Potential Published Instruments

After you have obtained information on each potential instrument, review it in the light of the following questions.

Table 14.2. Resources for Identifying Potential Published Instruments

Mental Measurements Yearbook (MMY) (Geisinger, Spies, Carlson, & Plake, 2007)	Available in many college libraries, this is an excellent source of information on instruments assessing all kinds of mental traits. It includes instrument information, contact information, research citations, and critical reviews by scholars. The Buros Institute of Mental Measurements Web site (http://www.unl.edu/buros) gives tips for using the *Mental Measurements Yearbook* and an index of all instruments reviewed by it since 1985.
Tests in Print (TIP) (Murphy, Spies, & Plake, 2006)	Also available in many college libraries, this is another excellent source for identifying potential instruments. It provides information on "all known commercially available tests that are currently in print in the English language" (Buros Institute of Mental Measurement, n.d.), so it is more comprehensive than the *Mental Measurements Yearbook,* but it lacks the yearbook's critical reviews and citations.
ETS TestLink (Educational Testing Service, 2008a)	This Web site has links to information on thousands of instruments.
National Postsecondary Education Cooperative (NPEC) Sourcebook of Assessment Information, Volume 1: *Definitions and Assessment Methods for Critical Thinking, Problem Solving, and Writing* (Erwin, 2000)	This has descriptions and analyses of a number of published tests and rubrics assessing critical thinking, problem-solving, and writing skills, although it is now somewhat dated and incomplete.
National Postsecondary Education Cooperative (NPEC) Sourcebook on Assessment: Definitions and Assessment Methods for Communication, Leadership, Information Literacy, Quantitative Reasoning, and Quantitative Skills (Jones & RiCharde, 2005)	This has descriptions and analyses of many published tests and rubrics assessing these skills.
First-Year Assessment Instrument Database (National Resource Center for the First-Year Experience and Students in Transition, 2002)	This Web site has information on many tests and surveys that can be used to assess learning goals germane to the first year of college.
Internet search engines such as Google	These can help identify potential instruments.
Professional journals, conferences, online disciplinary discussion lists, and colleagues at other colleges	While these can yield useful suggestions, keep in mind that an instrument used successfully at another college may not be suitable for your own circumstances.

Table 14.3. Helpful Information on Potential Published Instruments

A copy of the instrument or at least examples of items	Examining individual items helps determine if they are clear and measure what they purport to measure. Because of test security or copyright concerns, some publishers will not let you view the full instrument before purchasing it. Nevertheless, they should let you see enough examples of items—perhaps on an outdated edition of the instrument—to make an informed decision about whether to adopt the instrument. If the publisher is unwilling to do this, move on to another test (Banta, 2008).
Instructions for administering the instrument	These help determine if the instrument can be feasibly administered in your situation.
Ordering information and prices	These help determine if the instrument is affordable. There may be separate charges for purchasing copies of the instrument, getting results processed, and receiving the results in the format you need.
How completed instruments are scored	Some instruments can be self-scored; others must be sent to the publisher for processing, tabulation, and analysis; and still others offer both options.
How the results are reported and prices for each option	Some publishers offer a variety of report options and charge more for more detailed reports. Some offer reports or even full data sets in electronic formats as well as on paper, allowing you to analyze the results yourself, perhaps comparing residential and commuter students or looking only at business majors.
Technical information	This includes information on how the instrument was designed, how it was normed, and evidence of its quality (reliability and validity). This information may be available on the publisher's Web site, in a manual, or as a series of reports.

Do the Instrument's Stated Philosophy and Purpose Match Yours?

The publisher should have a statement on the instrument's philosophy and purpose, and that philosophy and purpose should match your own. Some faculty believe, for example, that general education courses in mathematics should emphasize the development of analytical reasoning skills through the study of pure mathematics, while others believe that such courses should emphasize the development of skills for solving real-life problems. Any quantitative reasoning test that you choose should match your faculty and staff's philosophy.

Do the Instrument's Content and Goals Match What You Emphasize?

The publisher should provide information on the specific kinds of knowledge and skills assessed by a published instrument. Some publishers provide a test blueprint or table of specifications (Chapter Eleven) that lists the content and skills covered by the test. Some publishers go further, identifying the individual test items that assess each learning goal. Review this information carefully to determine how well the instrument's goals and content correspond to your goals and curriculum. A writing test that focuses on grammar, for example, is inappropriate for writing courses focusing on developing well-reasoned arguments. If possible, examine some items on the instrument to verify its focus.

Does the Instrument Have an Appropriate Emphasis on Reading Skills?

Reading skills are essential for success in college and beyond, so it may be appropriate that a test of student learning includes considerable reading material to which students must respond. A test on English literature, for example, should certainly ask students to read and respond to literature passages.

If a test's reading level is too difficult, however, it becomes more a general reading comprehension test than a test of its purported subject. If students do poorly on a sociology test with a difficult reading level, for example, we can't tell if they did poorly because they don't understand sociology concepts or if they understand sociology concepts but are simply slow readers. Highly verbal tests are particularly likely to underrepresent the achievements of students who are not native English speakers and students from disadvantaged backgrounds. Tests that minimize text and maximize the use of charts, diagrams, pictures, numbers, and other non-verbal material may be fairer to these students, although they may give a less complete picture of their performance.

If you are looking for a published survey rather than a test, it is equally important to consider the reading skills required by the instrument. If the survey's reading level is too difficult, some students may misinterpret questions and give erroneous information.

Will the Results Be Useful?

Ask the following questions to determine if the results will give you useful feedback on your students. If the answers lead you to conclude that the results of a particular published instrument will not be useful, there is little point in using it.

How does the publisher recommend using the results?   The publisher should offer suggested uses of results and also describe inappropriate uses. A quantitative reasoning test designed to assess students' everyday problem-solving skills would be inappropriate for deciding whether to place students into calculus, for example. A test designed to demonstrate a college's overall effectiveness to public audiences (accountability, discussed in Chapter Four) would be inappropriate for identifying strategies to improve student learning in a particular program. Make sure that the publisher considers your planned uses of the results to be appropriate.

Does the publisher provide just one or two global scores or more detailed results?   See if the test or survey gives sufficiently detailed feedback to tell you what you're doing right and wrong and any problem areas that you should address.

How long is the instrument?   Some publishers, recognizing that neither students nor faculty and staff want to spend a great deal of time on tests and surveys, design relatively short instruments. These instruments can provide good information on how students are doing in general, but short instruments are often too imprecise to let us make sound decisions about individual students or even individual programs. A writing test designed to assess only the overall effectiveness of a writing program may have too little information to determine which students need remediation.

Is the instrument designed to be used with all students or just a sample?   Some published instruments are so expensive and cumbersome to administer that the publishers recommend administering them to samples of students rather than to all students. Information from a sample of students can yield information on how students are doing in general. But small samples do not yield enough information to let us examine subgroups of students, such as students in a particular program or with a particular background. Looking at these kinds of breakout results is often essential to understanding why we got the results we did and what we might do to improve student learning.

Does the Instrument Have Convincing Evidence of Its Quality?

A good-quality assessment instrument yields accurate, truthful information regarding whatever the instrument purports to measure (Chapter Three). Psychometricians refer to this attribute as *validity*. A valid instrument has evidence of the following.

Alignment with your learning goals.   The most important characteristic of a good-quality instrument is how well the instrument's content matches your learning goals, as discussed earlier in this chapter. You may find that a reputable instrument is inappropriate for your situation simply because it does not assess what you consider important.

Teachable traits.   If a test's scores have a strong relationship with measures of prior learning such as SAT or ACT scores, it may be more a measure of prior learning—or even innate aptitude—than of learning at your college. Check if the test publisher has calculated the proportion of the scores explained by prior learning, socioeconomic factors, and other factors that you cannot control. You may find that only a very small proportion of the instrument's scores are explained by the education your students receive at your college.

On the other hand, if the test assesses very concrete, teachable skills (such as how to perform certain mathematical calculations), your college may get wrapped up in teaching to the test: focusing on the skills assessed by the test at the expense of other skills that your faculty and staff value. This becomes a critical issue if someone has mandated that the results must be shared with public audiences or used to compare your students publicly against their peers. The challenges of peer benchmarks are discussed further in Chapter Fifteen, and Chapter Seventeen discusses communicating assessment results with public audiences.

Lack of bias.   A good-quality instrument is not biased against any particular group of people. A published instrument's technical materials often include information on steps the publisher has taken to reduce bias. Find out if the publisher has asked people from diverse backgrounds to review items for possible bias. Also find out if the publisher discards items on which students from particular backgrounds do unusually poorly. And ask people of diverse backgrounds to review potential instruments and advise you of any concerns they identify. Chapter Three has a more extensive discussion of fairness and bias in assessment.

Up-to-date content and aims.   A good-quality instrument is reasonably current. The publisher should periodically review and update it to ensure that it reflects current research, theories, and practices and does not contain obsolete material. How frequently an instrument should be revised depends in part on its subject. A test of technology skills obviously has to be updated very frequently, for example.

Consistency.   A good quality instrument has consistent or reliable results. Instruments can be consistent in several ways. Students should answer similar items within an instrument similarly; this is called *internal consistency.* Students who retake the instrument after a period of time without any intervening instruction should score about the same as they did the first time; this is called *test-retest reliability.* Publishers should provide statistical evidence that results are consistent in these ways.

Other evidence of validity.   This information can be quite technical, and you may wish to ask a psychology or education faculty member to help interpret it. Validity evidence may include:

- Correlations of instrument scores with scores on other, similar instruments

- Correlations of instrument scores with grades in appropriate courses

- Correlations among subscores (scores on related subtests, such as reading and writing, should have some degree of correlation, while scores on dissimilar subtests, such as writing and quantitative skills, should be less strongly correlated)

- Increases in scores after participating in an appropriate program (graduating engineering students, for example, should score higher on a test of engineering knowledge and skills than entering students)

Does the Instrument Have Adequate and Appropriate Norms?

If a published instrument will be used to benchmark students against those in peer programs or colleges (Chapter Fifteen), its value depends on the quality and completeness of the groups used to establish the instrument's norms (averages, percentiles, and the like). An instrument normed on students at highly selective liberal arts colleges, for example, would be inappropriate for benchmarking the performance of students at an open-admission community college.

Norms for any published test or survey—or any collaboratively developed rubric, for that matter—are based on students only from colleges and universities that have agreed to use the instrument. Furthermore, the samples are often only those students who have agreed to participate, and they may not be representative of all students at the participating colleges. The result is thus a norm group that is not a true random sample of—and maybe not representative of—students enrolled in all peer colleges and universities (Baglin, 1981).

An instrument's technical information should include information on how its norms were developed. Find out answers to the following questions:

- *How many colleges and students are included in the norms?* Obviously you can have greater confidence in norms developed from thousands of students at dozens of colleges than in norms developed from a few hundred students at a handful of colleges.

- *Do the norms represent your college?* Do the norms include an adequate number of students from colleges with missions and characteristics similar to yours?

- *Do the norms represent your students?* Do the norms include an adequate number of students similar to those at your college? If your college attracts commuters, part-time students, nontraditionally aged students, students of color, or students in particular majors, are such students well represented in the norms?

- *When did the norming take place?* Students today are different from students fifteen years ago, so norms created then and not updated since may not be useful.

Is the Instrument Practical to Administer?

Consider the following.

Incentives. Chapter Two discusses the significant challenges of motivating students to participate meaningfully in add-on assessments such as published tests and surveys that are not required for certification or licensure. As that chapter emphasizes, the major challenge with most add-on assessments—indeed, their major drawback—is convincing students not only to participate in them but also to give the assessment tasks serious thought and effort.

Time required to administer the instrument. Instruments that take longer than a standard class period require special administration periods that may be difficult for students to attend.

Administration requirements. Instruments administered online may be inappropriate if a significant number of your students do not have easy access to a computer or do not have strong experience using one.

What If There is Little or No Information on a Potential Instrument?

Because interest in assessment at the higher education level is relatively new, many published instruments aimed at the higher education market have been developed only recently, and their publishers may not yet have answers to all of the questions discussed in this chapter. Trudy Banta (2008) has noted that validity studies may be "sparse to non-existent," norms may be "based only on the small samples of institutions" (p. 4), and studies to tell if students attending college do better on the instrument than comparable students who have not been in college may not have been conducted.

Lack of information on an instrument does not automatically mean that it is poor quality and should be removed from consideration. It simply means that the instrument is unproven, and an unproven instrument may nonetheless be a useful addition to an assessment program. Some learning style inventories, for example, have few or no published validation studies, but faculty, staff, and students nevertheless have found them helpful. And locally developed instruments usually have little systematic evidence of their quality and nonetheless can be very useful.

But if you are considering an instrument whose quality is largely undocumented, let the buyer beware. You and your colleagues must rely on your own appraisals rather than the work of others to determine if the instrument is of sufficient quality to be useful. Review the instrument itself and whatever information you have about it, and ask the questions in Table 14.4.

You can try the instrument on a small scale, essentially conducting your own validation study. If you are considering a writing test, for example, you could give the test to some students

Table 14.4. Questions to Ask About Instruments with Little Published Information

Overall, does the instrument make sense? Does it appear to measure what it purports to measure?

Does the instrument look as if it would give us useful information? Does its content appear to match our learning goals?

Are the individual items clearly written? Will students have any difficulty answering them?

Does the instrument appear to be unbiased and fair? Does it have any stereotyped or offensive material?

What is the potential for harm if it turns out that the instrument is of poor quality and does not give accurate information? Any assessment tool—validated or not—should never be the sole basis for any important decision, as discussed in Chapters Three and Eighteen. It should simply add to the picture of student learning and growth that you are drawing from multiple sources.

completing a writing course and compare test scores against rubric scores of essays they've written in class or their grades in the course. If the scores correlate reasonably well and the results give you some useful insight, you may decide that the test is a worthwhile addition to your assessment program.

Is a Published Instrument Right for You?

Just because a particular published instrument is used at other colleges and universities doesn't mean that it's right for yours. At the same time, just as home buyers quickly learn that the perfect house does not exist (at least not within their budget), neither does the perfect published instrument. Probably no publisher will ever be able to answer all the questions posed in this chapter to the complete satisfaction of you and your colleagues.

Table 14.5 summarizes the fundamental questions to consider after you have assimilated the information you've collected and perused on potential published instruments.

If your answers to the questions in Table 14.5 for any published instrument are a resounding no, the instrument that you are considering does not meet your needs and should not be considered further. If you answer no to these questions for all the instruments you've identified and reviewed, turn your attention to designing and implementing a local assessment strategy.

Time to Think, Discuss, and Practice

1. One of Kingsway College's learning goals is that graduating students write effectively. Brainstorm three arguments for assessing this goal using a locally designed assessment

Table 14.5. Deciding if a Published Instrument Is Right for You

Does this instrument assess what we think is important?

Are we reasonably convinced that the instrument measures what it purports to measure?

Will students have compelling reasons to participate in this assessment and take it seriously?

Will the results help us understand what and why students are learning?

Is the instrument part of a multiple-measures approach to assessing student learning? Will we be collecting other evidence to corroborate what these results tell us?

Will the results help us decide how to improve students' learning experiences?

Will we have enough confidence in the results to be able to use them to help make decisions?

strategy and three arguments for assessing it using a published instrument.

2. A local community college aims for all its students to graduate with quantitative problem-solving skills.

   • Use the resources described in this chapter to identify three possible published instruments for assessing such skills.

   • Find whatever information you can on each instrument, and evaluate it. Which instrument would you recommend to the college, if any? Why?

Recommended Readings

The following readings are recommended along with the references cited in this chapter.

American Educational Research Association. (2000). *Standards for educational and psychological testing 1999* (2nd ed.). Washington, DC: Author.

Banta, T. W. (2007). The search for a perfect test continues. *Assessment Update, 19*(6), 3–5.

Borden, V.M.H., & Zak, J. L. (2001). *Measuring quality: Choosing among surveys and other assessments of college quality.* Tallahassee, FL: Association for Institutional Research.

Ewell, P. T. (2001). Statewide testing in higher education. *Change, 33*(2), 21–27.

Hawthorne, J. (2008). Accountability and comparability: What's wrong with the VSA approach? *Liberal Education, 94*(2), 24–29.

Hopkins, K. D. (1997). *Educational and psychological measurement and evaluation.* Needham Heights, MA: Allyn & Bacon.

Kubiszyn, T., & Borich, G. D. (2002). *Educational testing and measurement: Classroom application and management* (7th ed.). San Francisco: Jossey-Bass.

Rudner, L. M. (1994). Questions to ask when evaluating tests. *Practical Assessment, Research and Evaluation, 4*(2). Retrieved September 16, 2008, from http://PAREonline.net/getvn.asp?v=4&n=2.

Shermis, M. D. (2008). The collegiate learning assessment: A critical perspective. *Assessment Update, 20*(2), 10–12.

PART FOUR

Understanding and Using Assessment Results

CHAPTER 15

Setting Benchmarks or Standards

Some Valuable Ideas You'll Find in This Chapter

- There are many ways to set standards or benchmarks, and any one alone may give an incomplete picture of student learning.
- Comparing programs or colleges against peers is not always appropriate or useful.
- Employers are more supportive of faculty-evaluated assessments than tests comparing colleges against one another in terms of advancing students' thinking skills.
- What is often more important than value-added is whether students graduate with the competencies expected of college graduates.
- Any growth we see in students' skills may be due to extraneous factors rather than our curricula and pedagogies.

Many faculty and staff find that one of the most difficult parts of assessment is closing the loop: using the results to improve teaching and learning (Chapter Eighteen). Often this is because they have a hard time understanding the results. Imagine that Michael, one of your students, scored a 55 on a particular test. Did he do well or not? Or imagine that all students in your college averaged 55 on a published test. Did they do well or not in terms of this performance standard (Chapter One)? Answering these questions is critical to figuring out how to use the results. If we decide our students did well, we can celebrate, but if we decide they didn't do well, we have work to do.

A score or average of 55 alone tells us nothing about how well our students did. In order for the 55 to have meaning, we must compare it against something else—what has been called a *benchmark,*

Table 15.1. Ten Kinds of Benchmarks or Standards

Benchmark	Questions Each Benchmark Can Answer
Local standards	Are our students meeting our own standards?
External standards	Are our students meeting standards set by someone else?
Internal peer benchmark	How do our students compare to peers within our course, program, or college?
External peer benchmark	How do our students compare to peers at other colleges?
Best practices benchmark	How do our students compare to the best of their peers?
Value-added benchmark	Are our students improving?
Historical trends benchmark	Is our program improving?
Strengths-and-weaknesses perspective	What are our students' areas of relative strength and weakness?
Capability benchmark	Are our students doing as well as they can?
Productivity benchmark	Are we getting the most for our investment?

brightline, standard, or *criterion.* Setting that benchmark or standard is not easy. Standards and benchmarks are, after all, a continuation of the process that begins with articulating clear, meaningful goals—and articulating goals can be difficult. The process often continues with articulating the specific traits we value in a rubric or test blueprint, which can also be difficult. So it should be no surprise that it is also difficult to articulate the benchmarks or standards against which we judge student achievement of those goals and traits.

To complicate things further, setting a benchmark or standard is a multistep process:

1. Choosing the kind of standard or benchmark to set from among the ten kinds listed in Table 15.1 (Suskie, 2007)

2. Setting specific, appropriate standards or benchmarks for adequate, exemplary, and inadequate performance

3. Setting targets for students' collective performance

This chapter discusses these three steps, beginning with the ten kinds of benchmarks or standards from which you can choose. Discuss and decide on the kinds of benchmarks you want to use when you plan an assessment (Chapters Four and Seven) rather than when you're examining the results. Otherwise you may end up with an assessment that doesn't answer questions that you or others care about.

Local Standards

Local standards (or *competency-based* or *criterion-referenced* benchmarks) compare Michael's 55 against a standard established by those teaching in the course, program, or college. Suppose that your department colleagues agree that students should earn at least a 35 in order to earn a passing grade on the test. According to this standard, Michael did well.

An advantage of using local standards is faculty ownership (Chapter Five). Suzanne Pieper, Keston Fulcher, Donna Sundre, and T. Dary Erwin (2008) "have noticed that faculty pay much closer attention to assessment results when they have played a role in establishing performance expectations" (p. 7).

Another advantage of using local standards is that they are what many audiences want to see. Employers, legislators, and other public audiences are increasingly calling for evidence that college graduates have achieved an appropriate level of important knowledge and skills. Peter D. Hart Research Associates (2008) have found that employers are very supportive of faculty-evaluated assessments such as evaluations of field experiences, essay tests, electronic portfolios, and senior projects.

But if your results will be viewed by skeptical audiences, you will need to set local standards that are clearly defensible. Strategies to do this are discussed later in this chapter.

Because self-reported information can be unreliable (Chapter Twelve), the local standards perspective may not be appropriate for add-on assessments such as surveys in which students, alumni, and others self-report information about themselves.

External Standards

External standards (or *competency-based* or *criterion-referenced* standards) compare Michael's 55 against an externally established standard. Suppose that your disciplinary association has decreed that students should earn at least a 45 on the test Michael took in order to be considered worthy of a college degree in your discipline. According to this standard, Michael did fairly well.

External standards most often come from tests required for certification or licensure, such as the Praxis (Educational Testing Service, 2008b) for teachers and the NCLEX (National Council of State Boards of Nursing, 2008) for nurses. Employers, legislators, and other public audiences sometimes find external standards more compelling than local standards.

If external standards are appropriate for your situation, consult Chapter Fourteen for information on identifying and using published instruments, which are the source of many external standards.

Internal Peer Benchmarks

An *internal peer* (or *comparative* or *norm-referenced*) benchmark compares Michael's 55 against the scores of peers in his class or college. Suppose that the average score earned by all your students on Michael's test is 65. Under this benchmark, Michael didn't do very well with his score of 55.

Internal peers can be all the students at your college, all the students in Michael's program at your college, or all the students in programs at your college that are similar to Michael's. For example, if Michael is a Spanish major, his score might be compared against those of all foreign language majors at your college.

Internal peers can also be students who did not have the same experience. Suppose, for example, that Michael is in an online class. Comparing his class's scores against those of students who took the same class in a traditional setting would help us understand the effect of online instruction on student learning. If you do this, keep in mind that differences may be due not to the class format but to differences in the students enrolled in the two classes. Statisticians have tools that can help address this to a certain degree (Chapter Sixteen).

Peer benchmarks can be helpful because they add a fresh viewpoint. We may think that students in our class are not very good writers but learn that they're writing relatively well compared to other students at our college. Or we may think that students in our program are very satisfied with tutoring assistance, only to learn that they're less satisfied than students in other programs at our college.

External Peer Benchmarks

An *external peer* (or *comparative, normative,* or *norm-referenced*) benchmark compares Michael's 55 against the scores of his peers at other colleges. Suppose that the national average for the test Michael took is 70. Under this benchmark, Michael didn't do very well with his score of 55.

While external *standards* are usually specific targets set by some external organization, an external *peer benchmark* is often the average (Chapter Sixteen) of some peer group, although it need not be. Depending on your circumstances, an appropriate benchmark may be that your students surpass only a third of their peers, or you may aim for your students to be in the top 10 percent.

External peer benchmarks get us out of our ivory tower. They can also help inform faculty and staff discussions about setting appropriate local standards. If the average score for students in your course or program is 65, knowing that the national average is 70 can help faculty and staff decide whether an average of 65 is "good enough."

External peer benchmarks nonetheless have limitations:

External peer benchmarks are not appropriate or useful for everyone. Some colleges, such as those with specialized missions or serving unique student populations, may find it difficult or impossible to identify appropriate peers, making this an inappropriate benchmark. Even if appropriate peers can be identified, Peter D. Hart Research Associates (2008) have found that employers are far more supportive of faculty-evaluated assessments than "tests that show how a college compares to others in advancing students' critical thinking skills" (p. 7).

Relevant information on peers may not be available. While public information resources are increasingly available online (Table 15.2), available information may not be relevant to your college's learning goals.

Table 15.2. Public Sources of Information on Colleges and Universities

Resource	Sponsor	Web Site Address
College Navigator	National Center for Education Statistics	http://nces.ed.gov/collegenavigator/
College MatchMaker	College Board	http://collegesearch.collegeboard.com/search/index.jsp
College Results Online	Education Trust	www.collegeresults.org
National Survey of Student Engagement	*USA Today* and the National Survey of Student Engagement	www.usatoday.com
America's Best Colleges	*U.S. News & World Report*	http://colleges.usnews.rankingsandreviews.com/college
100 Best Values in Public Colleges	*Kiplinger's*	www.kiplinger.com/tools/colleges
Washington Monthly College Guide	*Washington Monthly*	www2.washingtonmonthly.com
College Portrait	Association of Public and Land-grant Universities (APLU) and American Association of State Colleges and Universities (AASCU)	www.voluntarysystem.org
U-CAN	National Association of Independent Colleges and Universities (NAICU)	www.ucan-network.org

Truly representative norms don't exist for many assessment instruments.   This topic is discussed in Chapter Fourteen.

People focus on the peer average even when it is inappropriate. Unless everyone in the peer group is performing identically, there will always be someone below average and someone above average, and it's mathematically impossible to expect everyone to perform at or above the average. Given colleges' varying missions and student backgrounds and needs, it may be completely appropriate for some colleges to be below average.

Publication of peer assessment results raises the specter of high-stakes testing.   Although collecting peer information and using it for internal discussions can be very helpful, publishing comparative assessment results, as many colleges and universities are being pressured to do, raises troublesome questions. Trudy Banta (2008) asks:

> Will some institutions be castigated publicly because their students are (supposedly) failing to gain as much in college as students at some other institutions? Will students ultimately be discouraged from attending these institutions? Will funding for these institutions be withheld, or corrective actions imposed by state or federal governments, as is the case in the K–12 sector? Will institutions develop prep courses to help students improve their scores on these tests? Will private consultants and companies profit from coaching students to help improve their scores? [p. 4]

Identifying appropriate peers.   If an external peer benchmark is appropriate for your situation, your first step is to identify appropriate peers. The key word is *appropriate*. It's not useful, for example, for an open-admission college to compare its students' quantitative skills against those of students at highly selective colleges. Table 15.3 gives some sources for identifying peer institutions in the United States.

Some colleges find it helpful to identify two sets of peers: current peers and aspirational peers. Others find it useful to identify several sets of peers, perhaps one set for the engineering school and another for the fine arts programs.

Once you have identified peers, find out what assessment information is available for them. The resources in Table 15.2 may be helpful in this regard. As noted earlier, in many cases public information will not relate to your college's learning goals. If so, try contacting potential peers and soliciting their cooperation in sharing information. Perhaps some peers might be willing to work collaboratively on assessing student learning.

Table 15.3. Sources of Potential Peer Institutions

Institutions using the same published instrument (Chapter Fourteen)

Information-sharing networks such as the Higher Education Data Sharing (HEDS) Consortium for private institutions

Institutions with the same or similar Carnegie classifications (Carnegie Foundation for the Advancement of Teaching, 2007)

Fellow members of a higher education organization or consortium, such as the American Association of Universities (AAU), the American Association of State Colleges and Universities (AASCU), the National Association of Independent Colleges and Universities (NAICU), or the Associated New American Colleges (ANAC)

Fellow members of a state or regional system (for public institutions)

Peer institutions that the institution identifies, perhaps by using tools such as College Results Online (Education Trust, n.d.)

Best Practice Benchmarks

Best practice (or *best-in-class*) benchmarks compare your results against the best of your peers. Suppose that you are at a community college whose students average 125 on the XYZ Quantitative Reasoning Test. The national average for all community college students is 112, but students at Hillcrest Community College average 148, one of the best college averages in the country. Under this best practice benchmark, although your students scored above the national average, you would nonetheless conclude that there is room for improvement because your students' average fell short of Hillcrest's.

While peer benchmarks are often the average of peers, best practice benchmarks are the very best of peers. If the faculty and staff of a best-practice course, programs, or college are willing to share what they are doing, you can gain valuable ideas on how you might achieve similarly outstanding results.

Use a best practice benchmark only if you and your colleagues have a strong commitment to further improving your course, program, or college, no matter how good it may already be. If a best practice benchmark is appropriate for your situation, your challenge will be to identify peers that have best practices and to obtain their cooperation in sharing information about what they do that makes them among the best in their class.

Value-Added Benchmarks

Value-added (or *growth, change, longitudinal,* or *improvement*) benchmarks compare Michael's 55 against his performance when he began his studies. Suppose that a year ago, Michael scored a 25 on the same test. Under this value-added benchmark, Michael shows considerable improvement.

The value-added perspective was embraced during the early years of the assessment movement in the 1980s, then fell out of favor because of the concerns discussed later in this section. Two recent forces have led to its resurrection. One is the heavily marketed Collegiate Learning Assessment (Council for Aid to Education, 2006), which presents its scores using value-added benchmarks. The other is the report of the Commission on the Future of Higher Education (U.S. Department of Education, 2006), which stated that "student achievement . . . must be measured by institutions on a 'value-added' basis" (p. 4). The concept of a value-added benchmark is appealing because if we assess students only at the end of a course or program using a local standard or peer benchmark, the students we identify as, say, superior writers may have been superior writers in high school who learned little from us.

Value-added benchmarks are not necessarily appropriate for several reasons (Suskie, 2007).

Value-added benchmarks may not be relevant or useful.   Perhaps the greatest concern with the value-added benchmark "is whether the question it answers is truly relevant. Is how much students learn in college more important than whether they graduate with the competencies we expect of a college graduate? Imagine an open-admission college whose mission is to educate a very underprepared student population. Students enter reading at the third grade level, and after Herculean work by the faculty and staff they graduate four years later reading at the eleventh grade level. This is tremendous value-added, but would employers want to hire graduates who are not reading at the college level?" (Suskie, 2007, p. 12). George Mehaffy, vice president of the American Association of State Colleges and Universities, has noted "a huge tension . . . between assessment that measures how far students have come and assessment that measures the absolute level they've reached . . . you can be satisfied with how far you've brought your students but not with the absolute level of their performance, or vice versa" (Miller, 2008, p. 11).

We can't be sure that improvement is the result of our efforts. Value-added advocates tend to think of it as a form of the pre-post research design used in social science experimental research. But assessment is not experimental research. It is instead action research (Chapter One), a distinct type of research whose purpose is to improve one's own work rather than make broad generalizations. And the value-added approach is not a pre-post design; we do not usually assign students randomly to treatments (colleges or programs) and a control group (who receive no college education at all).

Because assessment is not experimental research and the value-added perspective is not a pre-post experimental design, we cannot be sure that any growth is due to our curricula and pedagogies. It may instead be due to concurrent influences such as part-time jobs or even normal maturation. Growth in a student's oral communication skills, for example, may be due more to her part-time job as a restaurant server than to her speech communication course, and the refinement of her life goals may be due as much to normal maturation as to a special career exploration program.

Changes between entry and exit scores can be so imprecise that they mask the true amount of change or growth.   The error margin (Chapter Sixteen) of value-added scores is generally about twice as large as that of the scores themselves. Suppose that student essays are scored using a five-point scale. The average score for entering freshmen is 3.2, and the average for rising sophomores is 3.4—a discouragingly small gain. Part of the reason for this apparently small change may be that the five-point scale hides the growth of a student who scores, say, a very low 3—almost a 2—at entry and a very high 3—but not quite a 4—at exit. Under the five-point scale, the student would earn a 3 at both entry and exit and appear to have no growth at all.

Value added can be calculated in a number of ways, and statisticians have found that "value added statistics can differ significantly depending on the method of calculation used" (Banta, 2008, p. 4). This of course raises further questions about their meaning and accuracy.

Value-added assessments may not be available for students who transfer into or out of a college or program.   Value-added results for colleges or programs with many students transferring in or out may not be representative of all students in the college or program. Suzanne Pieper, Keston Fulcher, Donna Sundre, and T. Dary Erwin (2008) have noted that students persisting through the end of a program—those for whom value-added can be determined—"might be systematically stronger than those choosing to depart or delay completion" (p. 6).

Value-added results may be affected by the assessment's floor and ceiling.   An assessment with a relatively narrow range of possible scores may mask the growth of exceptionally well-prepared and underprepared students. Students who earn close to the highest possible score when they enter may not show much growth simply because they are so close to the assessment's ceiling. Students who earn the lowest possible score when they enter may not show much growth if their true entry-level performance is actually much lower than the assessment's floor.

It can be difficult to motivate students to do their best on preassessments at the beginning of a course or program. Indeed, there is a subliminal disincentive for students to do their best—after all, the worse they do at entry, the bigger the potential growth by exit.

Value-added benchmarks may nonetheless be a good choice if it is important to document that a course or program yields significant gains in student learning. You might be asked to justify, for example, that the $200,000 your college spends each year on mathematics tutoring improves students' mathematics skills significantly, and a value-added approach may provide the most convincing evidence.

Value-added benchmarks can also be helpful if your students are so different from typical students that peer benchmarks would be inappropriate. Suppose that you have many students who never studied algebra in high school, leaving them far behind typical college students in quantitative skills. With an external peer benchmark, you might conclude that your mathematics program is deficient, but with a value-added benchmark, you may learn your students' skills improve significantly and your programs are actually quite effective.

Value-added benchmarks can also be helpful if you have too few students to compare with confidence against local standards, external standards, or peers. If, for example, your program typically graduates only a handful of students each year, their average score on a particular assessment could fluctuate considerably from one year to the next, making it difficult to determine how successful the program is. In this case, it may be more useful to examine each student's individual growth. This is called an *ipsative* assessment.

Value-added benchmarks aren't needed in those disciplines about which most students know little or nothing when they enter, such as occupational therapy or aeronautical engineering.

Historical Trends Benchmarks

A *historical trends* benchmark compares current students against peers in prior classes. Suppose that on Michael's test, all students this year averaged 65, while students last year averaged 50 and students the year before averaged 40. According to this benchmark, this year's class did quite well.

Historical trends benchmarks differ from value-added benchmarks because they look at changes in successive groups of students rather than change within one group or one student. They are particularly helpful in evaluating the effectiveness of changes in courses or programs. They can also be useful if your students, courses, or programs are very different from those of peer institutions. With external standards or peer benchmarks, relatively low scores might lead you to conclude that your courses or programs are inadequate, but with a historical trends benchmark, you may learn that this year's course or program is significantly more effective than last year's and you are making good progress.

The shortcoming of historical trends benchmarks is that meaningful historical data are not always available. Students change, their needs change, curricula change, and pedagogies change. A survey conducted a few years ago may not have asked the questions that concern us today. Students writing research papers a few years ago may not have had access to the information resources and technologies that students use today, so we might want to use a different assessment now than we did then.

If you are considering a historical trends benchmark, it is thus important to balance your need for historical information with your need for information that's relevant to your current course, program, or college. Review your assessment tool on a regular basis, and revise any items or sections that are outdated or irrelevant, even if that means losing some historical trends information.

Strengths-and-Weaknesses Perspectives

A *strengths-and-weaknesses* perspective compares the subscores of a particular assessment against one another. Suppose that Michael's 55 was based on a test with two halves. He scored a 65 on the half addressing conceptual understanding and a 45 on the half addressing applying that conceptual understanding to real-life situations. Under this perspective, Michael was relatively strong in conceptual understanding but relatively weak in his capacity to apply that understanding.

The strengths-and-weaknesses perspective answers the question, "What are our students' relative strengths and areas for improvement?" which is of great interest to many faculty and staff. The shortcoming of this approach is that many assessments are not designed to yield comparable subscores. But many rubrics and some published instruments do provide meaningful subscores.

Capability Benchmarks

A *capability* (or *potential*) benchmark compares assessment results against what students are capable of doing. Caitlyn is tone-deaf but loves to sing, so she's taking a choral class to meet a general education performing arts requirement. She is conscientious with her classwork and practice, but by the end of the course, she still can't sing in tune. Raj's kicks still miss the goal most of the time, despite a semester of hard work in a fitness class emphasizing soccer. Are these students successes or failures? By the criteria of most benchmarks, they are clearly deficient in some respects that faculty value. But perhaps they are doing as well as they possibly can, given their inherent capabilities.

Now consider Lakisha, who won first prize at her state's high school science fair for two straight years. As a college senior, she has scored at the sixty-fifth percentile on a national science test, and faculty have judged her senior research project good, not outstanding. Is she a success or a failure? By the criteria of local standards and peer benchmarks, she is successful, but a nagging thought remains: she could be doing better.

A capability benchmark can be helpful for understanding these kinds of outliers—students whose capabilities are significantly above or below those of typical students. The challenge to using this benchmark is determining students' capability accurately. "Identifying those students who lack [soccer] talent, as opposed to those who simply aren't trying very hard, is highly subjective and would be difficult to quantify precisely" (Suskie, 2007, p. 13). Some published test batteries for basic (K–12) education are normed so that achievement scores can be compared against aptitude scores, but these kinds of tests are rare at the higher education level. This perspective is therefore seldom used in higher education, except informally.

Another shortcoming of the capability benchmark is that it is often not relevant (Suskie, 2007). We do not want to graduate students who, despite trying as hard as they can, still write at a precollege level.

A capability benchmark might be useful, however, in some terminal general education courses or elective courses whose primary goal is not to develop specific competencies but simply to increase the student's interest in and comfort with the subject.

If a capability benchmark is appropriate for your situation, try to collect information systematically on student capability as well as achievements.

Productivity Benchmarks

Let's suppose that it cost Michael's college four hundred dollars to provide him with the education that led to his score of 55. Carmen enrolled in another section of the same course and also earned a 55 on the same exam, but at a cost of three hundred dollars, perhaps because she was in a larger class or taught by a junior faculty member earning a lower salary. The cost of instruction might be called a *productivity* perspective that answers the question, "Are we getting the most for our investment?"

While this perspective is of great interest to some audiences, it can draw attention away from educational effectiveness. Some policymakers might be tempted to focus on the lowest-cost approach, even if the quality of the student learning suffers.

Which Kind of Benchmark or Standard Should You Use?

Conclusions about Michael's performance have varied considerably in the examples throughout this chapter. Whether Michael did well or not depended on the kind of benchmark or standard against which his score was compared. The implications of this variability may be explained as follows:

> In essence, the perspectives that have been described here can be thought of as a set of lenses through which an object—assessment results—can be viewed. While each perspective or lens can give us a view of the object—student learning—the view through each lens is somewhat incomplete, because each looks at the object from only one angle, and somewhat distorted, because no assessment tool or strategy is completely accurate. Viewing assessment results using only one perspective thus gives us an incomplete and somewhat distorted perception of student learning. We saw this when we examined Michael's results; according to some benchmarks he did well, but according to others he didn't. Examining student learning through multiple lenses, from multiple angles, or at least having the latitude to choose the lenses that provide the most meaningful view, gives us the best chance of answering the complex question of what our students have learned and whether they have achieved our goals for them. [Suskie, 2007, p. 13]

Thus, if you are examining the performance of your students on a certification examination, you might look at how they compare against national norms, against students in the best programs in the country, and against your students who took the examination a few years ago. If you are using a locally developed rubric to evaluate student writing samples, you might look at how they compare against a standard that your faculty and staff have identified and also against students a couple of years ago. Considering multiple benchmarks will give you a more balanced picture of your students' achievements.

Setting Specific, Appropriate Performance Standards or Benchmarks

Once you have identified the kind of benchmark or standard that is most appropriate for your situation, the next challenge is setting a specific, appropriate performance standard against which actual performance is compared. For example, if you are comparing Michael against his peers, is your goal for him to surpass just 10 percent of his peers, half his peers, or two-thirds of his peers? Or do you want him to be the very best?

Unless your benchmark is an external standard, such as those set by licensure boards, deciding what target level is good enough is essentially a subjective decision—and therefore difficult. How can you justify that your standards are truly appropriate and truly college level? The following steps may help.

Do some research. Perhaps appropriate disciplinary associations have issued statements on standards for graduates of particular programs. A simple Web search may turn up examples of rubrics and benchmarks, particularly for common learning goals such as writing, science laboratory skills, and information literacy. Colleagues in peer programs or colleges may have set standards that might be adapted to your situation, even if you don't plan to use a peer benchmark approach.

Involve others in the standard-setting process. These may include employers, students, faculty teaching in your program, and faculty teaching in more advanced programs.

Use samples of student work to inform your discussion. Some assessment practitioners advocate setting standards as part of the assessment planning process, before assessments are undertaken. But while it's important to identify the kind of benchmarks you will use when planning an assessment, setting specific standards before an assessment is undertaken may lead to arbitrary and perhaps unrealistic standards. It may be more feasible to mirror the approach for developing a descriptive rubric (Chapter Nine). Implement the assessment on a small scale, and discuss just a few examples of student work, using the following questions as a springboard for conversation:

- Which examples represent exemplary work? Why? Would it be realistic to establish these as the targets we aim for in all students?

- Which examples are unacceptably inadequate? Which would embarrass you if they were from graduates of this program or college? Why?

- What kinds of student performance represent minimally acceptable work for a graduate of this program or college?

- How do the exemplary, acceptable, and inadequate examples differ?

Use other kinds of benchmarks and standards as corroboration. You might show, for example, that your local standards for college-level writing are comparable to those of peer colleges or to those your faculty used ten years ago.

A Note on Setting Local Standards with Rubrics

The easiest way to set local standards is by developing a rubric or holistic scoring guide in which you clearly articulate what is minimally acceptable performance, what is exceptional performance, and what is inadequate performance. Chapter Nine discusses how to create rubrics.

There are three models for setting standards with rubrics. (If you are grading student work, make sure your students understand which model you plan to use to arrive at a grade.) To understand your options, consider the rubric in Exhibit 15.1, which evaluates research papers in terms of seven criteria. The ratings shown in italics are the results for a paper written by a hypothetical student we'll call Melissa.

A minimum standard for every trait. Under this model, faculty and staff set a minimum standard that students must demonstrate on every trait in order to pass or be considered minimally adequate overall. For the rubric in Exhibit 15.1, faculty might decide that a paper would have to score Barely Adequate or better in every

Exhibit 15.1. A Scored Rubric for Research Reports in Speech-Language Pathology/Audiology

Melissa, a hypothetical student, earned the statements and numbers that are italicized.

	Exemplary (90–100 points)	*Good (80–89 points)*	*Barely Adequate (70–79 points)*	*Inadequate (0–69 points)*
Introduction (10 points)	The introduction smoothly pulls the reader into the topic, is organized, presents the main argument clearly, and states the author's views. (10 points)	The introduction is organized but does not adequately present the main argument or does not state the author's views. (8 points)	*The introduction presents the main argument and the author's views but is disorganized and does not flow smoothly. (7 points)*	The introduction is disorganized and difficult to follow. The main argument and the author's views are not introduced. (5 points)
Content (20 points)	Information is presented clearly, completely, and accurately across all sections. At least 3 major sections; at least 1 major section has 2–3 subsections. (20 points)	*Information is unclear and difficult to understand in 1 section. (18 points)*	Information is unclear and difficult to understand in 2–3 sections. (16 points)	The paper is unclear and difficult to understand across 4 or more sections. (12 points)
Organization (20 points)	*Organization is clear; good framework. Headers, preview paragraphs, topic sentences, and transitions aid in understanding main points. Information is presented logically. (20 points)*	Organization is unclear in 1 section (unfocused paragraphs, poor topic sentences, poor transitions). All other sections are logically organized. (18 points)	Organization is unclear in 2–3 sections OR headers and preview paragraphs or sentences are missing. (16 points)	Organization is unclear in 4 or more sections. (12 points)
Conclusion/ original thought (20 points)	Specific ideas for improving research or other ideas are presented in an organized manner with logical rationales. (20 points)	*Specific ideas are presented but the rationales for 1 idea may be weak. (18 points)*	Ideas are presented but in a vague, generic format OR rationales for 2 or more ideas are weak. (16 points)	Fewer than 3 original ideas related to the topic are presented OR all ideas are not well explained. (12 points)

	Exemplary (90–100 points)	Good (80–89 points)	Barely Adequate (70–79 points)	Inadequate (0–69 points)
Writing style (10 points)	Tone is professional, vocabulary and syntax are mature, and easy-to-understand terms are used throughout the paper. (10 points)	*Syntax or vocabulary is complex, awkward, or filled with jargon in 1–2 sections of the paper OR words are used incorrectly in 1–2 sections of the paper. (7 points)*	Syntax or vocabulary is complex, awkward, or filled with jargon in 3–4 sections of the paper OR words are used incorrectly in 3–4 sections of the paper. (5 points)	Writing style makes more than 4 sections of the paper difficult to read and understand. (3 points)
Writing use/ mechanics (10 points)	The paper is free of spelling, syntax, formatting, and punctuation errors. (10 points)	The paper has fewer than 5 spelling, punctuation, formatting, and syntax errors. (7 points)	The paper has 6–15 spelling, punctuation, formatting, and syntax errors. (5 points)	*More than 16 errors across the paper make it difficult to follow. (3 points)*
APA rules (10 points)	All APA rules are followed for citations, headers, numbers, series, quotes, references, and so on. (10 points)	*Fewer than 3 violations of APA rules, or 1–2 missing or incorrect citations and references. (7 points)*	4–10 violations of APA rules and/or 3–5 missing or incorrect citations and references. (5 points)	11 or more violations of APA rules and/or 6 or more missing or incorrect citations and references. (3 points)

Source: Adapted with permission from a rubric adapted by Sharon Glennen and Celia Bassich-Zeren, Department of Communication Sciences and Disorders, Towson University.

category in order to be considered at least minimally adequate overall. Under this model, Melissa's overall performance on this paper is Inadequate (failing), because her Writing Use/Mechanics score is Inadequate.

A minimum standard for the sum or average of all traits. Under this model, faculty and staff set a minimum standard that students must demonstrate on the overall rubric in order to pass or be considered minimally adequate. This allows poor performance in one category to be offset by good performance in another category. Under this model, Melissa's paper is Exemplary on one trait, Good on four traits, Barely Adequate on one trait, and Inadequate on one trait. If the seven categories are equally important, summing or averaging these seven ratings yields an overall rating of Good for Melissa's entire paper.

The seven categories don't have to be equally important, however. In the rubric in Exhibit 15.1, the faculty have decided that Content is twice as important as the Introduction, and they've indicated this by assigning a maximum of 20 points to Content and 10 points to the Introduction. Melissa earned 7 points for her Introduction, 18 points for Content, 20 points for Organization, and so on, for a total score of 80 points out of 100. This puts her overall paper (barely) in the Good category.

If you are using this model, make sure that the points you assign sum to totals that are appropriate for the performance levels they represent. In the rubric in Exhibit 15.1, someone scoring Barely Adequate in every category would earn a total score of 70, widely regarded as a C−, an appropriate grade for barely adequate work. Someone scoring Good in every category would earn a total score of 83, widely regarded as a B, an appropriate grade for good work.

A minimum standard for certain traits. Under this model, faculty and staff set a minimum standard that students must demonstrate on just certain attributes in order to pass or be considered at least minimally adequate overall. Suppose that, using the rubric in Exhibit 15.1, the faculty agree that students must score at least Barely Adequate in the Content category in order to pass or be considered at least minimally adequate on the overall paper. If the student passes this initial hurdle, the ratings for all categories can be summed or averaged to determine the paper's overall rating.

Under this model, Melissa scored Good on Content, so her paper passes the Barely Adequate hurdle. Her paper's overall rating would be Good, based on the sum or average of her ratings in all seven categories. But suppose that Kelly, another student, scored Inadequate on Content and Exemplary in every other category. Even though her paper was strong in most respects, her paper would still be considered inadequate (failing) overall.

A Note on Setting Local Standards with Multiple-Choice Tests

Many faculty set traditional standards for multiple-choice tests: 90 to 100 percent correct is an A, 80 to 89 percent is a B, and so on, with a target of 65 percent or so as minimally acceptable or passing performance. While this practice may be appropriate in some circumstances, it can also be arbitrary and difficult to substantiate. A more defensible practice is to set minimal standards for each test item or group of items, based on their difficulty and importance. You may want every student to answer all items on certain fundamental concepts correctly, but you may expect far fewer to answer some especially challenging items correctly. The 50 percent rule, discussed in Chapter Sixteen, may be helpful here: your targets should be that no less than 50 percent of your students answer any item or group of items correctly.

Setting Targets for Students' Collective Performance

Once you have decided on the kind of standard or benchmark that you will use and you've set specific standards for minimally acceptable, exemplary, and unacceptable performance, the next step is to set targets for students' collective performance. Suppose, for example, that you have set a standard of 35 as the minimally acceptable or passing score on Michael's test. How many students would you want to meet this standard? Do you want every student to meet this standard, or would you be satisfied if 90 percent met it? Would you be satisfied if every student earned a 35 but no students earned anything higher?

The strategies for setting defensible performance standards apply here. Involve others—students, faculty, and employers—in these discussions, and look at samples of student work to inform your thinking. Also consider the following suggestions.

Express targets as percentages rather than means. Percentages are usually more understandable and useful than means (Chapter Sixteen). If you plan to use a rubric, for example, a target that 90 percent of your students will earn at least a minimally adequate rating is more understandable and useful than a target that students will earn an average of 3.1 on a five-point rubric scale. Similarly, if you are using a test, a target that 95 percent of your students will earn at least a 65 is more understandable and useful than a target that they earn an average of 73.

Vary your targets depending on the circumstances. Certainly we want every student to graduate with fundamental skills, such as the ability to write in complete sentences. Similarly, if students are preparing for careers in which errors can have grave consequences, such as nursing or civil engineering, we want absolute assurance that every student is graduating with a certain base of knowledge and skills.

If you decide that every student should meet a standard, keep in mind that every assessment is an imperfect, incomplete sample of what students have learned. It's thus entirely possible that a few students who have truly mastered important learning goals will do poorly on one particular assignment or test. So as emphasized in Chapter Three, give students multiple opportunities to demonstrate their learning before deciding that they have failed to demonstrate minimal competence.

Despite our best efforts, sometimes a student with truly inadequate skills may slip through the cracks. Weigh the costs of perfection against the benefits. The occasional economics or biology student who slips through with, say, less-than-desired public speaking skills may nonetheless have a productive and satisfying career. For these kinds of goals, a target under 100 percent may be appropriate. And sometimes it's not realistic or appropriate to expect every student to meet a minimal standard. In these cases, a target well below 100 percent may be appropriate. You may be satisfied if only a quarter of your students achieve a goal that students think creatively.

Consider multiple targets.   Sometimes it's useful to set multiple performance targets for several performance levels. You might set a target that 90 percent of your students earn at least a minimally adequate rating or test score and another that at least 30 percent earn an exemplary rating or test score.

View Standard Setting as an Iterative Process

Once you have set initial standards and targets, see how a full group of students does, and be open to adjusting the standards and targets as advisable. As with every other aspect of assessment, view standard setting as a perpetual work in progress, something to be modified as you learn more about your goals, the assessment tools you're using, and your students' performance.

Time to Think, Discuss, and Practice

1. For each of the following scenarios, decide which kind or kinds of benchmark or standard would be most appropriate—and realistically feasible—for interpreting the results.

   • One of the foreign language department's goals is for its French seniors to be fluent in reading, writing, speaking, and listening.

   • One general education goal is for students to think critically and analytically.

- One institutional goal is for students to develop a stronger sense of self-identity, including a greater understanding of their personal values.
- One institutional goal is to have an "exceptional" first-year-to-sophomore retention rate.

2. For each of the following scenarios, discuss whether the department should conclude that it is achieving its goal. Can you decide this? If not, what more do you need to know to make a decision? Be specific.

- One of the foreign language department's goals is for its French seniors to surpass seniors nationally on the Major Field Test in French. This year, 55 percent of seniors scored above the national average on the test.
- One of the social work department's goals is for its graduates to succeed in graduate study. A survey of alumni who graduated five years ago shows that 40 percent have earned an M.S.W.

3. Faculty teaching first-year composition scored 200 student essays and obtained the following results: for Language Use, 100 essays scored Excellent, 50 scored Adequate, and the rest scored Unacceptable; for Content, 75 scored Excellent, 75 scored Adequate, and the rest scored Unacceptable; and for Organization, 25 scored Excellent, 50 scored Adequate, and the rest scored Unacceptable.

- What are the major conclusions you would draw about these students' writing performance? Why?
- What kinds of standards or benchmarks did you use to draw your conclusions?

4. If you teach, which kinds of standards or benchmarks do you use most often when you evaluate students' work in your classes?

- Why do you use this benchmark or these benchmarks? What does your choice say about you as a teacher? What does it say about what you value in your classroom?
- If you use a local standard, how do you decide on the cut-off point for each grade? What does this say about you as a teacher?

Recommended Readings

The following readings are recommended along with the references cited in this chapter.

Banta, T. W. (2007). If we must compare. . . *Assessment Update, 19*(2), 3–4.

Banta, T. W., & Pike, G. R. (2007). Revisiting the blind alley of value added. *Assessment Update, 19*(1), 1–2, 14–15.

Campbell, D. T., & Stanley, J. C. (1963). *Experimental and quasi-experimental designs for research.* Skokie, IL: Rand McNally.

Ewell, P. T. (2005). Power in numbers: The values in our metrics. *Change, 37*(4), 10–16.

Fulcher, K. H., & Willse, J. T. (2007). Value added: Back to basics in measuring change. *Assessment Update, 19*(5), 10–12.

Jones, D. P. (2002). *Different perspectives on information about educational quality: Implications for the role of accreditation* (CHEA Occasional Paper). Washington, DC: Council for Higher Education Accreditation.

Jones, E. A., & Voorhees, R., with Paulson, K. (2002). *Defining and assessing learning: Exploring competency-based initiatives* (NCES 2002–159). Washington, DC: U.S. Department of Education, National Center for Education Statistics.

Livingston, S. A., & Zieky, M. J. (1982). *Passing scores: A manual for setting standards on performance on educational and occupational tests.* Princeton, NJ: Educational Testing Service.

Pascarella, E. T. (2001). Identifying excellence in undergraduate education: Are we even close? *Change, 33*(3), 19–23.

Pike, G. R. (1992). Lies, damn lies, and statistics revisited: A comparison of three methods of representing change. *Research in Education, 33,* 71–84.

Pike, G. R. (2006). Assessment measures: Value-added models and the collegiate learning assessment. *Assessment Update, 18*(4), 5–7.

Pike, G. R. (2007). Response to Fulcher and Willse. *Assessment Update, 19*(5), 12–13.

Seybert, J. A. (2007). Benchmarking in community colleges: A current perspective. *Assessment Update, 19*(5), 3.

Shepard, L. A. (1980). Standard setting issues and methods. *Applied Psychological Measurement, 4*(4), 447–467.

Stufflebeam, D. L. (2000). *The CIPP model for evaluation.* In D. L. Stufflebeam, G. F. Madaus, & T. Kellaghan (Eds.), *Evaluation models: Viewpoints on educational and human services evaluation* (2nd ed., pp. 279–318). Norwell, MA: Kluwer.

Taylor, B. E., & Massy, W. F. (1996). *Strategic indicators for higher education.* Princeton, NJ: Peterson's.

CHAPTER 16

Summarizing and Analyzing Assessment Results

> **Some Valuable Ideas You'll Find in This Chapter**
>
> - Most assessment results can be summarized with simple tallies and percentages.
> - Error margins, which are easy to estimate, provide important information on the precision of assessment results.
> - Good multiple-choice items discriminate well between students who do well and poorly on the overall test.
> - Keep a sample of good, bad, and mediocre student work on file to provide firsthand evidence of your standards and rigor.

After weeks or months of careful planning, your assessments have finally been conducted. The completed rubrics, surveys, and test scores are piled up on your desk or saved in a computer. Now what?

Before you can share your results with others (Chapter Seventeen) and use them to launch conversations about their implications (Chapter Eighteen), you'll need to summarize them. If you've established standards and targets (Chapter Fifteen), you'll need to compare your results against them to see if there are any meaningful differences. You may also want to evaluate the quality of your assessment strategies to see if they're yielding reasonably accurate information. Depending on the kinds of results you have and what you would like to learn, you may also wish to analyze the results to explain, predict, or explore. And you'll need to do a little housekeeping to maintain records of your results. This chapter reviews all these steps.

Planning Your Summary and Analysis

How you summarize and analyze assessment results depends on the kinds of questions you would like your assessments to answer, the kinds of standards or benchmarks you are using, and the kinds of results you have.

What Questions Are to Be Answered?

Review why you conducted this assessment, including your audiences for the results, the questions you and your audiences would like answered, and the decisions that you and your audiences would like to make (Chapter Four).

What Kinds of Standards or Benchmarks Are You Using?

Your results will be more meaningful and useful if you compare them against a benchmark or standard (Chapter Fifteen). If you have set a target for student performance, you will need to summarize your results in a way that mirrors that target. For example, if your goal is that 75 percent of your students surpass some minimum performance level, you will need to summarize the results as the percentage of students who surpass that level. If your goal is that the average test score for your students is above the national average, you will need to summarize the results as an average.

What Kind of Results Do You Have?

Assessment results fall into five categories:

Qualitative results. Qualitative results (Chapter Twelve) are open-ended text-based results, such as reflective writing, notes from focus groups and interviews, and responses to open-ended survey questions. Strategies to summarize and analyze qualitative results are discussed later in this chapter.

Categorical (or nominal) results. These kinds of results break students into discrete categories. Students' majors, hometowns, and responses to individual multiple-choice questions are examples of categorical information. Responses can be tallied, but means or medians cannot be calculated, and because of this, categorical results can be used only in limited ways in statistical analyses designed to explain, predict, or explore.

Ordered (or ranked or ordinal) results. These results can be put in a meaningful order. Many rubrics and survey rating scales yield ordered results. Medians can be calculated, and results can be analyzed. If you or someone you know has expertise in nonparametric statistics, you can use ordered results to explain, predict, or explore.

Scaled (interval and ratio) results. Scaled results are numerical, and the difference between, say, a 1 and a 2 is the same as the difference between a 4 and a 5. Grade point averages, earned credits, salaries, and retention, graduation, and job placement rates are examples of scaled results. Means can be calculated, and results can be analyzed using a wide variety of powerful statistical techniques.

A topic of hot debate among social science researchers is whether results from Likert and other rating scales can be treated as scaled rather than ordered results, as doing so makes possible a far broader range of statistical analyses. Some researchers assert that we can't be sure that the degree of difference between Strongly Agree and Somewhat Agree is the same as the difference between Somewhat Agree and Slightly Agree, so rating scale results should be considered ordered, not scaled. Other researchers, however, argue that statistical analyses designed for scaled results are sufficiently robust that they can be used to analyze ordered results. These researchers point to the multitude of published journal articles using such analyses with ordered results as evidence that this approach is widely accepted.

Dichotomous results. Dichotomous results are those that have only two possible values. Gender and full-time/part-time enrollment status are examples of dichotomous results. Although such results are technically categorical, because there are only two values with only one interval between them, some researchers assert that they can be treated as scaled results and used to explain, predict, and explore.

Will You Use Technologies to Summarize and Analyze Your Results?

Unless you have just a handful of assessment results, you will probably want to enter the results into a computer to make them easier to summarize and analyze. Today many software programs facilitate data entry. They include database software, some statistical analysis packages, and software designed to support surveys, testing, and assessment. A scanner or optical mark reader can be used to enter results from bubble sheet tests and forms. Chapter Six offers suggestions for looking into assessment technologies. Technologies for qualitative results are discussed later in this chapter.

Review your data entry and analysis plans with your college's technical support staff before you finalize your tests, rubrics, and surveys and conduct your assessment. Otherwise it may not be possible to enter and analyze your results as you hope.

Five Basic Ways to Summarize Results

Tallies, percentages, aggregates, averages, and qualitative summaries can be used to summarize assessment results. Chapter Seventeen discusses how to present summarized results through tables and graphs.

Tallies

Tallies are straightforward counts of how many students earned each rating or chose each option. Exhibit 16.1 is an example of such a tally for twenty papers scored using the rubric in Exhibit 9.2. It's fairly easy to see that students are relatively strong at speaking clearly and loudly and that their biggest weakness is being well organized.

If you are using a test, you can tally how many students answered each test question correctly. If the test is multiple choice (Chapter Eleven), you can tally how many students chose each option of each test question. This information can be used to evaluate the quality of each test item, as discussed later in this chapter.

Percentages

Percentages are easier to understand and more meaningful than raw numbers. Few people will understand the implications that 125 students passed a test; more will care that only 23 percent did. Exhibit 16.2 provides percentages for the tallies in Exhibit 16.1.

Percentages make it easier to compare groups of different sizes. You might want to compare your current class against a class four years ago (the historical trends perspective in Chapter Fifteen) or your students against peers at other colleges (the external peer benchmark in Chapter Fifteen). Exhibit 17.3 is an example

Exhibit 16.1. A Tally of Results for the Rating Scale Rubric in Exhibit 9.2

The presenter . . .	Strongly Agree	Agree	Disagree	Strongly Disagree
Clearly stated the purpose of the presentation.	16	2	1	1
Was well organized.	8	5	4	4
Was knowledgeable about the subject.	13	4	0	3
Answered questions authoritatively.	10	4	3	3
Spoke clearly and loudly.	18	1	1	0
Maintained eye contact with the audience.	15	3	1	1
Appeared confident.	13	2	2	3
Adhered to time constraints.	17	1	1	1
Had main points that were appropriate to the central topic.	12	6	1	1
Accomplished the stated objectives.	13	3	3	1

Exhibit 16.2. Results in Exhibit 16.1 Presented as Percentages

The presenter . . .	Strongly Agree	Agree	Disagree	Strongly Disagree
Clearly stated the purpose of the presentation.	80%	10%	5%	5%
Was well organized.	40%	25%	20%	20%
Was knowledgeable about the subject.	65%	20%	0%	15%
Answered questions authoritatively.	50%	20%	15%	15%
Spoke clearly and loudly.	90%	5%	5%	0%
Maintained eye contact with the audience.	75%	15%	5%	5%
Appeared confident.	65%	10%	10%	15%
Adhered to time constraints.	85%	5%	5%	5%
Had main points that were appropriate to the central topic.	60%	30%	5%	5%
Accomplished the stated objectives.	65%	15%	15%	5%

of a peer comparison. Or you might want to compare students' answers to question 5 on a test with their answers to question 12 (the strengths and weaknesses benchmark). Percentages help you easily view such differences.

Aggregates: Summarizing Results into Overall Scores

Sometimes it's helpful to aggregate tallies into overall scores or subscores. Whether and how you do this depends on the purpose of the rubric, test, or survey and how its components align with your learning outcomes.

An overall score. Course rubrics and tests can be aggregated into a single score or grade. Doing so can help to give students feedback on their overall performance on the assignment and help faculty determine course grades. Some assessment audiences may want to know simply, "Can students write effectively by the time they graduate?" and aggregating ratings on various rubric criteria into a single score may be an appropriate response. Chapter Fifteen discusses several ways to do this.

Subscores. Sometimes several items on a rubric, test, or survey address a common learning goal. In these cases, it can be helpful to aggregate those item results into an overall subscore. Perhaps three survey items address students' attitudes toward diversity. Aggregating the results of the items into a single subscore can be helpful in understanding how well students are achieving a goal on diversity.

In order to understand the results of test items addressing a common learning goal, you'll need to aggregate the results according to the test blueprint you used to design the test (Chapter Eleven). This is called "mapping" the results back to the test blueprint. Suppose that the biology faculty have written a fifteen-item test for a general education biology course. The test has five items each on three topics: the scientific method, key vocabulary, and quantitative reasoning. Exhibit 16.3 summarizes the results mapped back to these three topics. In this example, the faculty are using the 50 percent rule, discussed later in this chapter, to decide if they are satisfied with the results.

Exhibit 16.3. Biology Test Results Mapped Back to the Test Blueprint

Topic	Test Items Addressing This Learning Goal	Average Proportion of Students Answering These Questions Correctly
Scientific method	4, 7, 11, 12, and 15	80%
Key vocabulary	1, 3, 6, 8, and 9	84%
Quantitative reasoning	2, 5, 10, 13, and 14	48%

Source: Adapted with permission from an example developed by Virginia Anderson, professor of biology, Towson University.

In this example, the faculty are satisfied with students' understanding of the scientific method and key vocabulary, but they are dissatisfied with students' quantitative reasoning skills. They might try to improve student learning by increasing the number of quantitative problems and questions in lab exercises.

Leaving things be. When a department assessment committee reviews senior theses to learn about seniors' writing skills, there may be no need to summarize the rubric's ratings of various attributes into an overall score or subscores. It may instead be sufficient simply to determine that, say, 84 percent of graduating students organize the paper effectively, 92 percent make compelling arguments supported with suitable information, and 78 percent use appropriate grammar and mechanics.

Averages

Averages are numbers that summarize the central tendency of assessment results. The best-known average is the *mean*: the arithmetic average we learned in grade school. It's appropriate for scaled results.

If your results are ordered, a more appropriate statistic is the *median*: the midpoint of all results when they are listed from highest to lowest. Medians are also a good choice when a few very high or very low results distort the mean. Suppose, for example, that twenty students take a national certification exam whose passing score is 80. Eighteen students score 85 and pass comfortably, but two students fail miserably, scoring 10. The mean of these twenty students is 77.5, which gives the incorrect impression that the "average" student failed the test. The median of 85 better reflects the performance of the "typical" student in this group.

If your results are categorical, the appropriate statistic is the *mode*: the most frequent result.

Qualitative Summaries

Qualitative assessment results such as minute papers, other reflective writing, open-ended survey questions, and focus group records (Chapter Twelve) can be summarized through quick read-throughs, grouped listings, and thematic analysis. These processes are more subjective than those used to summarize the results of quantitative assessments such as rubrics, ratings scales, and multiple-choice tests. Careful, consistent judgment in interpreting results is essential.

Quick read-throughs. The fastest way to get a sense of qualitative results is to read through them quickly for general impressions.

Simply reading through minute paper responses (Chapter Twelve), for example, will give you a good sense of what students are finding difficult. If you have too many responses to read them all, read through a random sample.

Grouped listings. If your qualitative assessment information is composed of brief statements that fall into reasonably discrete categories, you may wish to list the results grouped into categories. Exhibit 16.4 is a listing of qualitative feedback on an assessment workshop. This simple summary makes clear that participants mentioned rubrics most often as the most useful thing they learned at this particular workshop, with multiple-choice tests coming in second.

Exhibit 16.4. A Summary of Qualitative Participant Feedback on an Assessment Workshop

What was the one thing you learned in this workshop that you'll find most useful?

Rubrics (thirteen comments)
- Characteristics and advantages of different types of rubrics
- Descriptive rubrics seemed useful
- Examples of rubrics
- Reinforcing understanding and validity of rubrics
- Using rubrics
- Rubrics are a very good thing when instructors buy into using them.
- Developing rubrics
- Holistic scoring
- The three different kinds of rubrics and how to begin writing them (I'm going to begin soon!)
- How to construct a rubric—from basic to complex
- Creating rubrics may be an excellent collaborative exercise by which department colleagues establish common goals and compare their grading definitions (scales).
- The potential range and flexibility of rubrics
- Examples of different types of rubrics and examining purpose of rubric to select one

Multiple Choice (nine comments)
- Tips for writing multiple choice
- Creating multiple-choice questions
- Multiple-choice tests—I haven't used in a long while and will rethink.
- The criteria for writing good MC tests
- How to avoid pitfalls in the writing of multiple-choice exams

- Options for multiple-choice questions
- Interpretive exercises—I think these will be most useful.
- I learned how to use scenarios effectively!
- Interpretive exercises may work well in my comparative literature course—where I usually emphasize essay writing.

Self-Reflection (five comments)

- The self-reflection info will really work for my students.
- Reflective writing—I think these will be most useful.
- The role of self-reflection and metacognition
- Role of self-reflection in assessment as a strategy
- Examples of self-reflection questions

General and Miscellaneous (three comments)

- How to process and assess the assessment tools we use on a daily basis
- Great tips and tools for assessing student learning
- That assessment encompasses test design and grading

Thematic analysis. More extensive qualitative assessment results, such as reflective essays and transcriptions of focus group interviews, don't lend themselves to simple lists and groupings. Such results may be analyzed using thematic analysis, which synthesizes the results into a holistic description by looking for common themes, patterns, links, and relationships among results. For more information on thematic analysis, see the recommended readings at the end of this chapter.

A special note about summarizing minute papers. If you are summarizing the results of minute papers (Chapter Twelve), once you have grouped the responses, compare students' answers to the question, "What was the most useful or meaningful thing you learned?" against what you think are the most important ideas of the class or program. If students' answers match yours, you've delivered the curriculum with appropriate balance. But if a number of students mention ideas that you consider relatively trivial and few mention your biggest ideas, you have a clue that you may not be getting your main points across effectively.

Next, look at students' responses to the question, "What question remains uppermost in your mind as we end this?" If the responses are all over the map, you may be able to conclude that your class had no major sticking point. But if a number of students raise questions about a particular point, you have a clue that you may need to modify your curriculum or pedagogy to make that idea more understandable.

Ensuring consistent, fair qualitative summaries. Analyzing qualitative results is a subjective process that requires careful, consistent professional judgment. Suppose that one of the comments in Exhibit 16.4 was, "Using rubrics for student self-ratings." Would this be categorized under rubrics, self-reflection, both, or in a separate category? These kinds of decisions must be made deliberately and consistently.

Taking steps to ensure consistent, appropriate categorizations of qualitative results is particularly important if the results are part of a major, important assessment effort. Create some written "rules" or examples for categorizing ambiguous results. After all the results have been categorized, review your decisions to make sure they have been consistent. Better yet, consider having two people independently read and categorize results and compare their decisions. It's also a good idea to corroborate conclusions from qualitative assessments by comparing them against the results of other assessments (Chapter Three).

Technical support for qualitative assessments. If your qualitative results are voluminous, consider using qualitative research software to summarize them more efficiently. After responses are keyed in, qualitative research software typically highlights words and phrases and counts their frequency. Some software also organizes responses (groups all responses on one theme together) to facilitate review and analysis. For information on such software, consult the recommended readings at the end of this chapter. Or speak to a social science faculty member interested in qualitative research, or search online using terms such as "qualitative research" or "qualitative analysis."

If qualitative research software isn't available to help analyze voluminous results, develop a simple coding scheme to examine a sample (Chapter Three). You might, for example, code reflections mentioning writing as the most important thing learned as 1, code those mentioning oral presentation skills as 2, and so on. Or use an assortment of highlighting markers to code each theme.

Identifying Meaningful Differences

Once you have summarized assessment results, you may wish to compare them against performance targets (Chapter Fifteen). If your results are quantitative, statistical tests can help you decide if the differences are large enough to be significant. Keep in mind, however, that a *statistically* significant difference may not be large enough to have *practical* significance (Chapter Seventeen). Qualitative results and the capability benchmark (Chapter Fifteen) require subjective, professional judgment rather than statistical analysis to decide whether student performance results are acceptable.

Evaluating the Quality of Your Assessment Strategies

The questions presented in this section represent only a few of the many approaches to evaluate the quality of assessment strategies. To learn more about evaluating assessment quality, ask a psychology or education faculty member for information on reliability and validity.

How Well Does Your Sample Reflect All Your Students?

Sometimes it isn't practical to assess what every student has learned, especially in a program or college with hundreds or thousands of students. In such cases, we can assess a sample of student work, as discussed in Chapter Three.

The conclusions we draw from a sample of students are valid only if the students in the sample mirror the group from which they were taken. If 55 percent of all students are women, for example, roughly 55 percent of the students being assessed should be women. Similarly, the students in the sample should be similar to all students in terms of their grades, class level, major, full-time/part-time status, or any other factor considered important.

But how similar is good enough? If 55 percent of all students are women, for example, is it good enough that 52 percent of the sample are women? What if the sample is 50 percent women? 45 percent women? Fortunately, statistical analyses can help make these decisions. Consult someone knowledgeable about statistics for help conducting these analyses.

How Precise Are Your Sample Results?

Suppose that faculty and staff assess a sample of two hundred essays and find that 84 percent of them are at least "satisfactory" in terms of overall writing skill. You would like to be able to say that 84 percent of all students at your college write satisfactorily. Assuming that the students in your sample mirror all students, can you say this? No! It's very unlikely that exactly 84 percent of all students write satisfactorily. The real overall percentage may be

83 percent, 82 percent, or even 91 percent. The discrepancy between your 84 percent and the true percentage is called an *error margin* (Chapter Three). It's not really an "error," just a phenomenon that exists because even a good random sample is unlikely to mirror all students precisely.

When reporting results, you will be much more credible if you mention the error margin of your findings. Instead of saying that "84 percent of students write satisfactorily," you could say, "84 percent of students write satisfactorily with an error margin of plus or minus 7 percent." This means that you are 95 percent sure that between 77 percent and 91 percent of all students (84 percent plus and minus 7 percent) write satisfactorily.

Table 3.4 provides the error margins for some sample sizes. The error margin for other sample sizes can be estimated with this formula:

$$\sqrt{\frac{1}{n}} \times 100\% \text{ where } n = \text{your sample size}$$

If faculty and staff evaluate 200 essays, the approximate error margin is:

$$\sqrt{\frac{1}{200}} \times 100\% = \sqrt{.005} \times 100\% = 7\%$$

If you want a more accurate error margin, consult someone knowledgeable about statistics.

How Difficult Is Each Test Item?

It's often helpful to calculate the percentage of students who answered each item correctly or earned acceptable ratings on each rubric criterion. Software for processing bubble sheet and online tests can generate these percentages. If software isn't available, these percentages are easy to calculate.

Take a close look at any test items or rubric criteria that many students got wrong to see if they worked as intended. Try the 50 percent rule: if more than half the students got a particular test question wrong or fail a particular part of an assignment, the problem probably lies not with the students but with teaching methods, curriculum design, or the test or assignment itself (Chapter Eighteen). Often such assignments or test questions are flawed in some way, causing the better students to misinterpret them, or they assess some relatively trivial concept that most students have missed. Sometimes—and this is hard to admit—we simply didn't do a good job teaching that particular concept.

If the fault is with us—our goals, our curriculum (including placement), our teaching methods, or our assessment strategies or tools—students shouldn't be penalized. Give everyone credit for that part of the assessment.

How Well Does Each Test Item Discriminate Between High and Low Scorers?

An effective test item discriminates well between students who generally understand the test's subject and those who don't. Students who answer any one test item correctly should do better on the overall test than students who get the item wrong. Similarly, students who do well on any one rubric criterion or trait should do better on the overall assignment than students who do poorly on that trait. Items that do not follow this pattern are probably not working correctly; the top students are reading something into the item or assignment that wasn't intended.

Software for processing bubble sheet and online tests can calculate item discrimination. If software isn't available, these analyses aren't difficult to compute:

1. Sort the scored tests from highest to lowest total score.

2. Choose a manageable number of tests with the highest and lowest scores for further analysis. Depending on how many tests you have, you might choose the top and bottom thirds, the top and bottom fifths, or the ten tests at the top and bottom. Make sure you have exactly the same number of tests in the top and bottom groups.

3. For each group, count the number answering each item incorrectly (which is usually faster than counting the number answering each item correctly).

4. For each item, subtract the number of incorrect answers in the top group from the number of incorrect answers in the bottom group.

Exhibit 16.5 presents item discrimination results for a six-item objective test. Item 5 is an example of a question with very good discrimination. Only two students in the top group got this question wrong, while eight students in the bottom group got it wrong. This item clearly distinguishes the top students (as defined by this particular test) from the bottom ones. Item 4 is another example of a test question with good discrimination, although not quite as strong as for item 5.

Item 2 is an example of a question with no discrimination; in each group, four students got it wrong. Test experts would say that

Item Number	Number Incorrect in Top Group (Ten Students)	Number Incorrect in Bottom Group (Ten Students)	Difference (Bottom–Top)
1	0	0	0
2	4	4	0
3	0	1	1
4	2	5	3
5	2	8	6
6	6	2	−4

Exhibit 16.5. Examples of Item Discrimination Results

this is not an effective item—even a waste of testing time—because it doesn't help distinguish between the students who have learned a lot and the students who learned comparatively little.

Item 6 is an example of a question with negative discrimination: more top students got it wrong than bottom students. Items with negative discrimination are simply not working correctly. Because they unfairly penalize the top students who read too much into them, they should generally be thrown out and the tests rescored. They should definitely be discarded or revised when future editions of the test are prepared.

In order to interpret discrimination information correctly, the difficulty of each item must be taken into consideration. Item 1 is very easy (everyone in both groups got it correct), so of course there's no discrimination. Everyone in the top group got item 3 correct and only one person in the bottom group got it wrong, so while the discrimination of item 1 may not seem high, the item is so easy that this is the highest possible discrimination.

Rubric scores can be similarly analyzed for discrimination. If essays have been scored for organization, focus, and mechanics, for example, you can compare the papers with the highest overall scores against the papers with the lowest overall scores in terms of the ratings they earned on each criterion. If bottom-scoring papers generally score higher than top-scoring papers on, say, organization, you have an important clue that something isn't right with the assignment or with how faculty and staff scored the essays.

If you are stumped by why a particular multiple-choice question is so difficult or has poor discrimination, look at the number of top and bottom students who chose each option. Exhibit 11.3 includes an example of this kind of item analysis information. Sometimes one distracter is the source of the problem. Perhaps top students who really understood the tested concept misinterpreted and chose this distracter. Test questions with one or two poorly performing distracters can often be revised so the questions can be reused on future tests.

Do Other Assessments Corroborate Your Findings?

A student whose writing sample receives a high rubric score should also receive a high score on a published writing test and a high rating from her professor on her writing skills. Comparing results of various assessments against one another is called *corroboration* or *triangulation* and can be an important way to document the quality of an assessment strategy.

Do Results Fall in Appropriate Patterns?

Students at the end of a program should generally do better on an assessment than students at the beginning, and students with high grades should generally do better on an assessment than students with low grades. Some results should predict current or future performance; scores on a precalculus test, for example, should predict calculus grades at least somewhat accurately. And sometimes students should perform differently by major. Physics majors, for example, may appropriately score higher on a quantitative reasoning assessment, on average, than English majors.

Should You Analyze Your Results in Other Ways?

While many assessments are conducted simply to describe student learning, which can be done by summarizing results, others are intended to explain, predict, or explore, considering questions such as, "What kinds of students are most likely to drop out?" or "What instructional strategies most help students learn to think critically?" Using assessment results to answer these kinds of questions can be more interesting and useful than simply summarizing them. Examples of questions that can be answered through statistical analyses include the following:

- Why did students learn X but not Y?
- Why did some students master Z but others didn't?
- What high school courses best prepare students to do well in this program?
- Are there any relationships among results? Is there, for example, a relation between students' survey responses and

their grades? Is there a relation between students' test scores and whether they graduate or drop out?

Analyzing results to answer these kinds of questions generally requires a background in inferential statistics and a statistical software package. You may also need assessments that yield scaled or at least ordered results. If you're comfortable with inferential statistics, Chapter Six of *Questionnaire Survey Research: What Works* (Suskie, 1996) provides a series of charts to help choose an appropriate analysis. Keep in mind, however, that even statistical experts may disagree on the most appropriate analysis for particular results.

If you're not knowledgeable about inferential statistics, find people on your campus who can help. Ask your computer center, institutional research office, or faculty with backgrounds in educational or social science research methods for referrals to people with expertise in inferential statistics and appropriate software.

Documentation and Storage

The higher education community has way too many stories of assessment results that no one can find later, forcing everyone to begin anew and start everything from scratch. Make sure your results are securely saved, with backups. You may also wish to consider saving the following:

A listing of the raw data (each individual response or rating for each student). Once the results have been thoroughly checked and edited, you may want to delete identifying information, such as student names or ID numbers, to ensure confidentiality. If you want to preserve identifying information, store this list very securely. Don't leave it on a hard drive or server if there is any chance of unauthorized access. If you keep the list on paper, CD, or flash drive, store it in a locked drawer or cabinet.

Notes on coding. If any of your results are coded (say, "Excellent" is coded as 5), keep careful notes explaining the meaning of each code. The notes will minimize confusion and will be invaluable if anyone decides to repeat the assessment later.

Copies of completed student work, rubrics, surveys, tests, and the like. Sometimes an accreditor or other external audience expects or requires that these be kept on file. If so, you may want to explore technologies to store these documents electronically (Chapter Six). If these documents have identifying information, such as faculty name or student identification number, remove such information or store these documents very securely.

If you are not required to keep all these documents on file, think carefully about doing so, as maintaining these files can add significantly to the burden of assessment. Instead, keep just a few samples of student work on file. They can help you make sure your standards aren't inadvertently slipping over time, and they can provide firsthand evidence of your standards to accreditors and other external audiences ("This is an example of a paper we consider outstanding").

If you decide to keep samples of student work, be sure to keep a representative sample, not just your students' best work. Samples of student work that you judge barely adequate and inadequate are powerful evidence of your standards and rigor.

Time to Think, Discuss, and Practice _____

1. The business administration faculty have decided to use the rubric in Exhibit 9.2 to assess the oral presentation skills of students in the program's senior seminar. Decide if the results will be qualitative, categorical, ordered, scaled, or dichotomous.

2. Of three hundred Jameson College alumni responding to a survey, 74 percent said they were satisfied with the quality of their Jameson education. Calculate the error margin of this result, and write a sentence explaining the result and the error margin.

Recommended Readings _____

The following readings are recommended along with the references cited in this chapter.

Aronson, J. (1994). A pragmatic view of thematic analysis. *Qualitative Report, 2*(1). Retrieved September 16, 2008, from www.nova.edu/ssss/QR/BackIssues/QR2–1/aronson.html.

Carroll, S. R., & Carroll, D. J. (2002). *Statistics made simple for school leaders: Data-driven decision making.* Lanham, MD: Scarecrow Press.

Denzin, N. K., & Lincoln, Y. S. (2000). *Handbook of qualitative research* (2nd ed.). Thousand Oaks, CA: Sage.

Keller, D. K. (2005). *The Tao of statistics: A path to understanding (with no math).* Thousand Oaks, CA: Sage.

Krueger, R. A. (1998). *Analyzing and reporting focus group results* (Focus Group Kit, Vol. 6). Thousand Oaks, CA: Sage.

Mittler, M. L., & Bers, T. H. (1994). Qualitative assessment: An institutional reality check. In T. H. Bers & M. L. Mittler (Eds.), *Assessment and testing: Myths and realities* (pp. 61–67). New Directions for Community Colleges, no. 88. San Francisco: Jossey-Bass.

Patton, M. Q. (2002). *Qualitative research and evaluation methods* (3rd ed.). Thousand Oaks, CA: Sage.

Salkind, N. J. (2007). *Statistics for people who (think they) hate statistics* (3rd ed.). Thousand Oaks, CA: Sage.

Silverman, D. J. (2001). *Interpreting qualitative data: Methods for analyzing talk, text and interaction.* Thousand Oaks, CA: Sage.

Urdan, T. C. (2001). *Statistics in plain English.* Mahwah, NJ: Erlbaum.

CHAPTER 17

Sharing Assessment Results with Internal and External Audiences

---

Some Valuable Ideas You'll Find in This Chapter

- Look on sharing assessment results as an opportunity to tell an important story with a meaningful point.

- Use good teaching practices to share assessment results.

- The briefer your assessment information is, the more likely people will absorb it.

- Three kinds of information are most important to share with public audiences:

  - How you and your colleagues define a successful student

  - Whether you are satisfied with your evidence of student success

  - What you are doing about unsatisfactory results

- Tables, graphs, and other visuals may be more effective than traditional written reports.

Assessments are worthwhile only if the results are put to good use, and those uses can take place only after careful consideration and discussion. That consideration and discussion, in turn, can take place only if assessment results are communicated usefully, clearly, and accurately. How you share assessment results should therefore be planned as carefully as any other part of the assessment process.

When you share assessment results with an audience, you are in essence educating them about what you and your colleagues are doing and what you value. In other words, you are a teacher, and sharing results is, at its heart, a teaching process. Sharing results effectively thus means following good teaching practices (see Table 18.3), including the following, all discussed in this chapter:

- Understanding your audiences and their needs
- Helping your audiences see a synthesizing big picture
- Presenting your results in a variety of ways
- Actively involving your audiences

Be Open, Honest, Balanced, and Fair

A number of professional organizations engaged in the assessment of human performance have developed statements of ethical standards for assessment (Chapter Three). Virtually all of these statements agree that ethical assessment practices include sharing and using results in a fair and appropriate manner. This section describes strategies for doing so. Table 18.1 offers strategies to ensure that assessment results are used fairly, ethically, and responsibly, including discouraging others from making inappropriate interpretations.

Share only aggregated results. The suggestions in this chapter relate to sharing results for groups of students participating in an assessment. Results for individual students must be kept confidential, shared only with the student and the faculty and staff involved in his or her education (Chapter Three).

Present results completely, fairly, and objectively. This includes making available information on:

- The exact wording of survey and interview questions given to students
- How the participating students were selected and evidence that they are a representative, unbiased sample of the students you wanted to assess (Chapter Two)
- The number of students invited to participate, the number actually participating, and the participation rate (for example, "A random sample of fifty seniors was invited to participate in exit interviews. Twenty students, or 40 percent, of those invited participated")
- The precision of the results (Chapter Sixteen)

Give appropriate attribution to the work and ideas of others. Don't use items from someone else's test or survey in your own assessment instrument without obtaining permission from the author or copyright holder and acknowledging the contribution. If anyone provided financial support for your assessment, helped with the mechanics, assisted with data entry and analysis, or helped in any other way, it's only courteous to acknowledge that assistance and express appreciation for it—especially if you'd like that help again!

Document the author, originating office, and date. It's amazing how useless a report is if no one can remember who did it or when. For the sake of those pulling your results from a file or bringing up your Web site five years from now, note the author, the originating office, and the date of release. Consider carefully whom to list as author. While you may have done the actual work (and you should receive an acknowledgment of that), it may be more prudent to show the results as being released by, say, a committee or a dean's office. If these people are more visible than you are, the results may be given more attention. If the results are likely to be controversial, it may be wise to associate them with others.

Offer to make additional information available. As discussed later in this chapter, brief communications are more likely to engage your audiences in your findings. So you will need to balance the need to be complete and accurate with the need to be succinct. One way to do this is to offer to make available additional information on request. Your presentation might say that your findings are based on a review of a sample of fifty portfolios and that anyone interested in how the portfolios were chosen can contact you for more information. Don't be disappointed, however, by how few people take you up on your offer!

Understand Your Audiences and Their Needs _____

Planning an assessment begins with considering your audiences and their needs (Chapter Four). Review your plans to remind yourself of the answers to the following questions:

- Who are your audiences?
- What are their perspectives, needs, and priorities?
- What decisions do they need to make?
- What information do they need from your assessment in order to make those decisions?

Recall that your audiences may be external as well as internal and may be more interested in the accountability of your college or program than in improving it.

When in doubt, plan to share your results widely rather than narrowly. As Paula Gangopadhyay (2002) has noted, "The wider the outreach, the greater the impact." Richard Ekman and Stephen Pelletier (2008) have found that widespread reporting of results can engage entire campuses in conversations about how to improve student learning.

What Do Your Audiences Care About?

Connect your results to your audiences' interests and needs (Table 4.2). Within those interests, your audiences will be most concerned with the following:

Matters your audiences can do something about. If you are sharing results with faculty, point out results related to teaching and learning. If you are sharing results with student life staff, point out results related to out-of-class activities and student development. If you are sharing results with admissions staff, point out results that the staff might use to market the college or program to prospective students.

Interesting and unanticipated findings. Don't bother telling your audiences that science majors graduate with stronger math skills than literature majors, but do tell them that students who transferred from a local community college have stronger writing skills than students who started college at your institution. Don't bother telling your audiences that your Catholic students have largely Catholic parents, but do tell them that growing proportions of students are from upper-income households or that interest in extracurricular activities is well below the national average.

Meaningful differences. Don't emphasize, for example, that 15 percent of your program's students are African American when 16 percent of all students at your campus are African American. Keep in mind that a statistically significant difference may not be large enough to have any practical, meaningful significance, especially if you're assessing large numbers of students. In a survey of fifteen hundred students, for example, a 4 percent difference may be statistically significant but not large enough to merit special attention. It might be more appropriate to point out only differences of, say, 10 percent or more and thus focus your audiences on the major differences that deserve their consideration.

Table 17.1. Venues for Sharing Assessment Results Beyond Traditional Paper Reports

Web sites
E-mails and e-mail attachments
Newsletters
Alumni magazines
Department memos
Press releases to the student newspaper or regional media
Advertisements in the student newspaper
Brochures
Presentations at standing or special meetings of relevant campus groups
Handouts
Posters or banners

Also keep in mind that, as discussed in Chapter One, assessment is not controlled experimental research. Any significant differences—or lack thereof—may be due to factors beyond your control. If you are using a historical trends benchmark (Chapter Fifteen) and see an improvement in writing skills, for example, it may be that the improvement is simply because this year's class was better prepared in high school than last year's class.

How Do Your Audiences Prefer to Communicate and Receive Information?

Do your audiences prefer to receive information electronically, on paper, or at a meeting? Would they rather absorb information through text, numbers, or graphs? Observe which communication formats your audiences use most heavily, and take advantage of them. You'll probably find that the traditional report, written as a narrative and disseminated on paper, is the least popular communication venue. Table 17.1 suggests venues more likely to reach your audiences.

You may need to use different communication venues with different audiences. If you are assessing student learning in an academic program, you may want to prepare a detailed report for the department faculty, an executive summary for the dean, a Web page for prospective students and employers, a short summary for the college public relations office to use in press releases, and a visual presentation for the department's business advisory council. Sharing results with public audiences is discussed later in this chapter.

If you have multiple audiences, sketch out a dissemination plan listing who will receive information, what information will be shared with each group, in what venue and format, and when. This helps ensure that you don't inadvertently leave anyone out of the loop.

How Much Information Do Your Audiences Want and Need?

Are your audience members already familiar with the assessment, or will they need a complete description of what was done? Do they favor brevity or abundant information? Do they have time to study an extensive report? Will they want only findings and recommendations, or will they want to know how you arrived at your conclusions? Are they knowledgeable about empirical research methodology, or will you need to explain what you did in everyday language?

What If Your Audiences Will Feel Threatened by the Results?

No one likes to hear bad news. People who are directly affected by assessment results—or might be perceived as having had a role in them—will naturally feel threatened if the results are disappointing. Their instinct will be to "kill the messenger" by blaming the bad news on flaws in the assessment (Petrides & Nodine, 2005). If your assessment unearths a problem, get these audiences to focus on addressing the problem rather than attacking you or the assessment process. Try any of the following.

Consult with those who may feel threatened. People are less inclined to criticize something that they have helped to create. As discussed in Chapters Four and Five, include your audiences in planning the assessment. When you do so, discuss the possibility of disappointing results and how they might be communicated. Then, as soon as you suspect that your assessment may indeed yield disappointing results, talk to audience members with a stake in the results. (If students' general education quantitative skills are disappointing, for example, talk to faculty teaching those courses.) You may gain insight that explains your findings and modifies your conclusions. At the very least, you will have forewarned your colleagues so they can begin planning a response. If your colleagues have enough lead time, your report can include their plans to address those findings.

Balance negatives with positives.   Bad news is easier to digest if it's balanced with good news. Try sandwiching bad news between two positive outcomes, even if they're relatively minor.

Be gentle and sensitive.   Your audiences may bristle if you announce "bad news," a "serious problem," or a "failure." They may be more receptive if you present bad news as an "area of concern" or a "suggestion for further improvement." Rather than say, "The faculty is doing a poor job advising students," say, "Consider strengthening professional development opportunities for faculty on advising." Avoid pinning blame on individuals.

Provide corroborating information.   Additional information gathered on campus or through a review of research literature adds credibility to your findings.

Document the quality of your assessment strategy.   Chapter Sixteen suggests ways to do this. But be forewarned that no matter how extensive your efforts are to document the quality of your assessment strategies, you can never provide indisputable evidence of that quality to skeptics. You can never prove that your assessments are accurate and truthful; you can only collect evidence that your assessments appear to be accurate and truthful. In other words, no matter what you do, someone who wants to dispute your findings will always be able to poke a hole in your assessment strategy.

Acknowledge possible flaws in your assessment strategy.   Remember that all assessment methods are inherently imperfect and may not yield accurate information. Perhaps, through plain chance, you happened to sample the fifty worst student writing samples of the year. Assessments provide only indications of a problem, not proof of it. Often it's a good idea to repeat an assessment before concluding that changes are warranted, especially if the changes would be expensive or time-consuming.

Help audiences identify possible solutions.   Audiences may find bad news especially threatening if they see it as an insurmountable problem. Draw on research, your own experiences, and those of your colleagues to come up with practical suggestions for addressing problem areas. If you don't feel qualified to do this, sponsor a discussion of possible solutions.

Help Your Audiences See the Big Picture _____

Again remind yourself why you undertook this assessment. Then think about the big message you want to convey and the big things you want to accomplish by sharing the results. Perhaps you want to convince state officials of the quality of your college. Perhaps you want to initiate conversations across your campus on how best to improve the general education curriculum. Then help your audience clearly see your main message.

Tell a Story with a Meaningful Point

Assessment results should tell an important, coherent, interesting story. To give your results the most impact, try the following.

Make sure everything you include tells an important, interesting part of your story. Consider this paragraph from a hypothetical report on one fictitious college's participation in the Cooperative Institutional Research Program's annual Freshman Survey (2008):

> Between 78 percent and 80 percent of Lawndale College first-year students rely on family financial support. Lawndale first-year students are more likely to have student loans (48 percent) than first-year students nationally. Only 57 percent were dependent on grants, compared to 62 percent nationally.

What's the point of this paragraph? I don't know, and if I don't, the report's readers probably don't either, and they aren't going to spend time puzzling it out. Now consider these paragraphs on different results from the same survey at another fictitious college:

> First-year women at Kensington College have a stronger preparation for college than men. First-year women have, on average, earned higher grades in high school and have spent more time volunteering, studying, and participating in student clubs and groups. They are more likely attending college to "gain a general education," "learn more about things that interest me," "become a more cultured person," and "prepare for graduate study." It is more important to them to help others in difficulty, influence social values, and promote racial understanding.
>
> First-year men, on the other hand, are less likely than women to have completed high school homework on time and to have come to class on time. They have spent more time in high school playing sports, watching television, and working. Men are more likely attending to "make more money" and it is more important to men to

"be very well off financially." Despite their weaker preparation for college, men rate themselves higher in intellectual self-confidence, mathematics ability, competitiveness, originality, popularity, social self-confidence, physical health, and emotional health.

First-year men and women at this school both need help adjusting to college, but of vastly different kinds. Women need more self-confidence, while men need more help building academic skills and an appreciation of the broader benefits of a college education.

Because the Kensington report has a clearer point, people will probably pay more attention to it than to the Lawndale one, even though it's longer.

Use an engaging, meaningful title and headings. These help convince your audiences to read, view, or listen to your results. Headings should describe the point of an analysis ("Factors Affecting Grade Point Average") rather than the analysis itself ("Results of Multiple Regression Analysis"). Questions ("Why Do Students Drop Out?") can pique audience members' curiosity. Try writing your title and headlines like newspaper headlines that condense your principal findings. "Women Are Generally More Satisfied than Men" conveys more than "Differences Between Men and Women."

Open with something intriguing. Make your first statement or visual interesting and intriguing, like the lead sentence in a newspaper article.

Cascade from major points to details. Begin with an overall descriptive summary of the results. A simple table may be more effective than text. Include the error margin (Chapter Sixteen), which will help audience members judge which differences are truly meaningful.

Provide a context for your results. Explain very briefly why the assessment was done and what it was designed to find out. Summarize other information related to your assessment that's available from your campus or in research literature. If you are sharing results of a survey related to student retention, for example, give a brief summary of the research literature on student retention. If you are repeating an assessment conducted three years ago, compare past results with current findings. Explain how and why the contextual information supports—or doesn't support—your results.

Offer informed commentary. Make clear the implications of your results, as shown in the concluding paragraph above on Kensington College students. Explain how the results answer the questions that formed the purpose of the assessment and how the results relate to college or program priorities. Spur conversation by offering possible discussion questions suggested by the results.

You may even wish to suggest possible implications of the results for college and program policies and practices. Suggest possible conclusions and implications only if you don't mind being wrong about them! Before you offer them, discuss them with appropriate colleagues to make sure they seem logical and apropos. If you decide to offer recommendations, make them clear, well reasoned, practical, constructive, and concrete.

Keep Things Short

In today's busy world, few of us have time to wade through a lengthy report, sit through an extensive presentation, or click through endless Web pages. Most people want very brief summaries that highlight only key results. The shorter your communication, the more likely people will read, listen to, or view it, and the more likely your results will be put to good use.

Avoid the temptation, therefore, to report every result and every statistical analysis. While you may have found each detail of your assessment project fascinating, your audience probably won't. If a particular result doesn't make a meaningful contribution to your conclusions and will not help decision makers, leave it out. As Erin Harris and Suzanne Muchin (2002) have noted, "Most information is useless. Give yourself permission to dismiss it" (p. 4). Aim to give your audience just a quick overview of your principal findings and implications—no more than one or two pages, if you are conveying your results in writing. Exhibit 17.1 is an example of a brief but complete assessment report.

Exhibit 17.1. A Brief Assessment Report: The Effect of Learning Community Participation on First-Year Grade Point Averages

Does learning community participation compare first-year students' grades? The Office of Assessment compared the grade point averages (GPAs) of 177 learning community students against those of a random sample of 199 other first-year students. As shown in the graph below, the mean GPAs for *men* were 2.85 for those in learning communities and 2.30 for those not in learning communities, a statistically significant difference. The mean GPAs for *women* were 3.04 for those in learning communities and 3.01 for those not in learning communities, an insignificant difference.

Because students self-selected into the learning communities, we looked at some other possible factors. When we accounted for differences in high school GPA, our findings remained the same. Variations in SAT Verbal and Math scores and in student majors also did not affect our overall conclusions. Please let us know if you would like any details on these analyses.

Our overall conclusions are that, on average, (1) participating in a learning community improves the grade point averages of men and (2) women do well academically regardless of whether or not they're in a learning community.

Grade Point Averages of Men and Women In and Out of Learning Communities

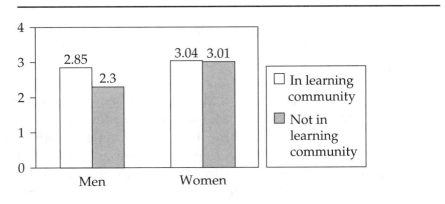

	Men		Women	
	In Learning Community	Not in Learning Community (Random Sample)	In Learning Community	Not in Learning Community (Random Sample)
Total number of students	58	75	119	124
Average GPA	2.85	2.30	3.04	3.01
Undecided major	31%	41%	22%	29%
Average high school GPA	3.28	3.20	3.49	3.49
Average SAT–Verbal	574	524	559	534
Average SAT–Math	582	564	536	541

Note: Percentages may not sum to 100 percent due to rounding.

Sometimes one brief report won't meet all your audiences' needs. You may need to prepare a series of brief reports or presentations, each targeted to a particular audience. If you have surveyed a sample of graduating seniors, for example, you might share their opinions of library resources only with the library staff.

Some audiences, such as assessment steering committees, accreditors, and state agencies, need comprehensive information on assessment activities and results. Some want to see representative samples of student work or other documented evidence of student learning, as discussed in Chapter Sixteen. But even these audiences benefit from a snapshot that orients them to the overall status of your college's assessment efforts. Exhibits 19.4 and 19.5 are examples of templates that might be used to provide such snapshots. Organize the supporting information carefully (perhaps with hyperlinks to online documents) so that your audiences have no problem finding whatever they want to see.

Keep Things Simple and Clear

Your audience members may not have time or inclination to scrutinize a scholarly missive filled with dense prose. Make it easy for your audience to discern your key points.

Avoid jargon. Some audience members may have a limited assessment vocabulary, so use language that everyone will easily understand. Avoid technical terms, formulas, statistical symbols, and research jargon such as *aggregate, variable, subject,* or *population.* Spell out every abbreviation the first time it is used. Explain statistical analyses in lay terms. The following paragraph describes a discriminant analysis without using that term:

> The analysis split the students responding to the survey into three groups: 462 students who returned or graduated, 50 students who were dismissed from the college for poor academic performance, and 92 students who voluntarily left without graduating. The three groups were then compared to identify distinguishing characteristics of each group.

Use numbers sparingly. Use figures only when they're necessary or inherently interesting. Mathphobes' eyes will glaze over a paragraph like the following:

> A greater percentage of Cape Anne College students are first-generation college students than nationally. Exactly 40% of fathers and 48% of mothers have never attended college, compared to 37% of fathers and 40% of mothers nationally. Over 36% of fathers of Cape Anne

freshmen are college graduates, while nearly 27% of mothers have college degrees.

Now consider this rewrite:

The parents of Cape Anne College students are not quite as well educated as those of students nationally; they are less likely to have attended college or earned a college degree.

The second paragraph, with no figures, communicates its point far more clearly than the first. Often it is sufficient to say something is more or less, or above or below average, without getting into figures. The rewritten paragraph is also more effective because it is more succinct; it tells in one sentence what the original paragraph said in three.

Round figures to the nearest whole number. Stating that 10.3 percent said X and 10.5 percent said Y encourages readers to focus on trivial, statistically insignificant differences and unnecessarily increases the number of digits that mathphobes must absorb.

Have a friend review your draft. Even if he or she knows nothing about assessment or statistics, a friend should be able to understand the purpose of your assessment, your basic findings, your conclusions, and why you drew them.

Present Your Results in a Variety of Ways

Not everyone learns best in the same way, as discussed in Chapter Three. Some people learn best by reading, others by absorbing visual information, others by listening, and others by interacting with one other. Your chances of getting your message across are therefore best if you use a variety of formats.

Face-to-face presentations and online presentations are especially effective communication venues, because they allow audience members to receive information through multiple formats. Online presentations let audience members read and view visuals such as tables, graphs, and slides. Face-to-face presentations also let audience members listen and discuss. These formats collectively create a better learning experience for your audiences than any of them would alone.

Multiple formats are especially effective if they build on rather than replicate each other. If you are giving an oral presentation accompanied by slides, for example, don't fill the slides with text and then read them aloud. Instead, put just a few key words on the slides and then elaborate on the points in your remarks.

Regardless of the presentation format you choose, you'll need to help your audiences absorb your results and not simply file or discard them. Today people increasingly expect to absorb information in short "bytes" from well-organized, eye-catching Web sites, short articles, brief video clips, and visuals such as simple charts and graphs. Emulate these media approaches to engage your audiences in your message. If you work with faculty in communications, tap their expertise for more ideas.

Tables and Graphs

Tables present series of tallies (Chapter Sixteen) succinctly and make comparisons easy. Line graphs can summarize ordered or scaled results (Chapter Sixteen) and show historical trends, while bar graphs can summarize virtually any type of quantitative assessment results. Tables and graphs can be created quickly using spreadsheet or presentation software. Exhibits 16.1 and 16.2 are examples of tables, and Exhibit 17.1 contains a table and graph.

A picture is worth a thousand words only if it is a good one! The key points of tables and graphs should almost jump out at the reader. Table 17.2 offers suggestions for creating good tables and graphs.

Exhibit 17.2 is an example of a poorly designed table of one fictitious school's results for a portion of the Cooperative Institutional Research Program's Freshman Survey (2008). The table's flaws?

- *There are too many columns*—so many that vertical lines must be inserted to make them readable.

- *The table presents too much information.* One can use this table to compare men to women, the entire class against two sets of national averages, men against two sets of national averages for men, and women against two sets of national averages for women.

- *The percentages are not rounded,* so some readers will focus on trivial differences, such as that 11.5 percent of St. Stephen's freshmen and 11.9 percent of freshmen at all universities expect to change career choice.

- *The table doesn't point out any meaningful differences.* The reader must do the math to decide which differences are big and which aren't.

- *The items aren't arranged in any particular order* (other than, perhaps, the order on the survey).

Because of these flaws, the table tells no story and has no apparent point. Few readers will derive anything meaningful from it.

Table 17.2. Tips for Creating Effective Tables and Graphs

Give each table and graph a meaningful, self-explanatory title. "Student Responses" won't do it; "Freshman Self-Ratings of Critical Thinking Skills" will.

Label every part of a table or graph clearly. Label each table column and each graph axis, avoiding abbreviations.

Make each table and graph self-explanatory. Some audience members won't read any accompanying text. Use headings or footnotes in the table or graph to provide definitions, assumptions, and notes to interpret the table or graph properly.

If there are many possible results, group them. Showing the percentages of students scoring 90–100, 80–89, and so on makes it easier for your audience to visualize the results of a 100-point test.

Make it easy for readers to see differences and trends. If a table is presenting results from this year's and last year's assessments, add a third column showing the amount of change. If your table is comparing male and female students, add a third column showing the differences between their results.

Avoid putting too much information into a table or graph. If you find that you must insert vertical lines into a table to make it clear, you have too many columns or figures. Break your results into two or more tables or simply delete some information.

Present your results in an order that makes sense to readers and helps convey your point. Listing results in their order on the original assessment instrument is neither interesting nor enlightening. Present your results with the most frequently chosen responses or highest scores at the top, so readers can quickly discern relative successes and areas of concern. Because people expect scales to increase from left to right, when you are presenting trends over time put the oldest information on the left and the most recent on the right.

Draw attention to the point you want your table or graph to make. Use boldface, italics, borders, colors, "bright lines" (highlighting), and fonts to draw attention to your most important figures. If you are comparing your college against peers, put your college's results in boldface. In a graph of student responses about proposed changes to current policies, use a different color for the bar representing current policy.

Don't assume a software-generated table or graph is readable. Some software default settings generate distorted tables and graphs or provide poor labels if any. Use software options to make your table or graph readable and distortion-free.

Date each table and graph and note its source. Readers may share tables and graphs with colleagues without the accompanying text.

Now compare Exhibit 17.2 with the revision in Exhibit 17.3. This has several improvements:

- *The gender results have been eliminated,* simplifying the table. (If the author wants to make a point of gender differences, those results can be put in a separate table.)

- *Only one set of national norms is presented*—the set that the author feels is of greatest interest.

- *The first column has been right justified,* so it's easier for the reader to read the correct figures for each item.

Exhibit 17.2. A Poorly Designed Table

Percentage of first-year students saying chances are very good that they will:	St. Stephen's University			All Universities			All Private Universities		
	Men	Women	All	Men	Women	All	Men	Women	All
Change major field	13.4%	13.2%	13.3%	11.7%	12.7%	12.2%	13.0%	13.4%	13.3%
Change career choice	10.9%	11.9%	11.5%	10.8%	12.8%	11.9%	11.4%	12.6%	12.1%
Get a job to help pay for college expenses	32.5%	42.1%	38.3%	35.2%	41.9%	38.8%	33.0%	41.1%	37.5%
Make at least a B average	48.3%	53.5%	51.4%	42.3%	44.3%	43.3%	40.8%	43.3%	42.2%
Need extra time to complete your degree requirements	7.9%	8.3%	8.1%	8.3%	9.7%	9.0%	9.6%	10.3%	10.0%
Get a bachelor's degree	72.5%	81.1%	77.7%	63.7%	69.0%	66.6%	70.5%	76.1%	73.6%
Be satisfied with your college	61.2%	75.2%	69.7%	44.2%	55.6%	50.4%	43.1%	53.2%	48.8%

Exhibit 17.3. An Improved Version of Exhibit 17.2

Percentage of first-year students saying chances are very good that they will:	St. Stephen's University	All Private Universities	Difference
Get a bachelor's degree	78%	74%	+4%
Be satisfied with your college	70%	49%	+21%
Make at least a B average	51%	42%	+9%
Get a job to help pay for college expenses	38%	38%	—
Change major field	13%	13%	—
Change career choice	12%	12%	—
Need extra time to complete your degree requirements	8%	10%	22%

- *All figures have been rounded* to the nearest whole percent, simplifying the table and encouraging readers to focus on only relatively sizable differences.
- *Differences between local results and national norms have been added* in a new column.
- *The items have been ordered* from greatest agreement to least agreement.

These changes make it much easier for readers to discern the major story the table is trying to tell: first-year students at St. Stephen's are generally more optimistic about college than their peers at other private universities.

Chapter Twelve describes ecosystem rating scales, a format that asks for two ratings, such as satisfaction with and importance of various services. The second rating gives information on the environment in which the first rating is made, thus helping to interpret the first rating. Ecosystem results are best presented in a matrix, such as Figure 17.1, which summarizes the results of the ecosystem rating scale in Exhibit 12.3.

This matrix shows four very different kinds of results:

Item 1: Students reported a high skill level and also a high degree of help from library sessions. This is the best possible response.

Item 2: Students reported a high skill level but a low degree of help from library sessions. While this outcome is good,

Figure 17.1. A Matrix for Summarizing Ecosystem Rating Scale Results

	Skill Level	
Library Session Help	Low	High
High	Item 3	Item 1
Low	Item 4	Item 2

the value of the library sessions is questionable. One could ask if the college's investment in these sessions is a wise use of its limited resources.

Item 3: Students reported a low skill level but a high degree of help from library sessions. While this outcome is disappointing, the library sessions appear nonetheless valuable to a certain extent. Perhaps one of the major outcomes of the sessions has been helping students realize how much they have to learn.

Item 4: Students reported a low skill level and a low degree of help from library sessions. This is the most disappointing outcome, of course.

This example shows how the second ratings help us understand the first ones. If we looked only at students' reported skills levels, we would have concluded that the first two items are good news and the second two identify problem areas. Adding context from the second rating shows that the results are more complex and call for different kinds of responses.

Reports, Executive Summaries, and Handouts

If you decide that a report or handout is an effective way to share assessment results with your audience, Table 17.3 offers suggestions on ways to make your message visually interesting and engaging.

If you are creating handouts to accompany a presentation, limit them to simple tables, graphs, and bulleted lists so readers can quickly digest them and grasp your point. If you have several handouts, considering duplicating them on paper in a variety of colors to help audience members locate them quickly ("Now please turn to the chart on green paper").

Slides and Posters

An increasingly popular means of sharing assessment results is through slides or posters created with presentation software either to accompany oral presentations or to be disseminated

Table 17.3. Tips for Creating Effective Reports and Handouts

Use plenty of headings and subheadings to help readers who will only scan the report to find quickly what interests them.

Use different fonts for headings, subheadings, and your key points to draw attention to them.

Use bulleted lists that readers can quickly scan.

Use "pull quotes": important statements taken from your text and repeated in a margin or sidebar to ensure that your major points aren't missed.

Insert simple tables and graphs.

electronically. These tips will help you create effectives lides.

Keep slides and posters simple, uncluttered, and readable. Use bulleted lists rather than paragraphs, limiting the number of bullets per slide to five or six. Use animation effects, such as fades and dissolves sparingly, only when they emphasize your main points or help the audience move from one point to the next. Frequent, dazzling animation effects will distract your audience, and your points will be lost.

Keep the text to just a few key words that emphasize your major points. If a slide accompanying an oral presentation has more than a few words, your audience will focus on reading it rather than listening to you.

Use large font size. For slides, use at least a 36-point font size for major headings and 24-point for text. Make sure that those in the farthest seats can easily read the projected slides. If the text, list, chart, or graph is too detailed to present on a slide using a large font size, share it through a handout instead.

Oral Remarks

Keep your remarks short and informal, and concentrate on your findings. Rather than read from a prepared text, keep your presentation fresh by using a bulleted list to remind you of what to say.

You may wish to consider asking someone else to make the presentation or copresent it with you. Having someone viewed as important (say, a dean or senior faculty member) make the presentation may help your assessment results be received more seriously. If you are uncomfortable with public speaking, having a dynamic speaker help with the presentation may make it more effective.

Actively Involve Your Audiences _____

We have all sat through lectures and presentations that were interesting and informative but didn't inspire us to change our thinking or actions. You want to do more than entertain: you want your audience to think about your findings and leave with a sense of commitment to act on them. The key to getting audience members to do this is to engage them in a structured discussion that will lead to action. The suggestions in Table 17.4 will help achieve this end.

Table 17.4. Tips to Engage Your Audiences

Plan to speak for no more than half of the time that you've been allotted, allowing the rest of the time for questions and discussion.

Remain in charge. While it's fine to allow questions and comments during the presentation portion of your allotted time, don't let such remarks eat up your time and derail your presentation. Don't be shy about saying, "This are great questions, but I'm afraid I have time for only one more," or "This is a great discussion and I hate to interrupt it, but I have several more points that I want to share with you."

Launch a structured conversation when you conclude your remarks by listing a few discussion questions on your last slide, such as:

What was the most important thing you learned today?

What one thing most surprised you?

How can we use this information to help our students?

If your group is too large for you to call on everyone, use minute papers (Chapter Twelve) or break your audience into small groups to discuss your questions. Each small group can then share its key responses with the entire group.

Record the answers to discussion questions on a flip chart, white board, or other medium visible to everyone in the audience. If you can't write legibly, ask someone else to do this for you.

Transcribe the answers and send them to the participants, who can use them as the starting point for an action plan.

Sharing Results with Public Audiences

Public audiences, particularly those more interested in accountability than improvement (Chapter Four), may not be familiar with your college or program and may not have the time or inclination to get thoroughly acquainted with it. Calls for accountability represent an opportunity to educate them. As Lee Shulman (2007) has noted, "The current quest for accountability creates a precious opportunity for educators to tell the full range of stories about learning and teaching" (p. 25). Jo Allen (2006) has endorsed this, noting that "assessment results offer tremendous potential to speak proactively to legislators and the general public about excellence, value, and the results of self-imposed accountability in higher education" (p. 5).

It is especially important to convey to your public audiences—clearly, compellingly, and briefly—your college's or program's aims, including your goals for your students and how you define success. Table 17.5 provides a list of questions that colleges might wish to answer when they tell the story of their effectiveness to audiences interested in accountability. Table 17.6 offers tips on how to tell the story in a way that best suits your college's mission, culture, and values.

Try to tell your story in the context of what your public audience wants to hear. Table 4.2 lists the questions and decisions of greatest interest to various internal and external audiences. If

Table 17.5. Key Information to Share with Public Audiences

How do we define a successful student? What knowledge, skills, and competencies does he or she have? Why do we think these are important?

What evidence do we have that students meet our definition of success?

How effective are we in ensuring that students are achieving their goals (for example, earning a degree or a promotion at work) in a timely fashion?

Are we satisfied with our results? Why or why not? If not, what are we doing about it?

How else do we define institutional success? What else is in our mission? What evidence do we have of institutional success? Are we satisfied with the results? Why or why not? If not, what are we doing about it?

Possible additional questions for prospective students and their families:
 What makes our college distinctive?
 What kinds of students do we aim to serve? What kinds do we actually enroll?
 What are we doing to provide students with optimal learning experiences? To what extent do we engage in research-based teaching-learning practices?

Possible additional questions for policymakers, as appropriate to the college's mission:
How effective are we in making our college affordable? Being efficient and cost-effective? Ensuring access to the disadvantaged? Meeting local, regional, and national needs?

Table 17.6. Tips for Telling the Story of Your College's Effectiveness

Justify why this story is appropriate for your college.

Provide a brief narrative and analysis, as well as numbers and facts.

Make the story easy to find. This usually means a Web page that's easy to find and reach from the college's home page.

Make the story easy to understand. Use very short, simple charts and graphics rather than long tables and lengthy text.

Keep the story succinct. Many audiences want the story in twenty-five words or less!

Resist calls to use particular prescribed measures—such as particular retention or graduation rates, particular published instruments, comparable measures, and value-added measures—without considering how appropriate they are for your circumstances. Remember that every measure of effectiveness is imperfect, as discussed in Chapter Three.

Feel free to direct audiences to public information resources on your college if you think the information is appropriate and helpful. Table 15.3 lists some public information resources that may include information on your college. Generally, though, these resources won't be sufficient to tell the story of your college. You will need to provide additional information germane to your college's distinctive mission, goals, student body, and culture.

your audience is especially interested in the cost of an education at your college, tell the story of what students learn in terms of "return on investment."

Sharing Positive Results with Public Audiences

Surprisingly, this may be easier said than done! The higher education community has a long-standing culture of keeping its light under the proverbial bushel basket and not sharing the story of its successes with its public audiences. Because of this culture, it can be remarkably difficult for faculty and staff to see successes for what they are and to share them with public audiences in clear, understandable ways. Table 17.1 suggests venues for sharing assessment results with various audiences. Consider the following.

- *Include positive results in materials for prospective students and employees.* They will be attracted to your program or college when they see solid evidence of its quality. As Jo Allen (2006) has noted, "People like to be associated with excellence" (p. 5).

- *Send a brief summary to prospective employers.* They will be more likely to hire your graduates when they see convincing evidence of their knowledge and skills.

- *Send a brief summary to your fundraising staff and your president.* They will be delighted to have solid evidence to share with prospective donors that your program or college is worthy of investment.

- *Ask the campus public relations office to send a press release* of especially exciting results to local media and policymakers.

Sharing Disappointing Results with Public Audiences

Because public audiences may not have the time or inclination to digest results thoroughly, they may misinterpret disappointing results or respond rashly, perhaps by imposing mandates or moving their support elsewhere. To compound the problem, media may spread misleading information further.

Two strategies are especially important in telling any potentially disappointing parts of your story. First, balance negatives with positives. As suggested earlier in this chapter, try sandwiching bad news between two positive outcomes. Second, present disappointing results as the basis for improvement initiatives. Announcing that students have unsatisfactory writing skills is one thing; announcing a major initiative to improve student writing skills, based on assessment results, sends a very different message. As Larry Braskamp and Steven Schomberg (2006) have noted, assessment "always needs to point to some action." Reporting not only your findings but also plans to address those findings gives your public announcements a very positive "problem-solved" spin.

Time to Think, Discuss, and Practice _____

1. The writing skills of students completing the first-year composition course at your college have been assessed using

the ABC Writing Test. The results have come back, and they're very disappointing: on average, students score well below the national mean on every characteristic of effective writing assessed by the test. Discuss how you might constructively communicate this information to the faculty who teach first-year composition.

2. Review exercise 3 in Chapter Fifteen:

- What are the main points that you would want the college's board of trustees to understand about the results of this assessment?

Table 17.7. Selected Results from the 2008 National Survey of Student Engagement: How Often Students at Rodney College Report Engaging in Various Learning Activities During Their Senior Year

	Average Frequency[A]	
	At Rodney College	At All Institutions Participating in the Survey
Asked questions in class or contributed to class discussions	3.02	3.10
Made a class presentation	2.91	2.81
Prepared two or more drafts of a paper or assignment before turning it in	2.46	2.50
Worked on a paper or project that required integrating ideas or information from various sources	3.33	3.33
Worked with other students on projects during class	2.65*	2.45
Worked with classmates outside of class to prepare class assignments	2.70	2.72
Put together ideas or concepts from different courses when completing assignments or during class discussions	2.77	2.82
Participated in a community-based project (e.g., service learning) as part of a regular course	1.53	1.59
Used an electronic medium (Listserv, chat group, Internet, instant messaging, etc.) to discuss or complete an assignment	2.92*	2.76
Used e-mail to communicate with an instructor	3.13	3.07
Discussed grades or assignments with an instructor	2.85	2.81
Discussed ideas from your readings or classes with faculty members outside of class	1.97	2.09
Received prompt written or oral feedback from faculty on your academic performance	2.75	2.81

*Difference between Rodney and national averages is statistically significant ($p < .05$).
[A]4 = Very often, 3 = Often, 2 = Sometimes, 1 = Never.

- Develop a summary (table, graph, slide, text, or some combination of these) that conveys those main points clearly, succinctly, and understandably.

3. Table 17.7 presents part of results of the National Survey of Student Engagement (Indiana University, 2007) for seniors at a fictitious college. You have been asked to prepare a short summary of these results for the college's senior administrators.

- What are the main points that you would want the college's senior administrators to understand about these results?

- Develop a summary (table, graph, slide, and/or text) that conveys those main points clearly, succinctly, and understandably.

Recommended Readings

The following readings are recommended along with the references cited in this chapter.

Bers, T. H., with Seybert, J. A. (1999). *Effective reporting* (Resources in Institutional Research, no. 12). Tallahassee, FL: Association for Institutional Research.

Eline, L. (Ed.). (1997). *How to prepare and use effective visual aids.* Alexandria, VA: American Society for Training and Development.

Fraenkel, J. R., Wallen, N. E., & Sawin, E. I. (1999). *Visual statistics: A conceptual primer.* Needham Heights, MA: Allyn & Bacon.

Hendricks, M. (1994). Making a splash: Reporting evaluation results effectively. In J. S. Wholey, H. P. Hatry, & K. E. Newcomer (Eds.), *Handbook of practical program evaluation* (pp. 549–575). San Francisco: Jossey-Bass.

Kuh, G. D. (2007). Risky business: Promises and pitfalls of institutional transparency. *Change, 39*(1), 31–35.

Lilley, S. (2002). *How to deliver negative evaluation results constructively: Ten tips for evaluators.* Retrieved September 16, 2008, from www.chebucto.ns.ca/ ~LilleyS/tips.html.

Pike, G. R. (2008). Assessment measures: Making accountability transparent: Next steps for the voluntary system of accountability. *Assessment Update, 20*(2), 8–9, 12.

Statistical Services Centre. (2000). *Informative presentation of tables, graphs and statistics.* Reading, UK: University of Reading.

Wainer, H. (1992). Understanding graphs and tables. *Educational Researcher, 21*(1), 14–23.

Wainer, H. (Ed.). (1993). Making readable overhead displays. *Chance: New Directions for Statistics and Computing, 6*(2), 46–49.

Wainer, H. (2000). *Visual revelations: Graphical tales of fate and deception from Napoleon Bonaparte to Ross Perot.* Mahwah, NJ: Erlbaum.

Wallgren, A., Wallgren, B., Persson, R., Jorner, U. K., & Haaland, J-A. (1996). *Graphing statistics and data: Creating better charts.* Thousand Oaks, CA: Sage.

CHAPTER 18

Using Assessment Results Effectively and Appropriately

Some Valuable Ideas You'll Find in This Chapter

- Actively discourage inappropriate interpretations or uses of assessment results.
- Prevent problems with closing the loop by carefully planning your assessment.
- While positive assessment *results* should be celebrated, even more recognition and reward should go to exemplary and improved assessment *efforts.*
- Students learn and remember more when we focus on just a few key learning goals than when we address many superficially.
- Hands-on practice and visual information are far more effective ways to learn than listening to lectures.
- Give funding priority to pervasive rather than isolated problems to encourage collaboration rather than competition over scarce funds.

Assessment reports that end up briefly perused and then filed without any resulting action are, to be blunt, a waste of time. Chapter Three opened by noting that good assessments are those whose results are *used* to improve teaching and learning and inform planning and budgeting decisions.

Making good use of assessment findings can be one of the most difficult phases of assessment. Recall a characteristic of assessment first discussed in Chapter One: assessment results should never dictate decisions; we should always use our professional judgment to interpret assessment results and make appropriate decisions. This is not easy! Getting everyone to agree on what changes should be made can be daunting.

This chapter provides some frameworks and considerations to guide your thinking on how best to use results to improve teaching and learning and inform planning and budgeting decisions. Using results to demonstrate accountability is essentially sharing results with relevant public audiences, which Chapter Seventeen discusses.

Use Results Fairly, Ethically, and Responsibly

The principles of good practice stressed throughout this book and summarized in Table 18.1 are essential to ensuring ongoing assessment efforts. Lisa Petrides and Thad Nodine (2005) have found that how assessment results have been used in the past has a significant effect on people's willingness to participate in gathering and using assessment information.

Know What You're Looking For

It's all too easy to plunge into assessment without a clear sense of what you're trying to find out or how the assessment you're undertaking relates to what you're trying to teach. Suppose that Strasburg College has decided, without much discussion, to administer the XYZ Critical Thinking Test to its students. The tests are scored, and the college community learns that its students average 145, far lower than the national average of 175. The community is plunged into a quandary, and questions fly:

- Why did our students do so badly?
- Why are we testing critical thinking?
- Why did we choose this particular test?
- What is critical thinking, anyway?
- Whose fault is this? Who is supposed to be teaching critical thinking, and in what courses?
- How are we supposed to teach critical thinking?

Table 18.1. Using Assessment Results Fairly, Ethically, and Responsibly

Make assessments planned and purposeful. Start with a cogent understanding of why you are assessing (Chapter Four), including a clear sense of the decisions your assessment results inform.

Focus assessments on important learning goals.

Assess teaching and learning processes as well as outcomes, because they help us understand the outcomes (Chapter Two).

Actively involve those with a stake in decisions stemming from the results (Chapter Five). Involve them in planning the assessment as well as discussing and using the results.

Communicate assessment information widely and transparently (Chapter Seventeen). People who aren't aware of assessment results certainly can't use them.

Discourage others from making inappropriate interpretations or otherwise false or misleading statements about assessment results. Make clear that every assessment strategy is imperfect and imprecise, along with any other appropriate qualifiers and caveats regarding your conclusions. You might want to caution your audience, for example, about a low participation rate, possible student misinterpretations of a test question, or the underrepresentation of men in the students you surveyed.

Don't hold people accountable for things they cannot do (Ewell, 2002), such as failing to meet an inappropriately high graduation rate target.

Don't penalize faculty and staff whose assessment results are less than positive.

Don't let assessment results dictate decisions. Using a single assessment score as a sole gatekeeper graduation or progression requirement is an unethical use of assessment results (Chapter Three). Assessments should only advise us as we use our professional judgment to make suitable decisions. *Failure to adhere to this maxim is one of the major shortcomings of many high-stakes testing programs.*

Promote the use of multiple sources of information when making any major decision (Chapter Three).

Keep faculty, students, and staff informed on how assessment findings support major decisions.

- How can we possibly boost critical thinking scores in all our students when no required courses emphasize critical thinking?

Most of these questions could have been avoided if the college had begun its assessment work with clear answers to at least the following questions, all addressed earlier in this book:

- Why are we assessing (Chapter Four)? Are we aiming to improve our program or validate it? Who are our audiences for this assessment (Table 4.1)? What decisions will this assessment help us and our audiences make (Table 4.2)?

- What are our most important student learning goals (Chapter Eight)? Do we have a common understanding of what fuzzy terms like *critical thinking* mean?

- Do we have a clear strategy in place to ensure that every student has adequate opportunity to achieve each of our major goals (Chapter Seven)?

- Do the assessment tools and techniques that we're considering clearly correspond to our student learning goals as we define them (Part Three)?

- Have we set targets against which to compare our results (Chapter Fifteen)? Do we know what level of student performance is good enough?

Much of the difficulty that campuses face in closing the loop could thus be prevented by focusing more on the kind of planning described in Chapters Four and Seven. Often the major outcome of an ill-conceived assessment strategy is bringing attention back to the need for careful planning, yielding a more useful assessment strategy on the second try.

Celebrate Good Assessment Results

Suppose that in blind reviews, faculty score 85 percent of anthropology senior theses "outstanding" in terms of clarity, organization, comprehensiveness of review of scholarly literature, and soundness of analysis and conclusions. Five percent are scored "very good," 5 percent "adequate," and 5 percent "inadequate." What might the anthropology faculty do with this information?

Because the purpose of assessment is usually to improve teaching and learning, it's easy to focus on problem areas and not see, let alone celebrate, positive findings. In this example, the faculty may need help recognizing that the results are very good on the whole. Once they acknowledge this, celebrate good results, perhaps in one or more of these ways:

- Provide a public forum for students to present their work, such as a student research conference

- Recognize students for outstanding work

- Host a party for students, faculty, and staff

- Make outstanding papers available to other students as models (first obtaining written permission from the papers' authors)

Good assessment results should be not only celebrated but also shared, and Chapter Seventeen suggests ways to do this.

While good results should be celebrated, think twice about rewarding them in substantial ways, such as with budget supplements. These can tempt faculty and staff to twist or distort their results to look as good as possible instead of focusing on results that identify areas for improvement.

Rewards for good results may also simply recognize the status quo. If one program is especially popular with students, it may be especially selective. If its students graduate with especially strong writing or thinking skills, this may be due solely to these underlying factors and not to any special effort by the faculty and staff.

Thus, while good assessment results should be celebrated, even more recognition and reward should go to exemplary and improved assessment *efforts*, as discussed in Chapters Five, Six, and Nineteen. On a regular basis, take time to recognize and honor those who have made significant contributions to creating an assessment culture on your campus. They are laying the groundwork for even stronger assessment efforts in the years to come.

What About the "Inadequate" 5 Percent?

Should the anthropology faculty be concerned about the "inadequate" 5 percent in the example above? Here are some questions to help faculty decide:

- *Are we certain that these papers are inadequate?* Score the inadequate papers twice, using separate scorers, to confirm the scores before taking any further action.

- *Does other evidence corroborate these results?* As noted in Chapters Three and Fifteen, consider multiple measures of student learning before making any major decisions. Look at other work these students have produced before coming to conclusions about their performance level.

- *How many students are we talking about?* If a program graduates twenty students a year, we are talking about only one student—hardly enough to warrant wholesale revisions in curriculum or teaching methods. Repeat the assessment next year, and possibly the year after, before deciding that this is an ongoing problem.

- *Is it appropriate to expect perfection?* Chapter Fifteen explains several reasons that it may be inappropriate to expect every student to demonstrate adequate performance.

Can Results Be Too Good?

Some faculty and staff might be concerned about the large proportion of students in this example who earned high scores. If 85 percent of senior theses are judged outstanding, are the standards too low? If the scores are based on clear, challenging criteria, high scores simply reflect a very successful learning experience. But it may be worthwhile to review those standards and discuss whether they should be ratcheted up a bit.

Address Disappointing Assessment Results _____

As the example of the XYZ Critical Thinking Test that opened this chapter demonstrated, causes of and solutions for disappointing results are rarely obvious. Any of four components of the teaching and learning process—learning goals, curriculum, teaching methods, and assessment strategy—may contribute to disappointing results.

Two ground rules for addressing disappointing results have been emphasized repeatedly throughout this book. First, don't try to brush disappointing results under the carpet. Remember that the primary purpose of assessment is to improve student learning, and addressing disappointing results can help achieve this aim. Second, don't be punitive. The fastest way to kill an assessment effort is to use less-than-positive results to deny tenure, promotion, or merit pay to individual faculty members or to cut a department's budget or program. Even the vaguest rumor of such a possibility will seriously impede assessment efforts.

Consider Your Learning Goals

Ask the following questions about your learning goals:

Do we have too many goals? Can a typical student truly be expected to achieve all the goals that have been identified for a course or program? Time on task is a major contributor to deep, lasting learning (Table 18.3). Students will learn and remember more if you focus on just a few key learning goals than if you address many superficially. If you have too many goals, you and your colleagues must decide which ones to emphasize and which to deemphasize. These discussions go to the heart of what faculty value, and discussions can become contentious. Chapter Eight offers suggestions for refining goals collaboratively.

Are our goals appropriate? It's unrealistic, for example, to expect to turn an incompetent writer into one capable of writing a senior thesis in just one semester. Similarly, faculty can't prepare a student who has taken only high school business mathematics to succeed in calculus in one semester—or even two. Student life staff can't expect students to become outstanding leaders in a one-week leadership program. Librarians can't expect students to master a full array of information literacy skills in a one-hour bibliographic instruction class. Consider whether your goals need to be scaled back to levels that challenge students but are realistic.

Should we clarify or refine our goals?   Suppose that Conestoga College biology majors score poorly on the botany section of the ABC Biology Test. Some biology faculty feel this is not a concern, because virtually all Conestoga biology graduates go on to careers in health fields, where they don't need a strong background in botany. Other faculty hold that grounding in botany is essential to being a well-rounded biologist. How might the faculty resolve this? Here are some strategies:

- Collect information to inform the discussion. Survey students to determine how many are planning careers that require an understanding of botany. Survey alumni to determine if they need or use botany in their careers.

- Investigate other tests and assessments that a majority of faculty might view as more relevant.

- Vote on whether to keep the goal of giving students a grounding in botany and whether to continue using this particular test. Or use the Delphi method (Table 8.7) to achieve consensus.

Consider Your Curriculum

Sometimes students perform poorly on an assessment because the course or program's curriculum gives insufficient attention to relevant learning goals. Students may have poor research skills, for example, because they've had few opportunities to develop and practice those skills. If a particular learning goal is truly a major priority, faculty and staff should ensure that students have many opportunities to study and practice it repeatedly and intensively. This means multiple learning opportunities within a course or program (Chapter Three).

Take a hard look, therefore, at how well your curriculum addresses each major learning goal. If you are assessing student learning in a course, examine its content and requirements, especially how much time students must spend achieving the course's major learning goals. If you are assessing student learning throughout a program, examine the following:

- Course offerings (both required and elective)
- Course content and requirements
- Course sequencing and prerequisites
- Admissions criteria
- Placement criteria

- Support services such as tutoring
- Cocurricular activities

It may also be helpful to review the transcripts of your best- and worst-performing students. Are there any patterns in the order in which they took required courses? In the grades they earned in those courses? In the elective courses they chose? Chapter Seven offers additional suggestions for curriculum review.

Most curricula are already packed to the gills, so how can faculty add more intensive study of a particular goal? Table 18.2 offers some suggestions.

Consider Your Teaching Methods

Sometimes we have to own up to a cruel fact: despite our best efforts, we simply didn't teach a particular skill or concept well. Improving teaching methods can be difficult because few faculty and staff have received formal instruction in contemporary

Table 18.2. Strategies to Add More Intensive Study of a Key Learning Goal

Make some tough choices regarding your priorities for student learning goals. Reduce attention to some less important goals to make room for more coverage for more important ones. Drop a less critical course requirement, or scale back coverage of less important concepts in some courses.

Increase the credit value of a key course, or spread its curriculum over two courses. Some students may be more successful in Calculus I, for example, if they can study it in two three-credit courses rather than in one four-credit course.

Replace a program elective with a required capstone course that reteaches a key learning goal.

Require students in their final semester to complete an independent project that emphasizes this goal. If you want to help students learn how to make oral presentations, require graduating students to make oral presentations on their projects at a department research conference.

Ask faculty to review—and assess—the skill or concept in several courses.

Require students to take an appropriate course in another department as a cognate or general education requirement if the goal is a generic skill, such as conducting statistical analyses or making oral presentations. If you elect this approach, you still need to build attention to these skills within your own curriculum so students learn the nuances of applying the skill to your discipline.

Give students more responsibility for learning on their own. Have students learn basic content knowledge outside class, perhaps by reading the textbook or working with peers, freeing up class time to focus on key learning goals. If students need to strengthen their writing skills but you don't have the time to read every draft, periodically ask students to read and comment on each other's drafts. Or have students strengthen their writing skills by composing summaries of concepts that the class can use as supplemental reading or study guides.

Look for ways to use class time more effectively. If students need to strengthen their oral presentation skills but you don't have time to hear individual oral presentations, have them hone their skills by teaching key topics to the class so your curriculum doesn't fall behind. Or have students make group rather than individual presentations.

teaching methods. As a result, many faculty and staff haven't a clue on how to teach more effectively. Fortunately, more and more colleges and universities are offering professional development resources such as teaching-learning centers, instructional technology centers, workshops, readings, and sponsored attendance at conferences on teaching and learning.

Another reason that it can be difficult to reconsider one's teaching methods is that today's students often learn in ways that are different from how we do. Many of us are in our careers because we came to college well prepared, we had good study habits, and our particular subject came to us easily. Many of us learned just fine from lectures and traditional textbooks, with minimal support from faculty.

Today's students are far different, partly because they are more diverse and partly because they are in a different generation, one that's used to multitasking and using technologies. They need us to engage them, help them learn good study habits, inculcate their sustained attention, and make class time intellectually meaningful (Jones, 2007). Fortunately, research over the past two decades on how students learn offers clues on teaching strategies that are likely to be effective. Table 18.3 offers many research-based ideas on ways to approach teaching and learning with today's students.

Consider Your Assessment Strategies and Tools

Sometimes disappointing student performance is due to the assessment itself. Sometimes test questions and assignments are so poorly written that students misinterpret them. Sometimes they're a poor match with major learning goals. Sometimes they're not administered appropriately (not allowing enough time, for example, or not allowing access to reference sources). And sometimes they're simply inappropriately difficult. In these kinds of situations, students may have learned more than is evidenced by their performance on the assessment. This is especially likely the first time a test or assignment is used. Chapter Sixteen discusses ways to analyze the results of a test or rubric and identify anything that is poorly written or overly difficult. Revise such assessments before using them again.

Isn't Poor Performance Sometimes the Student's Fault?

Of course. As the saying goes, you can lead a horse to water, but you can't make it drink. Despite our best efforts, some students will not make an adequate effort to learn, and they deserve to fail. But these students are usually in the minority. Most students generally want to do whatever is necessary to pass their courses and

Table 18.3. Strategies That Promote Deep, Lasting Learning

A growing body of research evidence indicates that students learn most effectively when:

They understand course and program goals and the characteristics of excellent work.

They are academically challenged and given high but attainable expectations.

They are graded on important goals. While students do pick up some things through faculty and staff modeling, discussions, and the like, they focus their time and energy learning what they'll be graded on and therefore learn those things more effectively than ungraded concepts.

They are taught with enthusiasm.

New learning is related to their prior experiences.

They spend significant time studying and practicing.

They use or apply memorized facts in some way, because facts memorized in isolation are quickly forgotten.

The diversity of their learning styles is respected. They are given a variety of ways to learn and to demonstrate what they've learned.

They spend more time actively involved in learning through hands-on practice and receiving information visually. They spend less time listening to lectures and reading long texts.

They engage in multidimensional real-world tasks in which they explore, analyze, justify, evaluate, use other thinking skills, and arrive at multiple solutions. Such tasks may include realistic class assignments, field experiences, and service-learning opportunities.

They spend more time interacting with others—either face-to-face or online. They receive individual attention from faculty and work collaboratively with fellow students.

They participate in cocurricular activities that build on what they are learning in class.

They reflect on what and how they have learned and see coherence in their learning.

They have a synthesizing experience such as a capstone course, independent study, or research project.

Assessments are learning activities in their own right.

They receive prompt, concrete feedback on their work.

They have opportunities to revise their work.

graduate. The 50 percent rule discussed in Chapter Sixteen is a good way to identify whether responsibility for poor performance lies with the student or elsewhere.

If the fault is with us—our goals, our curriculum (including placement), our teaching methods, or our assessment strategies and tools—students shouldn't be penalized. Throw out or give everyone credit for the part of the assessment that didn't work as it should have.

Use Assessment Results to Inform Planning and Resource Allocation

Sometimes assessment results suggest fairly simple, low-cost quick fixes:

- Faculty who realize that they're trying to cover too many learning goals in a course or program can agree to drop attention to some of them.

- Faculty who aren't satisfied with their students' quantitative reasoning skills can agree to incorporate work involving those skills in more courses.

- Faculty who aren't satisfied with their students' information literacy skills can try giving students collaborative rather than individual research assignments.

- Student life staff who find that some of their survey questions weren't clear to students can revise them for next time.

But sometimes assessment results point to a more significant problem that will take time, planning, and resources to address:

- A survey of employers shows that they need employees with a certain technological skill that, assessments show, students are not developing adequately. Considerable funds are needed to purchase updated versions of this technology along with online tutorials on how to use it. Faculty need professional development to learn how to use and teach the technology, and technical staff are needed to maintain it.

- Faculty dissatisfied with their students' critical thinking skills (the example at the beginning of this chapter) realize that they don't really know how to teach these skills. Professional development opportunities are needed to help them learn how to do this, along with time for them to redesign their course curricula and rethink their pedagogies.

- Faculty dissatisfied with their students' writing skills conclude that a multipronged strategy is needed, with more face-to-face tutoring and online tutorials for struggling students. Faculty need smaller classes so they have more time to grade papers and give students individual feedback.

- Faculty dissatisfied with their students' research skills conclude that students need a new sophomore-level course on research skills as well as the existing senior-level one. Creating a place for this course requires redesigning the entire curriculum.

All of these problems require considerable planning and resources and cannot happen without the strong support of campus leaders (Chapter Five). Campus leaders can help by doing the following.

Fold assessment results into campus planning discussions. Assessment evidence of students' critical thinking and writing skills can be considered when institutional goals and plans are rethought, for example. Should critical thinking and writing skills be a campuswide priority? Should there be a major campuswide push over the next few years to improve these skills?

Establish and promulgate clear funding priorities that are tied to institutional and unit-level plans. Once it's decided that improving students' critical thinking and writing skills is indeed a major campus priority, campus leaders can make clear to faculty and staff that funding priority will be given to requests that aim to do so.

Give funding priority—or exclusivity—to resource requests supported by assessment evidence. A request for a new staff position to support the technology education described above might receive priority.

Give funding priority to pervasive rather than isolated problems. This can foster collaboration rather than competition over scarce funds. For example, if there is pervasive evidence that student writing skills are inadequate—and strong consensus that this is a concern—funding priority might be given to strategies that will help students, faculty, and staff across campus address this.

Move programs engaging in serious assessment efforts to the top of the funding list. Another strategy is to eliminate from consideration those without assessment activities underway. Or release annual operating budgets or a portion thereof, such as travel funds, only to those programs that have submitted acceptable assessment reports.

———————

Using assessment results to inform these kinds of planning and resource allocation decisions is a powerful strategy to promote a culture of assessment (Chapter Five). Faculty and staff who don't receive requested resources will quickly learn that they need to provide assessment evidence to support future requests, and they'll get on the assessment bandwagon.

Time to Think, Discuss, and Practice

1. Faculty at Mountaintop Community College agree that graduating students should be able to think critically (which they define as analyzing, evaluating, and synthesizing), but they aren't satisfied with the critical thinking skills of their graduating students. Unfortunately, they can't find a place in the curriculum for students to practice these skills. They agree that they have so much content to cover in their courses that they don't have time to teach students

how to think critically and then grade critical thinking assignments. How might the faculty reconcile the need for content coverage with the need to help students learn critical thinking skills? Brainstorm practical, concrete advice!

2. One of the goals of the international business program is for students to be able to write clearly and effectively. Although international business majors are asked to write term papers in at least four courses, their writing quality is nonetheless generally still inadequate by the time they're seniors. Faculty are quick to point to the woefully poor writing skills of entering first-year students and equally quick to blame the English department for not bringing writing skills up to par in first-year composition classes.

- Who should have lead responsibility for helping international business majors develop their writing skills? Why?

- Brainstorm what might be done to improve students' writing skills by the time they graduate.

Recommended Readings

The following readings are recommended along with the references cited in this chapter.

Angelo, T. A. (1993). A "teacher's dozen": Fourteen general, research-based principles for improving higher learning in our classrooms. *AAHE Bulletin, 45*(8), 3–7, 13.

Astin, A. W. (1993). *What matters in college: Four critical years revisited.* San Francisco: Jossey-Bass.

Bain, K. (2004). *What the best college teachers do.* Cambridge, MA: Harvard University Press.

Butler, S. M., & McMunn, N. D. (2006). *A teacher's guide to classroom assessment: Understanding and using assessment to improve student learning.* San Francisco: Jossey-Bass.

Chickering, A. W., & Gamson, Z. F. (Eds.). (1991). *Applying the seven principles for good practice in undergraduate education.* New Directions for Teaching and Learning, no. 47. San Francisco: Jossey-Bass.

Gardiner, L. F. (2002). *Research on learning and student development and its implications.* In R. M. Diamond (Ed.), *Field guide to academic leadership* (pp. 89–110). San Francisco: Jossey-Bass.

Kuh, G. (2001). Assessing what really matters to student learning: Inside the National Survey of Student Engagement. *Change, 33*(3), 10–17, 66.

Kuh, G. D., Schuh, J. H., Whitt, E. J., & Associates. (1991). *Involving colleges: Successful approaches to fostering student learning and development outside the classroom.* San Francisco: Jossey-Bass.

McKeachie, W. J., & Svinicki, M. (2006). *Teaching tips: Strategies, research, and theory for college and university teachers* (12th ed.). Boston: Houghton Mifflin.

Mentkowski, M., & Associates. (2000). *Learning that lasts: Integrating learning, development, and performance in college and beyond.* San Francisco: Jossey-Bass.

Miller, M. A. (2007). Habits die hard. *Change, 39*(1), 7–8.

Pascarella, E. T., & Terenzini, P. T. (2005). *How college affects students: A third decade of research*. San Francisco: Jossey-Bass.

Steen, L. A. (1992). Twenty questions that deans should ask their mathematics department (or, that a sharp department will ask itself). *AAHE Bulletin, 44*(9), 3–6.

Strange, C. C., & Banning, J. H. (2000). *Educating by design: Creating campus learning environments that work*. San Francisco: Jossey-Bass.

Tagg, J. (2003). *The learning paradigm college*. Bolton, MA: Anker.

Wehlburg, C. M. (2006). *Meaningful course revision: Enhancing academic engagement using student learning data*. Bolton, MA: Anker.

What research says about improving undergraduate education. (1996). *AAHE Bulletin, 48*(8), 5–8.

CHAPTER 19

Keeping the Momentum Going

> **Some Valuable Ideas You'll Find in This Chapter**
>
> - Any campus requests for reports on assessment results should make clear the purpose of the reports, the audiences for the reports, and the decisions that reports may inform.
> - Faculty and staff benefit from constructive feedback on their assessment reports that tells them what they are doing well and how, if at all, they might be even more effective.
> - If an assessment activity is no longer providing useful information, stop using it, and try something else.

New initiatives can inspire bursts of energy, but it can be unrealistic to expect that energy level to continue indefinitely. How can you keep the momentum going when energies start to flag? Continue to foster a climate of assessment by employing the strategies suggested in Chapter Five: value campus culture and history, respect and empower people, value innovation and risk taking, and value assessment efforts—and do all of this in tangible, meaningful ways. Then consider the strategies for keeping the momentum going.

Celebrate and Honor Assessment Efforts

Why should good and busy faculty or staff continue to pile assessment onto an already full plate of work? Encourage them by recognizing and honoring strong, systematized assessment efforts with

Table 19.1. Strategies to Recognize and Honor Assessment Efforts

Base budget decisions in part on the presence of an effective assessment program, as discussed in Chapter Eighteen.

Allow faculty and staff who are fully engaged in assessment to submit reports less frequently. If you ask most programs for annual reports on assessment, for example, allow those clearly engaged in ongoing, systematized assessment to submit biennial reports.

Offer curriculum development grants to address disappointing assessment results (Chapter Five).

Give faculty and staff written recognition that might be placed in their personnel files or submitted with applications for tenure, promotion, or merit pay. This might be a certificate or a personalized letter of commendation signed by the president, chief academic officer, department chair, assessment committee chair, assessment officer, or a combination of these people.

Encourage faculty and staff to share what they are doing with their peers through journal articles, conference presentations, and the like.

Hold an annual event celebrating assessment efforts, perhaps an awards program, a special luncheon with a motivational speaker, or an assessment fair with exhibits of assessment activities.

Encourage campus leaders to commend publicly, in spoken and written remarks, those engaged in assessment.

Honor faculty and staff who obtain grants that will strengthen assessment.

convincing, meaningful, and ongoing incentives and rewards. Such strategies vary by campus culture but may include those in Table 19.1.

Make Assessment Part of Everyday Processes

Chapter Five notes that a culture of assessment is, at its heart, a culture of evidence-based planning and decision making. One of the keys to keeping the momentum going is to make assessment a natural part of everyday planning and decision making. If institutional leaders expect that important decisions are based on important goals, assessment becomes a habit and part of the fabric of institutional life. If someone has an idea for a new program to improve student retention, for example, everyone considering the idea should expect that the proposal will be accompanied with systematic, assessment-based evidence of the program's need, costs, and likelihood of success.

Assessment can be embedded into a number of routine processes.

Program review. Colleges and universities increasingly require programs to engage in periodic program reviews (Chapter One) in which the faculty and staff conduct a thorough review of the program, sometimes followed by an external review. If your campus has a program review process, make assessment results a high-lighted feature of it. If program reviews are conducted reasonably frequently—every three to five years or so—perhaps separate assessment reports are not needed, or perhaps annual assessment reports can be simple, brief updates. Just make clear that assessment should be a continual part of campus life, not conducted only when the program review is imminent.

Curriculum approval processes. Require new program proposals to include complete, feasible assessment plans.

Performance evaluations. Make assessment efforts a factor in evaluating deans and other appropriate administrators. Chapter Five discusses addressing assessment efforts in faculty tenure, promotion, and merit pay decisions.

Monitor Assessment Activities

As much as everyone hates writing reports, periodic written reports on assessment plans, activities, and results help in the following ways:

- Encouraging faculty and staff reflection on their overall assessment progress

- Spurring faculty and staff to keep working on assessment, making assessment an ongoing rather than sporadic effort

- Providing an opportunity to offer guidance and feedback before things go too far down the wrong road

- Making it easier to compile institutional accountability reports to governing boards, accreditors, state agencies, and other audiences

But edicts for elaborate, lengthy, rigidly formatted, and seemingly pointless plans and reports can alienate faculty and staff and stifle creativity and flexibility. If faculty and staff must spend considerable time preparing lengthy plans, they will loathe facing the seemingly monumental burden of updating or amending them.

So look at the need for reports as an opportunity to model good assessment practices. Take the time to articulate clearly the purpose of the reports and the decisions that the reports are to inform (Table 4.2). Then prepare written guidelines as you would a prompt for a class assignment (Chapter Ten). When you provide the guidelines, include any rubric used to evaluate the reports, such as the one in Exhibit 19.3.

Aim for plans and reports that are simple, supportive, flexible, and sensitive to workload as well as meaningful. Ask initially for too little information rather than too much; you can always request additional information in subsequent reports. Let faculty and staff know not only what the plans and reports should include but also when they are due and to whom they should be submitted. It's usually helpful if the reports include brief summaries of:

- The program's major learning goals
- How, when, and how frequently each major learning goal is being assessed
- What has been learned from each assessment
- How assessment findings have been used to improve teaching and learning
- Any additional information that helps the reader understand what's happening, such as plans to modify assessment strategies

Offer a Template

The job of report writing may be easier if you offer a simple template for faculty and staff to complete and submit electronically. A brief, straightforward word processing document or spreadsheet may be all that's needed. In subsequent years, you can simply ask the report writer to update it. Exhibits 19.1 and 19.2 are examples of simple templates for assessment plans and reports, respectively.

Keep in mind that faculty and staff who are not technologically savvy may view an electronic template—even if it's just a spreadsheet—as one more burden to struggle with. So offer a template, but don't make it mandatory, at least at first. Once faculty see firsthand that the template is faster and easier than preparing a separate report, they'll be more enthused about using it.

Some colleges and universities find it worthwhile to invest in technologies to record and maintain assessment plans and results. This can be an expensive proposition, and the decision should not be made lightly. Table 6.2 suggests steps to follow to make sure any investment in this kind of technology is a wise one.

Offer Options

Frame requests for assessment plans and reports as opportunities for faculty and staff to tell their assessment stories (Chapter Seventeen). Allow them to tell their stories in ways that best work with their aims and culture. This means being willing to bend the rules and be flexible in requirements and expectations, as discussed in Chapter Five.

Exhibit 19.1. A Template for an Assessment Plan

Key learning out-come: What should students be able to do after success-fully completing the program?	How do students learn how to do this? What class work and assignments help them learn this? In what courses?	How will you assess how well your students have learned this?	What kind(s) of benchmark or standard will you use to interpret your results?	When do you expect to begin collecting this assessment information?	How often will you collect this assessment information?
1					
2					
3					
4					
5					
6					

Exhibit 19.2. A Template for an Annual Assessment Report

Key learning outcome: What should students be able to do after completing the program?	Through what courses and assignments do you ensure that all students have the opportunity to learn this?	How are you assessing how well your students are learning this?[a] How often do you conduct this assessment?	Summarize the results of your assessments: What have you learned about how well you are achieving this goal? How do your results compare with your benchmark target?	How have you used this information to help your students?	Optional comments (such as changes to goals, assessments, or schedule)
1					
2					
3					
4					
5					
6					

[a]Please attach examples of your assessment tools (assignments, grading criteria, scoring guidelines, surveys, and the like).

Provide Feedback

Just as students benefit from constructive feedback on their work, faculty and staff benefit from feedback on their assessment reports that tells them what they're doing well and how, if at all, they might be even more effective. Feedback might, for example, offer suggestions on ways to fine-tune assessment strategies to keep them relevant. Or it might suggest that some assessments that aren't yielding new insight be moved to a back burner.

Who Should Provide Feedback?

Because faculty should have leadership responsibility for assessment, it's appropriate that faculty peers provide feedback. As Chapter Six suggests, these reviews are often best done by a faculty-led committee. If committee members don't feel qualified to generate feedback, the assessment coordinator might draft responses that the committee can review and finalize.

How Should Feedback Be Provided?

This is a good opportunity to model effective assessment practices by providing clear evaluation criteria and using them consistently. If you have developed a local statement of principles of good assessment practice, use it to create a rubric (Chapter Nine) delineating the characteristics of exceptional, sufficient, and inadequate assessment practices. Exhibit 19.3 is an example. Share the rubric with faculty and staff to help them prepare their reports.

Continue to model good assessment practices by keeping the review process as fast and simple as possible. Brief feedback provided within a couple of weeks is far more helpful than extensive feedback provided six months later. Frame the feedback as collegial advice rather than approval or disapproval.

Who Should Receive Feedback?

Obviously a program's assessment coordinator or assessment committee should receive feedback on the program's assessment report. Whether the feedback should be shared with all faculty and staff in the program or with the program's dean or vice president depends on campus culture. The aim of all communications should be to support assessment efforts, not to impede the process by creating problems or the perception of them.

Exhibit 19.3. A Rubric for Providing Feedback on Assessment Plans and Reports

Key Learning Goals

☐ *Best Practice:* In addition to meeting the standard described below, key program learning goals are clearly and actively communicated to students and faculty in the program.

☐ *Meets Standard:* Learning goals describe in explicit, observable terms, using action words, how students will be able to use their knowledge, what thinking skills and disciplinary dispositions they will have, and/or what else they will be able to do on completion of the program.

☐ *Needs Attention:* Learning goals do not meet the standard described above.

Teaching and Learning Strategies

☐ *Best Practice:* In addition to meeting the standard described below, it is clear that every student in the major has ample opportunity to master the learning outcome through multiple courses or intensive study in one course.

☐ *Meets Standard:* Every student has sufficient opportunity to master each learning outcome. Every student in the major takes at least one course that addresses the learning outcome.

☐ *Needs Attention:* Does not meet the standard described above.

Assessment Methods

☐ *Best Practice:* In addition to meeting the standard described below, evidence is provided that the assessment methods yield truthful, fair information that can be used with confidence.

☐ *Meets Standard:* Each assessment method clearly matches the learning outcome being assessed, and multiple assessments are used systematically (repeatedly, on a schedule) over time.

☐ *Needs Attention:* Does not meet the standard described above.

Use of Results

☐ *Best Practice:* In addition to meeting the standard described below, standards have been established that clearly describe performance levels considered minimally adequate for students completing the program, and positive assessment results are shared with faculty, students, academic administrators, prospective students, and other audiences as appropriate.

☐ *Meets Standard:* Assessment results are shared and discussed with faculty teaching in the program and are used to modify learning outcomes, teaching methods, curriculum, and/ or assessment strategies, as appropriate.

☐ *Needs Attention:* Does not meet the standard described above.

☐ *Not Applicable:* This is a plan that is not yet implemented.

Periodically Sit Back and Reflect

As discussed in Chapter Three, assessment is best considered a perpetual work in progress. It requires "a commitment to working out the kinks in the process. . . . It is important to implement and refine as you go" (Bresciani, 2007, p. 233). There's no point in continuing assessment strategies that aren't providing useful information or consume time and resources disproportionate to the value of the information they provide. So perhaps once every year or two, sit back and reflect on your efforts to date.

Inform these conversations by preparing a snapshot of where your campus or program is with assessment and where it's going. Exhibits 19.4 and 19.5 provide examples of charts that provide such snapshots. These kinds of charts may also be helpful in giving campus leaders, accreditors, state agencies, and other audiences an overview of the general state of your assessment efforts (Chapter Seventeen).

Another possibility is to develop some performance indicators (Chapter One): measurable outcomes of assessment efforts that can help faculty and staff can see how far they've come. Such measures might include:

Exhibit 19.4. An Example of a Completed Chart for Monitoring Assessment Progress Across an Institution

Program or General Education Requirement	Learning Goals Articulated? If Not, by When?	Assessment Strategies Identified and Developed? If Not, by When?	Assessments Implemented? When? Frequency?	Assessment Results Compiled and Shared? When? Frequency?	Assessment Results Used for Planning, Budgeting, and Decision Making? When? Frequency?
Academic Programs					
Accounting B.S.	Yes.	Yes.	Yes. Every spring, starting 2006.	Yes. Every fall, starting 2006.	Yes. Every spring, starting 2007.
Biology B.S.	Yes.	No. By 3/1/10.	No. Every year, starting 3/1/10.	No. Every year, starting 9/1/10.	No. Every year, starting 11/1/10.
History B.A.	No. By 4/30/09.	No. By 9/15/09.	No. Every fall, starting 2009.	No. Every spring, starting 2/1/10.	No. Every year, starting 4/1/10.
General Education Requirements					
Writing	Yes.	Yes.	Yes. Every semester starting 2007.	Yes. Every year, by 9/1.	Yes. Every year, by 12/1.
Social sciences	Yes.	Yes.	Yes. Every course once every three years, on a rotating schedule, starting fall 2008.	Yes. Even-numbered years, by 3/1.	Yes. Even-numbered years, by 9/1.

Exhibit 19.5. A Rubric for Evaluating Institutional Student Learning Assessment Processes

No plans   = The institution has no plans to do this.
No evidence = The institution is aware that it should do this, but this is not yet happening.
A few areas = This is happening in just a few areas (for example, only in programs with specialized accreditation).
Some areas   = This is happening in some but not most areas (for example, in a number of academic programs but not yet in general education).
Most areas   = This is happening in most but not all areas.
Everywhere = This is happening everywhere.

For academic programs, the general education curriculum, and institutional goals articulated in the mission statement, vision statement, or elsewhere:	No plans	No evidence	A few areas	Some areas	Most areas	Every-where
Institutional leaders demonstrate sustained support for promoting an ongoing culture of assessment and for efforts to improve teaching.	☐	☐	☐	☐	☐	☐
Clear statements of expected learning outcomes have been developed.	☐	☐	☐	☐	☐	☐
Standards or benchmarks for determining whether student learning outcomes have been achieved have been established.	☐	☐	☐	☐	☐	☐
Multiple measures of student achievement of expected learning outcomes, including direct evidence, have been collected.	☐	☐	☐	☐	☐	☐
The evidence of student learning that has been collected is clearly linked to expected learning outcomes.	☐	☐	☐	☐	☐	☐
Student learning assessment results have been shared in useful forms.	☐	☐	☐	☐	☐	☐
Student learning assessment results have been used to improve teaching and inform planning and budgeting decisions.	☐	☐	☐	☐	☐	☐
In any areas in which the above are not yet happening, concrete, feasible, and timely plans are in place.	☐	☐	☐	☐	☐	☐
There is sufficient momentum to provide assurance that assessment processes will be sustained indefinitely.	☐	☐	☐	☐	☐	☐

- The number of programs that have written assessment plans
- The number of multisection courses that have common learning outcomes for all sections
- The number of programs or courses whose learning outcomes, curricula, pedagogies, or assessment strategies have been revised in response to assessment findings
- Resources spent on assessment activities
- Resources spent on professional development activities that strengthen assessment skills

After a snapshot and perhaps performance indicators are compiled, ask yourself the kinds of questions listed in Table 19.2, and use the results of the discussion to fine-tune assessment strategies.

As you consider modifications, aim for a balance between necessary change and consistency. It can be frustrating when the rules of the game are constantly changing. So seek to fine-tune rather than dramatically overhaul your assessment processes unless your campus community acknowledges the need for wholesale change.

Table 19.2. Questions to Ask About Assessment Efforts

Goals and outcomes: How well has assessment in practice matched your intentions? Is everything working the way you intended?

Successes: What have been your major success stories? What has worked well?

Disappointments: What have been your biggest disappointments? What hasn't been helpful? What was more difficult than you anticipated?

Quality: Are assessment results generally of sufficient quality that you can have confidence in them and use them for improvements?

Value: Are assessments yielding useful information? If you find that a particular assessment is no longer giving useful information, stop using it and do something else.

Cost and benefits: What has been the cost of assessment efforts in terms of faculty and staff time, dollars, and other resources? What have been the benefits of assessment activities, and how do the costs measure up against the benefits? What has taken too much time or effort? If you find that a particular assessment is more time and trouble than it's worth, stop using it and do something else.

Resources and support: What resources and support would most help develop and implement better ways to assess student learning?

Changes in learning goals: Have student learning goals changed? Do your assessment tools still align with your learning goals?

Changes in context and culture: What new questions about student learning have emerged? How has the campus culture evolved since these assessments were first planned? How have students changed? How has current thinking on the nature and practice of assessment changed? How might these changes impact assessment policies and practices?

Possible modifications: What would you like to do over the next few years? Are plans to assess student learning still appropriate? How might you improve assessment efforts?

Time to Think, Discuss, and Practice

1. The community college president in Exercise 1 in Chapter Five is delighted with the work of the science faculty to assess student learning in the science requirement of the general education curriculum. She would like to recognize the faculty's work, but resources are very limited. Brainstorm up to three low-cost but meaningful ways that she might honor the faculty's work.

2. Brainstorm three practical, realistic ways to celebrate and reward assessment efforts that would fit well with your campus's culture.

3. Complete the chart in Exhibit 19.5 in terms of your program or college. What has been going well? What most needs attention at this point?

Recommended Readings

The following readings are recommended along with the references cited in this chapter.

Shepard, L. A. (1977). *A checklist for evaluating large-scale assessment programs* (Occasional Paper Series No. 9). Kalamazoo: Western Michigan University.

Stufflebeam, D. (2000). *Strategies for institutionalizing evaluation: Revisited* (Occasional Paper No. 18). Kalamazoo: Western Michigan University.

Suskie, L. (2003). Assessment at Towson University: Lessons learned on keeping assessment thriving. *Assessment Update, 15*(3), 8–9.

REFERENCES

Allen, J. (2006). Manias, pathologies, and alternative approaches to assessment: A response to doubting assessors. *Academic Leader*, 22(8), 4–5.

American Association of University Professors. (1940). *Statement of principles on academic freedom and tenure.* Washington, DC: Author.

Anderson, L. W., & Krathwohl, D. R. (Eds.). (2001). *Taxonomy for learning, teaching, and assessing: A revision of Bloom's taxonomy of educational objectives.* Needham Heights, MA: Allyn & Bacon.

Angelo, T. A. (1995). Reassessing (and redefining) assessment. *AAHE Bulletin*, 48(3), 7–9.

Angelo, T. A. (1999). Doing assessment as if learning matters most. *AAHE Bulletin, 51*(9), 3–6.

Angelo, T. A. (2000). A vision worth working toward: Assessment in support of learning communities. *Assessment Update, 12*(2), 3, 5.

Angelo, T. A., & Cross, K. P. (1993). *Classroom assessment techniques: A handbook for college teachers.* San Francisco: Jossey-Bass.

Association of American Colleges and Universities. (2002). *Greater expectations: A new vision for learning as a nation goes to college.* Washington, DC: Author.

Association of College and Research Libraries. (2000). *Information literacy competency standards for higher education.* Chicago: Author.

Baglin, R. F. (1981). Does "nationally" normed really mean nationally? *Journal of Educational Measurement, 18,* 97–107.

Banta, T. W. (2008). Trying to clothe the emperor. *Assessment Update, 20*(2), 3–4, 15–16.

Banta, T. W., Lund, J. P., Black, K. E., & Oblander, F. W. (1996). *Assessment in practice: Putting principles to work on college campuses.* San Francisco: Jossey-Bass.

Barr, R. B., & Tagg, J. (1995). From teaching to learning—A new paradigm for undergraduate education. *Change, 27*(6), 12–25.

Bauer, J. F. (2002). *Assessing student work from chatrooms and bulletin boards.* In R. S. Anderson, J. F. Bauer, & B. W. Speck (Eds.), *Assessment strategies for the on-line class: From theory to practice* (pp. 31–36). New Directions for Teaching and Learning, no. 91. San Francisco: Jossey-Bass.

Bloom, B. S. (Ed.). (1956). *Taxonomy of educational objectives, handbook 1: Cognitive domain.* New York: Longman.

Boyer, E. L. (1990). *Scholarship reconsidered: Priorities of the professoriate.* San Francisco: Jossey-Bass.

Braskamp, L., & Schomberg, S. (2006, July 26). Caring or uncaring assessment. *Inside Higher Ed.* Retrieved September 16, 2008, from http://insidehighered.com/views/2006/07/26/braskamp.

Bresciani, M. J. (2006). *Outcomes-based academic and co-curricular program review: A compilation of institutional good practices.* Sterling, VA: Stylus.

Bresciani, M. J. (Ed.). (2007). *Assessing student learning in general education: Good practice case studies.* Bolton, MA: Anker.

Bruff, D. (2009). *Teaching with classroom response systems: Creating active learning environments.* San Francisco: Jossey-Bass.

Buros Institute of Mental Measurements. (n.d.). *Publications catalog.* Retrieved September 16, 2008, from www.unl.edu/buros/bimm/html/catalog.html.

Butler, S. M., & McMunn, N. D. (2006). *A teacher's guide to classroom assessment: Understanding and using assessment to improve student learning.* San Francisco: Jossey-Bass.

Carnegie Foundation for the Advancement of Teaching. (2007). *The Carnegie classification of institutions of higher education.* Retrieved September 16, 2008, from www.carnegiefoundation.org/classifications/.

Carroll, J. (2004, May). *Fair assessment.* Paper presented at the University of Stirling, United Kingdom.

Cooperative Institutional Research Program. (2008). *Freshman survey.* Los Angeles: University of California at Los Angeles, Higher Education Research Institute.

Costa, A. L., & Kallick, B. (Eds.). (2000). *Discovering and exploring habits of mind.* Alexandria, VA: Association for Supervision and Curriculum Development.

Council for Aid to Education. (2006). *Collegiate learning assessment.* New York: Author.

Diamond, R. M. (2008). *Designing and assessing courses and curricula: A practical guide* (3rd ed.). San Francisco: Jossey-Bass.

Driscoll, A., & Wood, S. (2007). *Developing outcomes-based assessment for learner-centered education: A faculty introduction.* San Francisco: Jossey-Bass.

Eaton, J. (2007). Institutions, accreditors, and the federal government: Redefining their "appropriate relationship." *Change, 39*(5), 16–23.

Education Trust. (n.d.). *College results online.* Retrieved September 16, 2008, from www.collegeresults.org.

Educational Testing Service. (2008a). *TestLink overview.* Retrieved September 16, 2008, from www.ets.org/testcoll/.

Educational Testing Service. (2008b). *The Praxis series.* Princeton, NJ: Author.

Ekman, R., & Pelletier, S. (2008). Assessing student learning: A work in progress. *Change, 40*(4), 14–19.

Erwin, T. D. (2000). *The NPEC sourcebook on assessment, Vol. 1: Definitions and assessment methods for critical thinking, problem solving, and writing.* Washington, DC: National Center for Education Statistics.

Ewell, P. T. (1996). *Identifying indicators of curricular quality.* In J. G. Gaff, J. L. Ratcliff, & Associates, *Handbook of the undergraduate curriculum: A comprehensive guide to purposes, structures, practices, and change* (pp. 608–627). San Francisco: Jossey-Bass.

Ewell, P. T. (2002). *Perpetual movement: Assessment after twenty years.* Keynote address presented at the American Association for Higher Education Assessment Conference, Boston.

Gangopadhyay, P. (2002). *Making evaluation meaningful to all education stakeholders.* Retrieved September 16, 2008, from www.wmich.edu/evalctr/checklists/makingevalmeaningful.pdf.

Geisinger, K. F., Spies, R. A., Carlson, J. F., & Plake, B. S. (Eds.). (2007). *The seventeenth mental measurements yearbook.* Lincoln: University of Nebraska Press.

Graff, G. (2008, February 21). Assessment changes everything. *Inside Higher Ed.* Retrieved September 16, 2008, from www.insidehighered.com/views/2008/02/21/graff.

Harris, E., & Muchin, S. (2002). Using information architecture to improve communication. *Evaluation Exchange, 8*(3), 4–5.

Haswell, R. (1983). Minimal marking. *College English, 45*(6), 600–604.

Hollowell, D., Middaugh, M. F., & Sibolski, E. (2006). *Integrated higher education planning and assessment: A practical guide.* Ann Arbor, MI: Society for College and University Planning.

Hsu, C., & Sandford, B. A. (2007). The Delphi technique: Making sense of consensus. *Practical Assessment, Research and Evaluation, 12*(10), 1–8.

Huba, M. E., & Freed, J. E. (2000). *Learner-centered assessment on college campuses: Shifting the focus from teaching to learning.* Needham Heights, MA: Allyn & Bacon.

Indiana University, Center for Postsecondary Research. (2007). *National Survey of Student Engagement 2008.* Bloomington, IN: Author.

Johnstone, S. M., Ewell, P., & Paulson, K. (2001). *Student learning as academic currency.* Washington, DC: American Council on Education.

Jones, E. A., & RiCharde, S. (2005). *NPEC sourcebook on assessment: Definitions and assessment methods for communication, leadership, information literacy, quantitative reasoning, and quantitative skills.* Washington, DC: National Center for Education Statistics.

Jones, J. B. (2007, November 16). Start with a number . . . *Inside Higher Ed.* Retrieved September 16, 2008, from http://insidehighered.com/views/2007/11/16/jones.

Kirkpatrick, D. L., & Kirkpatrick, J. D. (2006). *Evaluating training programs: The four levels* (3rd ed.). San Francisco: Berrett-Koehler.

Lattuca, L. R., Terenzini, P. T., & Volkwein, J. F. (2006). *Engineering change: A study of the impact of EC 2000.* Baltimore, MD: Accreditation Board for Engineering and Technology.

Leveille, D. E. (2005). *An emerging view on accountability in American higher education.* Berkeley: University of California at Berkeley, Center for Studies in Higher Education.

Marzano, R., Pickering, D., & McTighe, J. (1993). *Assessing student outcomes: Performance assessment using the dimensions of learning model.* Alexandria, VA: Association for Supervision and Curriculum Development.

Meacham, J. (2008). The editor's desk. *Newsweek, 62*(17), 4.

Miller, M. (2008). The voluntary system of accountability: Origins and purposes: An interview with George Mehaffy and David Shulenberger. *Change, 40*(4), 8–13.

Murphy, L. L., Spies, R. A., & Plake, B. S. (Eds.). (2006). *Tests in Print VII.* Lincoln, NE: University of Nebraska Press.

National Council of State Boards of Nursing. (2008). *NCLEX examinations.* Chicago: Author.

National Resource Center for the First-Year Experience and Students in Transition. (2002). *First-year assessment instrument database.* Retrieved September 16, 2008, from http://nrc.fye.sc.edu/resources/survey/search/index.php.

Palomba, C. A., & Banta, T. W. (1999). *Assessment essentials: Planning, implementing, and improving assessment in higher education.* San Francisco: Jossey-Bass.

Peter D. Hart Research Associates. (2008). *How should colleges assess and improve student learning? Employers' views on the accountability challenge.* Washington, DC: Author.

Peterson, M. W., & Einarson, M. K. (2001). What are colleges doing about student assessment? Does it make a difference? *Journal of Higher Education, 72*(6), 629–669.

Petrides, L., & Nodine, T. (2005). Accountability and information practices in the California Community Colleges: Toward effective use of information in decision-making. *Journal: Insight into Student Services, 10.* Retrieved September 16, 2008, from www.ijournal.us/issue_10/ij_issue10_07.html.

Pieper, S. L., Fulcher, K. H., Sundre, D. L., & Erwin, T. D. (2008). "What do I do with the data now?" Analyzing assessment information for accountability and improvement. *Research and Practice in Assessment, 2*(1). Retrieved September 16, 2008, from www.virginiaassessment.org/rpaJournal.php.

Plucker, J., Beghetto, R. A., & Dow, G. (2004). Why isn't creativity more important to educational psychologists? Potential, pitfalls, and future directions in creativity research. *Educational Psychologist, 39*(2), 83–96.

Schneider, C. G., & Shulman, L. S. (2007). *Foreword.* In R. J. Shavelson, *A brief history of student learning assessment: How we got where we are and a proposal for where to go next.* Washington, DC: Association of American Colleges and Universities.

Shavelson, R. J. (2007). *A brief history of student learning assessment: How we got where we are and a proposal for where to go next.* Washington, DC: Association of American Colleges and Universities.

Shirley, R. C., & Volkwein, J. F. (1978). Establishing academic program priorities. *Journal of Higher Education, 49*(5), 472–488.

Shulman, L. S. (2007). Counting and recounting: Assessment and the quest for accountability. *Change, 39*(1), 20–25.

Smith, P. (2004). Curricular transformation: Why we need it . . . How to support it. *Change, 36*(1), 28–35.

Stein, S. (2001). *Equipped for the future content standards: What adults need to know and be able to do in the 21st century.* Washington, DC: National Institute for Literacy.

Stevens, D. D., & Levi, A. J. (2004). *Introduction to rubrics: An assessment tool to save grading time, convey effective feedback and promote student learning.* Sterling, VA: Stylus.

Suskie, L. (1996). *Questionnaire survey research: What works* (2nd ed.). Tallahassee, FL: Association for Institutional Research.

Suskie, L. (2006). *Accountability and quality improvement.* In P. Hernon, R. E. Dugan, & C. Schwartz (Eds.), *Revisiting outcomes assessment in higher education.* Westport, CT: Libraries Unlimited.

Suskie, L. (2007). Answering the complex question of "How good is good enough?" *Assessment Update, 19*(4), 1–2, 12–13.

Trustees of Hamilton College. (2008). *About the college.* Retrieved September 16, 2008, from www.hamilton.edu/about/.

Upcraft, M. L., & Schuh, J. H. (2002). Assessment vs. research: Why we should care about the difference. *About Campus, 7*(1), 16–20.

U.S. Department of Education. (2006). *A test of leadership: Charting the future of U.S. higher education.* Washington, DC: Author.

U.S. Department of Health and Human Services. (2005). *Code of Federal Regulations: Title 45: Public Welfare: Part 46: Protection of Human Subjects.* Retrieved September 16, 2008, from www.hhs.gov/ohrp/humansubjects/guidance/45cfr46.htm.

Walvoord, B. E., & Anderson, V. J. (1998). *Effective grading: A tool for learning and assessment.* San Francisco: Jossey-Bass.

Weaver, R. L., & Cotrell, H. W. (1985). Mental aerobics: The half-sheet response. *Innovative Higher Education, 10*(1), 23–31.

Wilson, C. D., Miles, C. L., Baker, R. L., & Schoenberger, R. L. (2000). *Learning outcomes for the 21st century: Report of a community college study.* Mission Viejo, CA: League for Innovation in the Community College.

Zubizarreta, J. (2004). *The learning portfolio: Reflective practice for improving student learning.* Bolton, MA: Anker.

RECOMMENDED READINGS

The following are some important resources on assessing student learning in addition to the references specifically cited in this book.

Bresciani, M. J., Zelna, C. L., & Anderson, J. A. (2004). *Assessing student learning and development: A handbook for practitioners.* Washington, DC: National Association of Student Personnel Administrators.

Leskes, A., & Wright, B. (2005). *The art and science of assessing general education outcomes: A practical guide.* Washington, DC: Association of American Colleges and Universities.

Maki, P. L. (2004). *Assessing for learning: Building a sustainable commitment across the institution.* Sterling, VA: Stylus.

Middle States Commission on Higher Education. (2003). *Student learning assessment: Options and resources.* Philadelphia: Author.

Suskie, L. (2000). Fair assessment practices: Giving students equitable opportunities to demonstrate learning. *AAHE Bulletin, 52*(9), 7–9.

Suskie, L. (Ed.). (2001). *Assessment to promote deep learning: Insight from AAHE's 2000 and 1999 assessment conferences.* Sterling, VA: Stylus.

Walvoord, B. E. (2004). *Assessment clear and simple: A practical guide for institutions, departments, and general education.* San Francisco: Jossey-Bass.

ASSESSMENT RESOURCES

Subscribe to *Assessment Update*. This peer-reviewed quarterly journal, published by Jossey-Bass, contains articles on cutting-edge practices by assessment practitioners. To subscribe, visit www.josseybass.com/WileyCDA/WileyTitle/productCd-AU.html.

Search *Internet Resources for Higher Education Outcomes Assessment*. This is sponsored by North Carolina State University (www2.acs.ncsu.edu/UPA/assmt/resource.htm). Among its hundreds of links are assessment handbooks, institutional assessment Web sites, and information on assessment of specific disciplines and skills.

Join the ASSESS Listserv. This is a fairly low-traffic but useful unmoderated online discussion list, sponsored by the University of Kentucky, in which higher education assessment practitioners share ideas on the nuts and bolts of assessment. To join or search the archives, visit http://lsv.uky.edu/archives/assess.html.

Attend a conference. They are the best places to network with colleagues and learn about the latest and best assessment practices. Some of the best-known conferences include the following:

- The Assessment Institute in Indianapolis, held in late October or early November, is the country's largest conference devoted solely to assessment in higher education. For information, visit http://planning.iupui.edu/conferences/national/nationalconf.html.
- The International Assessment and Retention Conference, sponsored by the National Association of Student Personnel

Administrators (NASPA) and held each June, focuses on integrating assessment and retention in academic and student affairs. For information, visit www.assessconf.net/.

- The Association for Institutional Research Annual Forum, held each May, devotes a track to assessment. For information, visit http://www.airweb.org.

- The National Conference on First-Year Assessment, sponsored by the National Resource Center on the First Year of College and Students in Transition, offers models and best practices than can often be applied beyond the first college year. For information, visit www.sc.edu/fye/index.html and click on Events.

- The North Carolina State Undergraduate Assessment Symposium (www.ncsu.edu/assessment/symposium/), the Texas A&M Assessment Conference (http://assessment. tamu.edu/conference/), and the New England Educational Assessment Network Fall Forum (http://neean.southernct. edu/activities/index.html) attract several hundred people from across the country. Their smaller size makes them ideal for networking.

For information on assessment of general education curricula, contact the Association of American Colleges and Universities (www.aacu.org).

For information on assessment in first-year-experience programs, two organizations with a wealth of resources on assessing these experiences are the Policy Center on the First Year of College (www.firstyear.org) and the National Resource Center for the First-Year Experience and Students in Transition (www.sc.edu/fye).

For information on assessment in student life programs, contact any of these organizations:

- Council for the Advancement of Standards in Higher Education (www.cas.edu)

- American College Personnel Association (http://myacpa.org/)

- National Association of Student Personnel Administrators (www.naspa.org/)

INDEX